Simone de Beauvoir and Her Catholicism

Joseph Mahon

Simone de Beauvoir and Her Catholicism
an essay on her ethical and religious meditations

Arlen House
2002

first published in October 2002 by

Arlen House
PO Box 222
Galway

and

42 Grange Abbey Road
Baldoyle
Dublin 13
Ireland

ISBN:

1-903631-27-0 paperback
1-903631-28-9 hardback

www.arlenhouse.ie
www.arlenacademic.com

House Editor:
Susan Bennett

Typesetting: Arlen House
Printed by ColourBooks, Baldoyle, Dublin 13

CONTENTS

FOR JAMES, ALYCE AND AMY MAHON

ACKNOWLEDGEMENTS

I am grateful to the following people for the following reasons: Rev. Colin Garvey, OFM for lending me, then making a present of, his copy of H. Davis, *Moral and Pastoral Theology: A Summary* (Sheed and Ward, 1952); Dr Alyce Mahon, Trinity College, Cambridge, for procuring for me various French editions of some of Beauvoir's works, and for drawing my attention to P. Assouline, *L'Epuration des intellectuals, 1944–45*: Dr Mark Shiel, University of Leicester, for helping to procure the photographs of Saint-Sulpice and Notre-Dame-des-Champs; Dr Evelyn Mahon, TCD, for reading the chapter on abortion, as well as for her reminiscences of travelling, as Evelyn Regan, with her mother and grandmother to Lourdes in the 1950s; MA students of Philosophy at NUI, Galway who took my course 'Studies in Feminist Philosophy', and made the lectures and seminars such a rewarding experience; Mrs M. Mahon for instructing me on some of the finer points of current Catholic devotional practices in Ireland; Alan Hayes, indefatigable, irrepressible publisher of Arlen House, for his enthusiastic, energising support for the manuscript; Susan Bennett for her extensive editing, and Angela Gallagher for the cover.

PREFACE

In 1997 I published a book with Macmillan and St. Martin's Press entitled *Existentialism, Feminism and Simone de Beauvoir*. When I was preparing the Index for that book I was struck by the number of words from the Catholic lexicon which kept appearing and reappearing. I decided to do some research on Beauvoir's Catholicism, research which has led to the present volume. The basic thesis of the monograph is that while Simone de Beauvoir ceased at an early age to be a practising Catholic, she continued to a significant extent to see the world through Catholic eyes. This thesis is developed and defended over ten chapters. They cover such topics as the body, modesty, pregnancy, abortion, punishment, God, and death. The second chapter concentrates on her Catholic formation.

Beauvoir scholarship can be divided into four phases: the orthodox phase, the revisionist phase, the archival phase, and the definitive phase.[1] The orthodox phase is dominated by the view that Simone de Beauvoir's philosophy is derivative and second-rate; that her existentialism is essentially a Sartrean existentialism, so that her work cannot even be understood without first having an extensive familiarity with Sartre's *Being and Nothingness*. For these reasons, Beauvoir does not deserve a place in the pantheon alongside Sartre, Heidegger, Merleau-Ponty and others. This line of thought – which climaxed during the 80s – can be found in a work as recent as Genevieve Lloyd's *The Man of Reason: Male and Female in Western Philosophy* (1993, 2nd edition), as well as in Moira Gatens' *Feminism and Philosophy* (1991).

The revisionists argue that Beauvoir's philosophy is not just a diluted version of Sartre's; that she made a substantial contribution to existentialism, especially to existentialist *ethics*, as well as to the understanding of human sexuate nature. Revisionists insist, then, that Beauvoir deserves to be considered a major philosopher in her own right. This phase begins with Michelle Le Doeuff's *Hipparchia's Choice: An Essay Concerning Women, Philosophy, Etc.* (1991, first published in French in 1989), and continues to the present day with Nancy Bauer's *Simone de Beauvoir, Feminism and Philosophy* (2001).

The archival phase concentrates on Beauvoir's unpublished work, especially her diaries, and seeks in them confirmation of the revisionist thesis. Much of the credit for this initiative must go to Margaret A. Simons [Southern Illinois University at Edwardsville], co-editor with

Beauvoir's adopted daughter Sylvie Le Bon de Beauvoir of a promised six-volume English-language edition of Beauvoir's philosophically significant texts.

The final, definitive phase will be that which produces an unquestionably authoritative account of Beauvoir's contribution to philosophy, when, for example, someone produces a book to match Jerry Cohen's first book on Marx, his *Karl Marx's Theory of History: A Defence* (1978).

My own 1997 book, *Existentialism, Feminism and Simone de Beauvoir*, belongs to the revisionist phase of Beauvoir scholarship. It argues for all of the following propositions:

(i) that Beauvoir's writings, and especially her works of the 1940s, merit inclusion in the existentialist canon, and that to exclude her from the pantheon is to do her a singular injustice.

(ii) that her philosophical monographs *Pyrrhus et Cinéas* (1944) and *The Ethics of Ambiguity* (1947) make a substantial contribution to existentialist thought, and especially to existentialist ethics.

(iii) that of the three *defences* of existentialism offered in the immediate post-war period – Beauvoir's, Sartre's and Merleau-Ponty's – Beauvoir's is the most philosophically sustained and impressive.

(iv) that the philosophical seeds of *The Second Sex* are to be found in these earlier philosophical essays, rather than in Sartre's *Being and Nothingness*.

(v) that Beauvoir's philosophical thought differs extensively, and profoundly, from contemporaneous works by Sartre, including the *Carnets* and the *Cahiers*.

(vi) that it is time for a revaluation of *The Second Sex*; in effect, that it should be reinstated as the master-text of feminist thought.

The present work is revisionist in the sense in which I have defined this term. It presses home the attack on the 80s orthodoxy, arguing that some of Beauvoir's deepest beliefs and attitudes have their provenance in the period of her Catholic formation. The book may also be read as a study of Beauvoir's meditations on a range of fundamental philosophical topics, such as freedom, the body, God, punishment, and death. In that sense it could be called an essay on her ethical and religious meditations.

Note
1   See L. McNay, 'Sartre's sex slave?' *Times Literary Supplement*, 12 October 2001, for an authoritative two-stage account of Beauvoir scholarship.

Chapter One

INTRODUCTION

Consider the lilies of the field, how they grow; they labour not, neither do they spin. But I say to you that not even Solomon in all his glory was arrayed as one of these.

– Matthew, 6, 28–29. Luke, 12, 31.

We flourished, in fact, like the lilies of the field, and circumstances fostered our illusions. We were bursting with good health, and our bodies objected to no demands we made on them unless we pushed things to extremes.

- Simone de Beauvoir, The Prime of Life, p. 363.

We should expect to find, in a work by a Catholic author, an imagination permeated by Catholicism. This is the fundamental idea in Conor Cruise O'Brien's critical work *Maria Cross*, subtitled 'Imaginative Patterns in a Group of Catholic Writers'. The writers in question are François Mauriac, Georges Bernanos, Graham Greene, Sean O'Faolain, Evelyn Waugh, Charles Péguy, Paul Claudel and Léon Bloy. Simone de Beauvoir's name does not feature on the list, though neither does it contain the name of any other female author.

Presumably one of the reasons Simone de Beauvoir was not included was that, notwithstanding the fact that she had received a strong

Catholic formation, her works have long been considered hostile to Catholic teaching; so hostile, in fact, that her feminist classic *The Second Sex* merited inclusion in another list, the Catholic Church's *Index Librorum Prohibitorum*, its official list, at the time,[1] of proscribed books. It is also well known that Beauvoir championed many causes, such as the campaign for free, safe and legal abortion in France, in the teeth of Catholic opposition. It would be deliciously ironic, then, should it emerge that she was, when all is said and done, a very Catholic author, that she had, in O'Brien's sweet phrasing of it, an imagination 'permeated by Catholicism'.[2]

The attractions of irony are nothing if not seductive. But to make credible the ironic truth just identified, it will be necessary to substitute more rigorous criteria for the application of the predicate 'Catholic' to an author than that proposed by O'Brien. For the purposes of this monograph, I propose to call an author Catholic when her writing meets all of the following three criteria:

(a) It is replete with terms and phrases belonging to the Catholic lexicon

(b) The author's obsessions are typically Catholic, and

(c) A significant proportion of her stances and attitudes are recognizably Catholic in content and tone.

Judged by these criteria Simone de Beauvoir's writing, I will argue, is luminously Catholic, despite her own disclaimers. Her Catholicism is obvious, as well as to be expected, in such very early writings as the collection of short stories *When Things of the Spirit Come First*. But the Catholic vernacular and disposition shine, like a Lourdes statuette in the dark, in much later works such as *The Second Sex*, the opening volume of her memoirs, *Memoirs of a Dutiful Daughter*, and in the much shorter, moving record of her mother's dying, *A Very Easy Death*.

The peculiarly Catholic *flavour* of Beauvoir's writing is not always sufficiently conveyed, or conveyed with adequate accuracy, by many of the standard English translations of her writings. The following are some illustrations of this statement, drawn from the opening volume of her memoirs. Kirkup translates the sentence *elle dirigeait mes lectures, m'emmenait à la messe et au salut* as follows: 'She supervised my reading, and accompanied me to Mass and compline'. But generally Catholics did not (and do not) go to Mass and compline, they went and go to Mass and Benediction.[3] Compline, or Night Prayer, is the last monastic office of the day, and is included as the prayer before sleep in a recently published Benedictine Prayer Book.[4] But the vast majority of Catholics do not, and did not during Beauvoir's childhood, belong to a religious order. They typically went to Mass, to Confession, and to Devotions. They did not 'say their office'; it was solely the priests and nuns who ministered to them, and who educated them, who did so.[5]

As Kirkup translates it, the sentence *je préparai ma communion privée* becomes 'I prepared my communion in private'. But for anyone reared in the Catholic tradition, it would be more appropriate to say 'I prepared for my First Holy Communion in private', since that is what would have been said. Neither would such private preparation have involved going 'into retreat', but going 'on retreat'. (In fact, in general, first communicants did not go on retreat at all, being too weak in every way to endure the rigours of lengthy bouts of prayer, meditation and fasting).

On page 72 of the standard English translation are printed the words 'and He would smile down upon me as He had smiled upon the Magdalene'. But Catholics always say 'Mary Magdalene' rather than 'the Magdalene' for both cultural and biblical reasons. For biblical reasons, so as to distinguish Mary Magdalen from Mary, the mother of Jesus, first of all, as well as from Mary the mother of James and Joseph, and the wife of Zebedee. 'The Magdalen' is a cultural shorthand for notoriously grim houses of detention for unmarried mothers and women otherwise considered sexually wayward, as well as the laundry service – secured under conditions of forced labour – which such institutions provided.

On page 78 of the Kirkup translation we find the sentence 'we would all climb into the dog-cart and go to hear Mass at Saint-Germain-les-Belles'. But Catholics 'go' to Mass, they don't 'hear' it; Catholic priests 'hear' Confession. Writing about Zaza's mother, and the coarseness of the sex education she had imparted to her daughter, Beauvoir says:

> Sa mère l'avertit très tôt, et avec une crudité très méchante, des réalités sexuelles: Zaza comprit précocement que Madame Mabille avait haï dès la première nuit et à jamais les étreintes conjugales.[6]

We have here – with the phrase *les étreintes conjugales* – an unmistakeable reference to a core concept in Catholic teaching on sex and reproduction, to what is variously called 'conjugal relations', 'the conjugal act', 'conjugal union', 'marital union' and 'marital love and communion'. Such behaviour is, by definition, restricted to spouses, whose married status does not confer on them a right to have children, but confers, somewhat differently, the right to perform 'natural acts which are *per se* ordered to procreation'. Only the child which is carried and born as a consequence of conjugal union, i.e. of sex between married partners which is continuously open to procreation, can be 'the living image of their love'.[7] This, as Mary Holland observed in the context of writing about Catholic strictures on *in vitro* fertilisation:

> is an extraordinarily harsh message to thousands of women who have been through the long trauma of trying to conceive and who may well feel that the ultimate test of conjugal love is the determination needed to overcome all medical obstacles to have a child,[8]

not to mention all those parents who are not married at all. But for present purposes, I wish merely to point out that Kirkup's translation of the sentence ending with the words *étreintes conjugales* into the following English:

> Zaza had a precocious understanding of why Madame Mabille had hated the first night of her marriage and had loathed *her husband's embraces* (my emphasis) ever since[9]

fails dramatically to capture the nuances, and in particular the moral undertones, of the Catholic vernacular which Beauvoir so effortlessly employs.

The works mentioned at the outset, viz. *The Second Sex, Memoirs of a Dutiful Daughter, When Things of the Spirit Come First*, and *A Very Easy Death*, positively bristle with words and phrases which are drawn from the Catholic lexicon. The following is a list of these same words and phrases, a list which has no pretensions to being exhaustive: 'the Virgin', 'limbo', 'the Infant Jesus', 'beatification', 'Lenten procession', 'fruit of thy womb', 'the confessional', 'His glory', 'the gospel', 'the will of God', 'Calvary', 'Benediction' (*salut*, which Kirkup translates as 'compline'), 'submission', 'pleasures of the body', 'resignation', 'appetites', 'revelation', 'forgiveness', 'pharisaiasm', 'sacraments', 'missal', 'mortal sin', 'conjugal relations' (*étreintes conjugales*, which Kirkup translates as 'the embraces of her husband'), 'Holy Communion', 'Confession', 'miracles', 'sacred', 'celibacy', 'the soul', 'sermons', 'Mass', 'offering up', 'immodesty', 'illicit', 'the body', 'that immaculate host, the soul', 'chastity', 'the Incarnation', 'damned', 'pray for my salvation', 'resigned', 'sacrifice', 'charity', 'body and soul', 'devotion', 'exhaltation', 'a vocation', 'renewed my vows', 'flesh and blood', 'hymns' (*cantiques*, translated by Kirkup as 'canticles'), 'litanies', 'psalms', 'prophecies', 'sanctified', 'the spirit', 'grace', 'blessed', 'renunciation', 'a soul in mortal peril', 'saved from damnation', 'worship', 'apostle', 'received Holy Communion', 'went on retreat', 'Mary Magdalen', 'martyrs', 'hope', 'faith', 'mystery', 'forsake', and 'eternity'. These words and phrases do more than describe a form of life; they are also constitutive of the uniquely Catholic experience. In many cases they refer to experiences which only Catholics enjoy; in such cases they mark out activities which only Catholics engage in; they fashion a world which Catholics alone inhabit. This is the world in which Simone de Beauvoir grew up, and which she describes in consummate, exquisite detail in her memoirs and short stories. It is also a world which, in some very real senses she left, and, in other senses now documented in this book, she never left and never could leave behind her.

She ceased in late adolescence (and later than is commonly supposed) to attend the sacraments, but she continued to see the world through Catholic eyes. Her vocabulary remains richly Catholic. Her ongoing obsessions with sex, motherhood, reproduction, death, God, the virtues and vices, the body, and so on, are deeply Catholic. Above all, perhaps, her attitudes remain strikingly Catholic, not least her attitude towards modesty. In a passage which has gone completely unnoticed by Beauvoir scholars, she recalls – soon after she had met Sartre for the first time – that there was nothing 'worldly' in his ambitions. She then informs us that 'He reproved me for making use of (a) religious vocabulary, but he, too, was really seeking "salvation" in literature'.[10] So Sartre not only noticed, but (typically) also 'reproved' Beauvoir for her use of the Catholic vernacular (one which she continues to use in her narrative of the event!). Evidently, and unsurprisingly, he thought it unworthy of a philosophy graduate of the Sorbonne that she should still be viewing the world through Catholic eyes. It is always possible that there was nothing very personal intended by his rebuke, that he (merely) took exception to all religious discourse, Simone de Beauvoir's therefore included. No doubt he did, but it seems more likely that he was reproving *her* for not having outgrown her Catholic inheritance. At all events, it is my contention in this monograph that she never did outgrow her childhood. Her quite intense Catholic formation left an indelible mark on her, and nothing she did or experienced in later life could ever quite extinguish its influence.

II

The second chapter of this monograph begins by describing a typical Catholic childhood in a closed Catholic milieu. It then offers a second insight into this type of religious formation, one derived on this occasion from the Irish novel of the 1960s, particularly the early novels of John McGahern and Edna O'Brien. Then using the memoirs and prose fiction, it documents the account of her Catholic upbringing which Simone de Beauvoir herself has left us. This account is conventionally taken to conclude with the sentence 'The break had been sudden, but complete'. I argue, against this orthodoxy, that this sentence is misleading, not least since Beauvoir continued for some time afterwards to attend the sacraments, for reasons which she herself supplies.

In the second half of the chapter I reflect on the narrative of her Catholic formation, and explore at some length her apparent lack of devotion to the Blessed Virgin. I argue that the most convincing explanation of this surprising detail, which can be given, is that suggested by Julia Kristeva's masterful essay *Stabat Mater*.

Chapter 3 provides a comparative study of the narratives of a Catholic childhood provided by Simone de Beauvoir, Kate O'Brien and Mary McCarthy. I first of all reconstruct Kate O'Brien's account of the formation received by an upper-middle class girl in a boarding convent school in Limerick, and then summarise the account given by Mary McCarthy of her education at a Sacred Heart school in Seattle. In the third and final section I bring together the three narratives of a Catholic childhood supplied by these authors – Simone de Beauvoir, Kate O'Brien and Mary McCarthy – for the purposes of comparison and further comment. In doing so I pay particular attention to the experience of a 'crisis of faith' as chronicled by Beauvoir and McCarthy, as well as to the institutional attempts at fostering vocations in the way that Kate O'Brien documents it.

Chapter 4 begins by distinguishing two different theoretical perspectives on the body, which, following current practices, I call *essentialism* and *constructivism*. Essentialism is the claim that human beings have bodies, that human bodies are sexed, and that we can identify the characteristics of each sex with great precision. Constructivism is the view that gender (the division into feminine and masculine) is socially created and socially sustained. I argue that Beauvoir is an essentialist about sex and a constructivist about gender. Thus, on the one hand, she writes (in *The Second Sex*) that 'The division of the sexes is a biological fact, not an event in human history', while on the other, she also (famously) writes that 'One is not born, but rather becomes a woman'. Chapter 2 examines at length the extent to which Beauvoir is an essentialist about the sexed body, and a constructivist about gender.

Modesty is not a uniquely Catholic virtue, but it is a characteristic Catholic obsession. It is linked in Catholic teaching with an elaborate virtue ethics, which itself belongs to an even more elaborate moral theology. In the fifth chapter I first of all provide an account of the concept of modesty such as it is understood and presented in orthodox Catholic teaching. Then I document the accounts of the modest body, and of modest feelings, which feature extensively in Simone de Beauvoir's writings, but especially in the memoirs and in the early prose fiction. In her memoirs, Beauvoir gives detailed information concerning the Catholic way of regulating sexual behaviour, on this occasion by getting the laity to internalise the virtue of modesty. But it is considerably more interesting to discover that she *adopts* the Catholic attitude towards modesty, as well as towards sexual intimacy, in her prose fiction.

The sixth chapter begins with anecdotal, and then documented, evidence of the Catholic Church's vision of fecundity as the natural end of conjugal love. Simone de Beauvoir's Catholic formation, coupled with her exposure to the large families favoured in the Catholic circles from which she came, gave her many insights into the social and domestic features of fecundity, while writing *The Second Sex* forced her to research the more biological and evolutionary dimensions of reproduction among humans and non-humans alike. Her writing on the subject of pregnancy and fecundity is, I argue, outdated and literally dangerous for the expectant mother. In this chapter on the pregnant body I venture to substantiate all of these claims comprehensively.

To present Beauvoir's stance on abortion, I distinguish between the following two questions:

(1) Is it morally acceptable to procure, or to assist in the procurement, of an abortion?

(2) How should the law, and the Health Services, respond to the demand for abortion?

Question (1) treats abortion as an issue in *personal morality*, while Question (2) treats it as an issue in *social morality*. As I see it, Beauvoir's answer to (1) is: Yes, abortion is morally permissible, even though there are strong moral reasons against it. However, the reasons against it are not those standardly adduced in Catholic moral theology, but are reasons drawn from the feminist ethics which she herself adumbrates in *The Second Sex*. Beauvoir's answer to (2), an answer with which many readers will be vastly more familiar, is that abortion should be fully legalised, and at this end of things she remains, of course, stridently and recusantly anti-Catholic.

The chapter on abortion is divided into the following six sections:

[i] A short history of Catholic teaching on the morality of abortion, especially in the post-war period.

[ii] The account provided in the secondary literature of Beauvoir's views on abortion.
[iii] Beauvoir on abortion in *The Second Sex*.

[iv] A summary of her views on abortion as expressed in her later writings for the pro-choice organization *Choisir*.

[v] A review of the conclusions to be drawn from [iii] and [iv].

[vi] Some tentative remarks on the feminist ethics which is adumbrated in *The Second Sex*, and some speculation on whether there are echoes here of a Catholicism still beckoning from afar.

In chapter eight I set out to provide answers to the following questions:

[i] What is Simone de Beauvoir's theory of punishment?

[ii] Does she make a convincing case for punishment?

[iii] Does she make a convincing case for *capital punishment*?

[iv] How does her theory of punishment, and in particular her stance on the death penalty, compare with that of her contemporary Camus?

[v] Does her theory of punishment – as found in her post-war essay *Oeil Pour Oeil* – synchronise with her other ethical writings of the 1940s?

In reply to these questions I answer:

(a) that her theory of punishment is best described as a social justice theory of punishment;

(b) that she does make a convincing case for punishment;

(c) that she does not make a convincing case for capital punishment;

(d) that her stance on the death penalty is diametrically opposed to that of Camus, and

(e) that her theory of punishment does mesh comfortably with her other ethical writings of the 1940s, though this is neither widely known nor acknowledged.

For someone who so vehemently protested she had rejected God, Simone de Beauvoir wrote an extraordinary amount about Him. She did so in her memoirs, short stories, journal articles, and philosophical monographs. In chapter nine I present a detailed account of Simone de

Beauvoir's understanding of God, and conclude with reflections on her theology. As I perceive it, her theology is, in essence, a paean to the power of faith. Faith precedes reason, first of all, since the truths of religion are compelling only to those who are already convinced, i.e. who place all their trust in God (*Les faits religieux n'étaient convaincants que pour les convaincus*). Second, faith precedes Philosophy, since the content of faith provides a much more reliable guide to the nature of God than do the conclusions of the philosophers. The 'God of the Faithful' (an expression I have coined for these purposes) is the only God with whom the people of God are capable of having a meaningful relationship. This God appears in many guises. He is Lord and Master. He helps and protects. He enlightens and saves. He is a Father whose will always gets done. A wife can confide in Him things she could never repeat even to her husband.

The God that Beauvoir herself seems most comfortable with is the God whose powers are in some way limited by His reliance on His human creatures. She quotes with much approval, in her *Pyrrhus et Cinéas,* the words of the mystic Angelus Silesius, who said 'God needs me, just as I need Him'. This concept of a sovereign, but somehow dependent God, makes many appearances in her writings.

In the tenth and final chapter I focus, and comment on, Simone de Beauvoir's contribution to the philosophical debate about death. A preoccupation with death is something to be noted throughout her writing. In early childhood she learned to distinguish between death and personal extinction, i.e. between death and *her* death, but she could derive immense comfort and reassurance from the promise of eternal life which, as a devout young Catholic, she had been given by her Maker:

> God had given me the promise of eternity: I could not ever cease to see, hear, talk to myself. Always I should be able to say: 'Here I am'. There *could* be no end.

But by the time she was eighteen, Simone was much less confident about the promise of eternity, at least so far as it concerned others. She had watched her uncle Gaston die of 'an intestinal occlusion', and the violence of the despair which this event occasioned 'surprised everyone, including myself'. 'I couldn't bear to think', she says, 'of that despairing glance which my uncle had cast at his wife just before he died, and in which the irreparable was already an accomplished fact'.

Then by the time she comes to compose her lengthy work on aging and the elderly, *Old Age,* she appears to have decisively sided with Sartre.

She quotes, with much approval, Sartre's claim that death is an *unrealizable*, that it is not a possible project for us as human beings. She herself phrases it as follows:

> the for-itself can neither reach death nor project itself towards it; death is the external limit of my possibilities, and not a possibility of my own.

This is eerily reminiscent of Wittgenstein's aphorism that we do not live to experience death. Death is the end of all experience, and one cannot, logically, experience the end of all experience. This is but one of the possible meanings attached to the view, to which Sartre and Simone de Beauvoir both subscribed, that death is not a *natural* occurrence.

Notes

1   The *Index* was abolished in 1967.
2   *Maria Cross*, p. ix.
3   *The Concise Oxford French Dictionary* translates *salut* as follows: '(Cath. liturg.) benediction'. I am informed by my mother that these days committed Catholics do 'The Miraculous Medal', and that Benediction is celebrated far less frequently than in the past.
4   *The Glenstal Book of Prayer*. The Columba Press, 2001. J.C. Whitehouse distinguishes, carefully and usefully, between Catholic *writing* and Catholic *literature*. He sees Catholic writing as 'work intended, whatever its methods and approach, to persuade, influence and perhaps even convince. It is epitomized in theology, apologetics and polemics', *Catholics on Literature*, p. 15. Catholic literature, on the other hand, 'is fundamentally artistic, the fictional expression of idiosyncratic and subjective insights rather than general and analytical ratiocination', *Ibid.* Some of Beauvoir's work belongs to the category of Catholic literature, as Whitehouse has defined this term, but the remainder, I would want to say, while not polemical, amounts to something more than 'the fictional expression of idiosyncratic and subjective insights'.
5   It has been pointed out to me (by Mr Fred Kelly of the Dept. of French, NUI, Galway) that 'as a *grande bourgeoise*', Simone de Beauvoir might well have been directed away from such 'common' Catholic occasions as Benediction. It is true that she received religious instruction in private as a child; but she went to Mass and Communion with her mother in local churches.
6   *Mémoires*, p. 117.

7   See M. Holland, 'The Pope's laws on love and test-tube babies', *The Observer*, 15.3.87. See also '"In vitro fertilisation dehumanises procreation", say bishops', *The Irish Times*, 4 February 1986.

8   *The Observer*, 15 March 1987.

9   *Memoirs*, p. 115.

10 *Memoirs*, p. 342.

Chapter Two

A CATHOLIC FORMATION

Morality which is no particular society's morality is to be found nowhere.

— Alasdair MacIntyre, *After Virtue*, pp 265, 266.

It is a universally known, but equally a universally ignored, fact that Simone de Beauvoir received a strong Catholic formation. Just how strong a Catholic formation she received is a question which has guided the research on which this book is based. That she received such a formation is not open to doubt, not least since she herself documented the experience, in copious detail, in the first volume of her memoirs – *Memoirs of a Dutiful Daughter* – a volume which has had both a very wide circulation and readership. Yet the subject of her Catholicism has received no serious attention from Beauvoir scholars; indeed, a mere mention of Beauvoir's 'Catholicism' can be calculated to evoke venomous responses from some of these same sources. This is not surprising, since quite apart from Beauvoir's status as a feminist icon, she herself has, seemingly, left us in no doubt about the matter. Towards the end of her *Memoirs of a Dutiful Daughter* she declares:

> I came to vehemently detest Catholicism; watching Lisa and Zaza fighting for their lives against 'this self-martyring religion', I was more and more thankful that I had escaped from its clutches.[1]

So there we have it in plain print: she both detested Catholicism and had fled from it. But it is instructive to read the next few lines of the text. She continues:

> in fact, I was still contaminated by it; the sexual taboos still haunted me to such an extent that I longed to become a drug-addict or an alcoholic, but never for a moment did I contemplate sexual indulgence.[2]

We are alerted here to a psychic phenomenon which I propose to explore at length in this book: that Simone de Beauvoir had abandoned Catholicism, but it had not abandoned her. In this chapter I am going to look at the early stages of this psychic odyssey. I shall begin with a very short account – based on personal experience – of growing up in a closed Catholic milieu. Then I shall offer a second, much longer, account of this same formative experience, based on the 'sociological' novels of John McGahern and Edna O'Brien. Then I shall reconstruct the account of a Catholic childhood which Simone de Beauvoir herself has left us. Finally, I shall offer some reflections on this same narrative.

I

A Catholic childhood is spent essentially in three places: in a Catholic home, in a Catholic school, and in the local parish church. Each of these domains of experience imprints itself easily on the mind of a child because of its proximity and pervasiveness: either you are at home, at school, or at Mass, another of the sacraments such as Confession, or at Devotions. Where Catholicism is the religion of the overwhelming majority of the population,[3] where the Catholic Church functions, for all practical purposes, as a State within the State,[4] and where there are really no major cultural alternatives to Catholicism such as television and rock 'n roll, then not only is there no avoiding Catholicism, but the very *idea* of organising life differently will not materialise. The same holds true for any of the major religions, of course, but my concern in this chapter is with the Catholic faith.

Many Catholic homes will have a Catholic name, such as *San Michele, St. Mary's, St. Jude's, Prague,* and *St. Bernadette's.* Catholic hospitals and nursing homes also follow this practice, adopting such names as *The Bon Secours, St. John of God's, The Mater, Calvary,* and *St. Bride's.* Catholic schools are very frequently named after the saints: for example, *St. Ignatius', St. Ita's,* and *St. Jarleth's,* to mention but three. Inside these dwellings and institutions, with their Catholic names on the main door will be encountered, in large or small amounts depending on the level of piety of the occupiers, a representative selection of the Catholic iconography: but especialy pictures of the Sacred Heart, pictures of the Immaculate Heart of Mary, statues of the Blessed Virgin, usually dressed in long flowing robes of light blue and white (and sometimes a miniature one, in a light shade of jade, of our Lady of Lourdes), a Brigid's Cross or some other such devotional object of strictly ethnic origin. During the month of May, children are encouraged to construct small shrines to our Blessed Lady, using cowslips, primroses and especially bluebells for this purpose.

A Catholic education is, in practice, a secular education onto which is grafted a very defined, recurring set of Catholic practices. For example, a prayer is said at the start of each class, and not just at the start of each schoolday. At the Jesuit school which I personally attended for ten years, there was a rosary each day in the Boy' Chapel (in addition to the period of religious instruction), and on Saturdays Mass in the early morning and Benediction at 1 o'clock. Afterwards you were expected to go to Confession, so that your soul would be in a fit state to receive Holy Communion the following day. A full assembly singing of hymns was an integral part of these activities.

In every Catholic education system there are periods of intense activity when it is necessary for children to receive instruction over and above that which they would normally receive in the rudiments of the Catholic faith. These are the months before children make their First Holy Communion, and later their Confirmation. On each occasion they must be able to satisfy the religious authorities that their specifically religious education has reached an appropriate standard for partaking of the sacrament in question. During these months, the children preparing for their First Holy Communion do little else all day long except sing the praises of God, the Virgin Mary, and the Church, as well as engage in endless recitation of prayer and catecheses. At a more advanced educational level, it is customary for three days to be set aside each year for going on retreat, i.e. for engaging in prolonged bouts of prayer, meditation, reading of canonical texts, and listening to homilies on carefully selected topics.

Writing about the novels of John McGahern, John Walsh maintains that:

> their depiction of Irish family life, the claustrophobic press of home
> and Church, the poignant carousel of fieldwork and harvests and
> weddings and funerals and exile ... form the truest picture since
> Joyce of a nation where the Angelus bell calls the people to prayer
> at 6 pm ...[5]

There are at least two manifestations of Catholicism mentioned in this sentence:

> (a) Catholicism understood as a religion which, in ways left unspecified, is
> highly restrictive of people's behaviour; and

> (b) Catholicism understood as the religion of the people.

In this section of this chapter I want to explore the way and the extent to which the Irish novel of the early 60s develops these two concepts of Catholicism. It will be my contention in these pages that the novels in question provide an even more complex sociology of Catholicism than that suggested by Walsh's elegant sentence; it can also be argued – thought I don't propose doing so here – that they also capture the onset of that secularisation which would become almost as endemic in later decades.

Ireland is a Catholic place in the Irish novel of the early 1960s, its Catholicism so deeply embedded and omnipresent that it requires no special attention from the writer. This religion of the people has four main functions:

> (1) It introduces a formal structure into daily existence, particularly in the
> form of set prayers before the start of a meal, and as a way of ending the
> day with the family rosary and the 'trimmings' immediately afterwards.

> (2) It provides a means of social convergence at the end of each working
> week, with the celebration of Sunday Mass, and on special occasions
> throughout the year, such as at Easter and Lent, when there are additional
> religious ceremonies.

> (3) It functions as a moral code, not least by offering a clearly defined
> means of regulating sexual behaviour, curbing sexual excess and, at the
> same time, ensuring the replacement of the population.

> (4) It provides an answer to all of life's deep questions, and in particular
> fortifies people against the ravages of disease and death.

I shall now illustrate some of the ways in which the Irish novel of the early 1960s offers us these images of Catholicism. The main focus will be on John McGahern's *The Barracks*, and Edna O'Brien's *The Country Girls*, but some of the other novels of the period will also be utilised.

The sense of a Catholic place is notified on the very first page of *The Barracks* as follows:

> The bright golds and scarlets of the religious pictures on the walls had faded, their glass glittered now in the sudden flashes of firelight, and as it deepened the dusk turned reddish from the Sacred Heart lamp that burned before the small wickerwork crib of Bethlehem on the mantelpiece.[6]

This sense of a Catholic place finds expression on the second page of *The Country Girls* as follows:

> He was our workman and I loved him. To prove it, I said so aloud to the Blessed Virgin who was looking at me icily from a gilt frame.[7]

The following are some examples of the *formality* that Catholicism introduces into people's lives, as well as the ways in which it encourages social convergence:

> (i) He made the sign of the Cross as he finished his meal. He'd never known mental prayer, so his lips shaped the words of Grace as he repeated them to himself.[8]

> (ii) He took a little cloth purse from his watch pocket and let the beads run into his palms. He put a newspaper down on the cement floor and knelt with his elbows on the table, facing his reflections in the sideboard mirror ... They blessed themselves together and he began: 'Thou, O Lord, will open my lips', 'And my tongue shall announce Thy praise', they responded.[9]

> (iii) And the last prayer, the last terrible acknowledgement, the long iambic stresses relentlessly sledged: 'O Jesus, I must die, I know not where nor when nor how, but if I die in mortal sin I go to Hell for all eternity'.[10]

> (iv) She'd been brought up in the fear of God but what remained most powerful in the memory was the Church services, always beautiful, especially in Holy Week; witnessed so often in the same unchanging pattern that they didn't come in broken recollections but flowed before the mind with the calm and grace and reassurance of all ritual, a nameless priest in black and white moving between the stations of the Cross with a breviary, the altar boys in scarlet and white and the lights of the candles they carried glowing on the young faces, a small crowd beneath the gallery in one of those eternal March twilights. That was her religion. The soul went before the Judgement Seat as dramatically after death as it did in the awful scarlet and gold and black of the pictures on the walls in every house, as concretely as the remains that went across the bridge to the graveyard in a motor hearse.[11]

(v) We put on our berets and went in. The chapel was almost dark, except for the light from the sanctuary lamp up near the altar. We prayed for the souls in Purgatory. I thought of Mama and cried for a while. I put my face in my hands so that the girls next to me would think I was praying or meditating or something. I was trying to recall how many sins she had committed from the time she was at Confession to the time she died.[12]

In *The Barracks*, Elizabeth reflects that the ethics enjoined by Catholicism was essentially a matter of keeping the observances, i.e. of going to Mass, Confession and Holy Communion on a regular basis:

Though it had never much to do with their lives, except the observances they had to keep: if they kept these their afterlife was as surely provided for as toil and marriage and care and a little luck would provide for the one here on earth. Everything was laid out and certain, no one needed to ask questions, and there was nothing to offer anyone who stumbled outside its magic circle.[13]

In her first novel, however, Edna O'Brien gives a far more definite content to Catholic ethics than McGahern. In addition to the observances, there was also the practice of the virtues, especially the virtue of *modesty*. Females, in particular, were obliged to keep hidden what ought not to be revealed:

The new girls won't know this, but our convent has always been proud of its modesty. Our girls, above anything else, are good and wholesome and modest. One expression of modesty is the way a girl dresses and undresses. She should do so with decorum and modesty ... Upstairs, the senior girls have separate cubicles; but, as I say, in an open dormitory like this, girls are requested to dress and undress under the shelter of their dressing-gowns. Girls should face the foot of the bed, doing this, as they might surprise each other if they face the side of the bed.[14]

For adolescent males, the great sin was masturbation, the details of which had to be confessed to a priest:

'Were there impure actions with yourself or someone else?'
'With myself, father'.
'You deliberately excited yourself?'
'Yes, father'.
'Did you cause seed to come?'
'Yes, father'.
'How many times?'
'Sometimes seven or eight times and other times not at all, father'.
'Could you put a number on them?'
'More than two hundred times'.
'And the thoughts?'
'More times than the actions, father', it was all out now, one pouring river of relief.

'That is all you have to tell, my child?'

'That's all father'.

'You must fight that sin, it'll grip you like a habit if you don't, if you don't break it now you may never be able to break it. You must come often to Confession. Come every week if you can. You must pray for grace. You must make up your mind to break that sin once and for all now, tonight. Confession is worthless if you're not firmly decided on that'.[15]

When Edna O'Brien's heroines are in their late teens one of them takes up with a separated, but still married, much older man in Dublin. She receives the following lecture in correct behaviour from the parish priest when she visits home:

'You are walking on the path of moral damnation'. 'Why, Father?' I said, quietly, folding my hands on my lap to try to look composed. I longed to cross my legs but still held to the belief that it was disrespectful. 'This man is dangerous company. He has no faith, no moral standards. He married a woman and then divorced her – whom God hath joined together, let no man put asunder', he said.[16]

The final function of Catholicism, as it is presented here, is to bring a human life to a fitting end on earth. This is accomplished in the following two ways chiefly:

(i) by the performance of recognized rituals, such as the anointing of the dying, and

(ii) by offering a system of beliefs in which members of the faithful can find their deepest questions about life and death answered.

In Elizabeth's case, we are told the following:

The priest came constantly and soon after she'd been taken bad he gave her Extreme Unction, it seemed awful ordinary, the touching of nostrils and eyes and ears and lips, the hands and feet with the yellow oil, smell of the 65 per cent wax candles burning, the wooden crucifix, the vessel of ordinary water, the host in the little pyx on the table.[17]

As she approaches her end, she reflects repeatedly on her situation, sometimes in religious terms, such as the following:

Christ on the road to Calvary, she on the same road; both in sorrow and in ecstasy; He to save her in Him, she to save herself in Him – both to be joined forever in Oneness. She'd gone to these devotions all her life, she'd only once fallen away, some months of bitterness in London. She saw her own life declared in them and made known, the unendurable pettiness and degradation of her own failings raised to dignity and meaning in Christ's passion; and always the ecstasy of individual memories breaking like a blood-vessel, elevated out of the accidental moment of their happening and reflected eternally in the mirror in this way.[18]

III

When I say, then, that Simone de Beauvoir had a Catholic childhood, what I am saying is that this is the kind of world in which she was reared; in the words of Hans Küng, this is the kind of 'faith movement' that formed her.[19] These narratives of the Catholic formative experience, and others which I propose to provide in the next chapter, are intended also to authenticate the account of her childhood that Beauvoir has left us.

In the first volume of her memoirs Simone de Beauvoir speaks of her 'Catholic upbringing',[20] and how it had taught her 'never to look upon any individual, however lowly, as of no account'.[21] Everyone, she continues, in a tone at once religious and metaphysical, 'had the right to bring to fulfilment what I called their eternal essence'.[22] Later, writing about Maurice Merleau-Ponty, she observes that they had much in common; 'Brought up, like myself, in a pious home', she explains, 'and now an unbeliever, he had been branded by Christian morality'.[23] As she closes the first volume of her memoirs, she reflects on her strong residual resistance to, her 'virtuous revulsion' of, 'the things of the flesh', and she then draws attention to the following lines in her diary:

> Is it my Catholic upbringing which has left me with such a fixation on purity that the slightest allusion to fleshly things causes me this idescribable distress? I think of Alain Fournier's Colombe, who drowned herself in a lake before she would sully her purity. But perhaps that is pride.[24]

In these pages I wish to reconstruct and explore Beauvoir's account of her 'Catholic upbringing'. What was it like, for her, to be brought up 'in a pious home' and how did this experience mark her in later life? The general argument of this book is that while she would cease to be a practising Catholic, she would remain a Catholic in other crucial ways, continuing, for instance, to see the world through Catholic eyes. In a passage which has gone completely unnoticed by Beauvoir scholars, she recalls – soon after she had met Sartre for the first time – that there was nothing 'worldly' in his ambitions. She next informs us that 'He reproved me for making use of (a) religious vocabulary, but he, too, was really seeking "salvation" in literature'.[25] So Sartre not only noticed, but also 'reproved' Beauvoir for her use of the Catholic vernacular: evidently, and understandably, he thought it unworthy of a former student of Philosophy at the Sorbonne that she should still be observing the world through Catholic eyes. It is not clear whether he took exception to religious discourse as such, or whether he was reproving *her* for not having outgrown her Catholic inheritance. Probably both. At all events, I shall argue that she never completely outgrew her childhood influences, no more than any of us do. Yet to make this claim a convincing one it is essential to document the Catholic experience which she actually had.

As soon as she could walk, confides Simone de Beauvoir, her mother had taken her to church, where she had been shown:

> in wax, in plaster, and painted on the walls, portraits of the Child Jesus, of God the Father, of the Virgin, and of the angels, one of which, like Louise, was assigned exclusively to my service. My heaven was constellated with a myriad benevolent eyes.[26]

In October 1915, when she was over five and a half years of age, she was sent to school, a private Catholic 'secondary top' 'with the alluring name of Le Cours Désir',[27] and 'More or less affiliated to the Jesuit order'.[28] She remembers her first day at school, as many of us do, for the kind of solemnity with which she was introduced to the Principal:

> The head of the elementary classes, Mademoiselle Fayet, received me in an awe-ispiring study with padded doors. All the time she was talking to my mother, she kept stroking my hair. 'We are not governesses', she explained, 'but educators'.[29]

Beauvoir had looked forward with intense eagerness to going to school because, she used to surmise, it would give her a certain independence from home, 'a life of my own'. She was not, she claims, disappointed by school:

> Every Wednesday and Saturday I participated in an hour-long ceremony whose almost religious pomp transfigured the whole week. The pupils took their places round a large oval table; the gathering was presided over by Mademoiselle Fayet, enthroned in a sort of professorial chair; from the rarefied heights of her gilded frame, Adeline Désir, our foundress, a stony-faced lady with slightly hunched shoulders who was in the process of beatification, gazed down upon us.[30]

But there would be no escaping her mother, for on these self-same occasions:

> Our mothers, installed on black imitation leather settees, did their embroidery or their knitting. According to whether we had been more or less well-behaved they bestowed good-conduct notes upon us which we had to give out at the end of the lesson. Mademoiselle

entered them in her register. Mama always gave me ten out of ten: to give me only nine would have brought, we felt, disgrace upon us both.[31]

In return for these good-conduct notes, the pupils received either 'Excellent' or 'Satisfactory' tokens from Mlle Fayet, and at the end of term were rewarded with gilt-edged prize books for having amassed a sufficiency of these same tokens. Moreover, as she was precocious, the young Simone quickly went to the head of the class:

> I could read and write already, and count a little: I was the star turn of the 'O' class. Towards Christmas, I was garbed in a white robe bordered with gold braid and represented the Infant Jesus: all the other little girls had to come and bend the knee before me.[32]

She loved the academic life of school, coming to view the world depicted in books as the truly real world, unlike the messy, imperfect world outside:

> The gospel story seemed to me much more amusing than Perrault's fairy-tales because the miracles it related had really happened. The maps in my atlas enchanted me. I was moved by the solitude of islands, by the boldness of promontories, by the fragility of those tenuous stips of land that connect peninsulas to continents ... The world of severe and unimaginable shapes, of stories firmly carved in the marble of the centuries, was an album of brilliantly coloured pictures that I looked at with rapturous delight.[33]

When war was declared, she became 'an adorable little patriot',[34] standing in her sky-blue overcoat, with a collection box:

> outside the door of a Franco-Belgian institution on the grand boulevard which was run by a friend of my mother.

She also:

> walked in procession with other little girls in the basilica of the Sacré-Coeur, singing and waving the sacred banner of St Denis. I offered up litanies and recited endless rosaries as special intentions for our dear, brave lads at the front.[35]

One section of the school had been fitted out as a hospital, so that the usual stale odour of lead pencil and stacked, new copybooks was replaced by:

> an edifying pharmaceutical odour mingled with the smell of floor polish. Under the white head-dresses, neatly spotted with blood, our teachers looked like saints and I was deeply moved when they kissed my forehead.[36]

This air of saintliness was contagious. The young Simone:

> hit on the idea of putting in a box all the nice things I was given to eat: when it was full of stale cakes and slightly mouldy chocolate and dry prunes, Mama helped me wrap it up nicely and I took it to the ladies of mercy. They took care not to thank me too effusively, but I couldn't help overhearing some very flattering whispers.[37]

Now was also the time to abandon the tendency to capricious rages which had so marked her very early childhood, and to graduate to the life of Catholic virtue. She was taken in hand by the chaplain at the Cours Désir, and under his tutelage became 'an exemplary little girl'.[38] The chaplain, Abbé Martin, 'was young, pale, infinitely suave'.[39] He played a significant role in her Catholic formation:

> He taught me my catechism, and introduced me to the sweet delights of confession. I knelt down before him in a little chapel and replied to his questions and promptings with dramatic fervour. I can't think what I could have told him, but, in the presence of my sister, who told me about it later, he congratulated Mama upon the radiant beauty of my soul.[40]

Like all good Catholic children she wanted, needed, her soul to be whiter than white. As she puts it herself:

> I fell in love with this soul which I imagined to be white and shining like the host itself, exposed in a silver monstrance. I piled up good deeds. Abbé Martin distributed to us at the beginning of Advent pictures representing the Infant Jesus: whenever we did a good deed we had to prick with a pen the outline of a figure, which was drawn in violet ink. On Christmas Day, we had to go and place our pictures round the crib at the end of the church, where the light played through the pin-prick holes. I invented every kind of mortification, sacrifice and edifying behaviour in order that my picture might be richly bedight with pinpricks.[41]

She also became a member of a children's sodality, with the alluring name of 'The Angels of the Passion'. [*Les anges de la Passion*] [42] Membership of this prayer group conferred on her:

> the right to wear a scapular, and it was my duty to meditate upon the seven sorrows of Our Lady.[43]

She prepared for her First Holy Communion in private, she declares, 'In accordance with the recent instruction of Pius X'.[44] In practice, this meant going on retreat. She gives the briefest description of the day itself and, unlike her counterparts in other Catholic jurisdictions, its associations for her are strictly devotional and sartorial:

Dressed in white tulle with my head covered with a veil of Irish lace, I swallowed my first consecrated wafer.[45]

From that day forward, she continues, her mother took her three times a week to communion at Notre-Dame-des-Champs:

In the grey light of early morning, I liked to hear the sound of our feet on the flagged floor of the church. Sniffing the fragrance of incense, my eyes watering with the reek of the candles, I found it sweet to kneel at the foot of the cross and dream vaguely of the cup of hot chocolate awaiting me when we got home.[46]

So it is hardly a surprise that she became, to use her own words, very pious. She provides the following details:

I made my confession twice a month to Abbé Martin, received Holy Communion three times a week and every morning read a chapter of *The Imitation of Christ*; between classes, I would slip into the school chapel and, with my head in my hands, I would offer up lengthy prayers; often in the course of the day I would lift up my soul to my Maker.[47]

She became infatuated with Jesus Christ, the only Son of God, and does not find it embarrassing to describe this infatuation in the language of romantic endearment:

I adored Christ to distraction. As supplements to the Gospels, I had read disturbing novels of which He was the hero, and it was now with the eyes of a lover that I gazed upon His grave, tender, handsome face; I would follow, across hills covered with olive groves, the shining hem of His snow-white robe, bathe His naked feet with my tears; and He would smile down upon me as he had smiled upon the Magdalen.[48]

Each year, she confides, she went on retreat for several days. She gives the following account of this singular event in the Catholic education calendar:

All day long, I would listen to the words of a preacher, go to Mass and Devotions, say my rosary, and meditate: I would remain at school for a frugal repast, and during the meal someone would read to us from the life of a saint. In the evenings at home, my mother would respect my silent meditations. I wrote down in a special notebook the outpourings of my immortal soul and my saintly resolutions. I desperately wanted to grow closer to God, but didn't know how to go about it. My conduct left so little to be desired that I could hardly be any better than I already was.[49]

The next logical step was to submit her entire life to God and the Church; in short, to become a nun. The thought did, in fact, cross her mind:

> It suddenly became obvious to me one morning that a Christian who was convinced of his eternal salvation ought not to attach any importance to the ephemeral things of this world. How could the majority of people go on living in the world as it was? The more I thought about it, the more I wondered at it. I decided that I, at any rate, would not follow their example: my choice was made between the finite and the infinite. 'I shall be a nun', I told myself. The acitivities of sisters of charity seemed to me quite useless; the only reasonable occupation was to contemplate the glory of God to the end of my days. I would become a Carmelite ... I knew that an implacable logic led me to the convent: how could you prefer having nothing to having everything?[50]

But there was another side to her nature, which she herself calls masochistic, that sometimes drove her to seek not just union with God, but martyrdom; moreover, she sought not a silent or unrecognized martyrdom, but a suffering which would become the stuff of legend:

> The majority of real or legendary heroines – Saint Blandine, Joan of Arc, Griselda, Geneviève de Brabant – only attained to bliss and glory in this world or in the next after enduring painful sufferings inflicted on them by males. I willingly cast myself in the role of victim. Sometimes I laid stress upon her spiritual triumphs: the torturer was only an insignificant intermediary between the martyr and her crown ... At times I was a nun confined in a cell, confounding my jailer by singing hymns and psalms. I converted the passivity to which my sex had condemned me into active defiance.[51]

But she also enjoyed the pain, or at any rate the fact that it was sure to be pleasing to her Maker:

> But I often found myself revelling in the delights of misfortune and humiliation. My piety disposed me towards masochism: prostrate before a blond young god, or, in the dark of the confessional with suave young Abbé Martin, I would enjoy the most exquisite transports: the tears would pour down my cheeks and I would swoon away in the arms of the angels. I would whip up these emotions to the point of paroxysm when, garbing myself in the blood-stained shift of Saint Blandine, I offered myself up to the lions' claws and to the eyes of the crowd.[52]

Sometimes this sacrificial masochism transmutes comfortably into the imagery of hard-core pornography:

> I was always extraordinarily moved by the fate of that captive king whom an oriental tyrant used as a mounting block; from time to

time, trembling, half-naked, I would substitute myself for the royal slave and feel the tyrant's sharp spurs riding down my spine.[53]

This sado-masochistic reverie reappears in the short story entitled *Marcelle*, about which Beauvoir said:

> I had come to realize that when I was a child there was a very close connection between my piety and the masochism of some of my games. I had also learnt that the most devout of my aunts used to make her husband whip her heartily by night. I had fun drawing a picture of piety gradually shading off into shameless appetite.[54]

Marcelle's favourite heroine is the woman who, though cruelly and harshly treated by her master, eventually wins his heart by her submission and forbearance. She imagines this heroine in a variety of guises, but more often than not in the role of a woman quivering with repentance at the feet of a sinless, beautiful and terrible man:

> He had the right of life and death over her, and she called him 'Lord': he made her strip herself naked before him, and he used her body as a step when he mounted his splendidly decked charger. With a sensuous delight she drew out this moment of feeling the harsh spur flay her servile back as she knelt there, her head bowed, her heart full of adoration and passionate humility. And when the stern-eyed avenger, vanquished by pity and by love, laid his hands over her head as a sign of forgiveness she clasped his knees in an exquisite swoon.[55]

Writing about her loss of faith in the first volume of her memoirs, Beauvoir says that 'The break had been sudden, but complete'.[56] But this short sentence is a bit misleading. In truth, she ceased going to confession to Abbé Martin. He had scolded her one day in the confessional about her behaviour at home, and only then did it dawn on her, to her horror, that this was not God's representative to whom she was confessing her sins, but her mother's secret ally. She left the confessional, she says, 'determined never to set foot in it again'. But she did go to confession again, to Abbé Roulin:

> I went back to Saint-Sulpice, kneeled down at his confessional, and told him I had not partaken of the sacraments for several months because I had lost my faith.

The priest was astounded, she says, and with a disconcerting brutality asked her:

> 'What mortal sin have you committed?' I protested that I had not committed any sin. He did not believe me and advised me to pray hard. I resigned myself to the life of an outcast.[57]

In the fictional narrative of these same events which is provided by the short story *Marguerite*, the eponymous heroine remarks that she was sick of these spiritual consultations. But there was more to come:

> That same year I went through my terminal classes with a fat, apopleptic priest who thought me cold-hearted and sceptical; without suspecting it, he certainly helped liquidate the last vestiges of religion in me.[58]

Like many other ex-Catholics, Beauvoir did not have the choice of immediately ceasing to practise her faith; social circumstances dictated that any loss of faith would not be accompanied by a change of behaviour. As she puts it herself, at greater length:

> The awkwardness of my situation was aggravated by dissimulation: I still went to Mass and took Holy Communion. I would swallow the host with complete indifference, and yet I knew that, according to the faith, I was committing a sacrilege. I was making mine all the worse by concealing it; but how could I have dared confess it? I would have been pointed at with the finger of scorn, expelled from the school; I would have lost Zaza's friendship; and how terribly upset my mother would have been! I was condemned to live out a lie. It was no harmless fib: it was a lie that cast a shadow over my whole life, and sometimes – especially with Zaza, whose forthrightness I admired – it weighed upon my spirits like a secret disease.[59]

IV

To anyone brought up as a Catholic there is much that is excessively, and even painfully, familiar in Simone de Beauvoir's narrative of her Catholic formation. The alliance between church, school and home in the provision of a Catholic education, the nearly sole responsibility assumed by the mother for the inculcation of the faith in the home, the arduous preparation for making First Confession and First Holy Communion, the annual retreats, the processions, the rosary, confession, the intensity of the meditations on the Holy, and on Christ, the abhorrence of anything remotely sexual: these experiences are universally constitutive of the uniquely Catholic formation. One can even get the *smell* of Catholicism from her description of the churches:

> on holidays Mme Drouffe took her to admire the wax Infant Jesuses in their cradles or to breathe in the scent of the shrines.[60]

While her formidable mother took sole responsibility for the transmission in the home of the Catholic inheritance, apparently this responsibility did not extend as far as the furnishing of the apartment. At any rate there is no reference, either in the memoirs or in the short stories, to Catholic iconography in the home. There is nothing, for instance, to compare with the following description of an Irish Catholic home, given in Frank McCourt's memoir *Angela's Ashes*:

> There are two pictures, the Sacred Heart of Jesus and the Immaculate Heart of Mary. Jesus is showing His heart with the crown of thorns, the fire, the blood. His head is tilted to the left to show his great sorrow. The Virgin Mary is showing her heart and it would be a pleasant heart if it didn't have that crown of thorns. Her head is tilted to the right to show her sorrow because she knows her Son will come to a sad end.[61]

There are some further interesting omissions. I am unable to locate any reference to the Friday abstinence from meat, the Lenten fast, Holy Days of Obligation, Hours of Adoration, or the twelve-hour fast before Holy Communion the following morning. Neither is there any reference to Confirmation, the third of the sacraments of Catholic initiation. In post-war Ireland this was a sacrament of great significance. By means of it you graduated to becoming 'a soldier of Christ', or as the *New Catechism* puts it:

> it gives us a special strength of the Holy Spirit to spread and defend the faith by word and action as true witnesses of Christ, to confess the name of Christ boldly, and never to be ashamed of the Cross.[62]

Lourdes has a special place in the collective psyche of the Irish. Holidays abroad during the heyday of Catholicism were frowned upon, since foreign travel – other than for the purpose of emigration – implied an interest in unalloyed pleasure. But a pilgrimage, with its twin associations of pleasure and pain, was tolerated. Lourdes met these purposes admirably, combining as it did foreign travel with prayer, and continuous exposure to the sick, the disabled, and the dying. As described in one contemporary report:

> Hundreds of infirm, some so ill or near death that they cannot sit up, are borne on bier-like stretchers – so much sadness and hope and so few miracles.[63]

Simone de Beauvoir mentions Lourdes on three occasions in the first volume of her memoirs. Her best friend Zaza's family went to Lourdes each year, she confides:

> on the occasion of the national pilgrimage ... the boys served as stretcher bearers; the girls washed dishes in hospital kitchens.[64]

The next reference to Lourdes occurs as part of the account of her loss of faith. She had lost her faith in her confessor, but her faith in God had remained intact, if only just. Her father, she reports, was not a believer; indeed 'the greatest writers and the finest thinkers shared his scepticism'.[65] Returning in the same paragraph to the subject of her father's scepticism, she reports him exclaiming 'The greatest miracle at Lourdes is Lourdes itself',[66] which she takes to mean that the truths of religion are convincing only to those who are already convinced. Back then she did not doubt that the Virgin had appeared, 'in a blue and white robe', to Bernadette, but even then she wondered whether she might come to change her mind at some time in the future.

Beauvoir mentions *going* to Lourdes when she was eighteen, though it seems from her narrative that she had not been there before. Before going on to Meyrignac, she says, her sister Hélène and herself spent two days at Lourdes:

> It gave me a shock. Confronted with that ghastly parade of the sick, the moribund, the lame and the goitrous, I made the brutal discovery that the world was not just an expression of the human soul. Human beings had bodies and their bodies were full of suffering. As I followed a procession, indifferent to the squalling of hymns and the sour body-smells of church hens on the loose, I began to feel ashamed of my self-complacency. This human misery was the only truth. I felt vaguely envious of Zaza who, when she went on a pilgrimage to Lourdes, washed the dirty dishes in hospitals.[67]

Yet these confrontations with mortality did not have the effect of restoring her faith; as she puts it herself:

> Tragedy, disguised by grotesquely smiling masks of hope, was here too completely devoid of meaning to make the scales fall from my eyes. For a day or two I supped on horrors; then I took up the threads of my own worried existence again.[68]

As I see it, the most remarkable feature of Beauvoir's memoir of her Catholic childhood is the absence from it of any reference to a devotion to Our Lady. This suggests two possibilities:

(1) The young Simone did not have any special devotion to Our Lady, so that there was simply nothing to record in the memoirs; or

(2) She did have a devotion to Our Lady during her childhood, but chose to suppress this fact in her autobiography.

It is difficult to say which of these two alternatives comes closer to the truth. On the one hand, it would be most unusual for a girl who – by her own words – was very pious and seriously contemplated becoming a nun, *not* to have a devotion to Our Lady. On the other hand, why should she want to suppress all reference to such a devotion when she could so easily have included it among all the other religious baggage she jettisoned in later life?

In her illuminating essay *Stabat Mater*, Julia Kristeva addresses the general question of the rejection of 'the virginal myth' in recent times; but in the early section of her essay, on the construction and power of the cult of the Virgin, she ridicules, in passing, Beauvoir's understanding of the 'virginal maternal'. Among its several accomplishments, she argues, the figure of the Virgin 'also served as a mooring point for the humanization of love'.[69] She explains that:

> It was again in the thirteenth century, that this tendency took shape, producing representations of Mary as a poor, modest, and humble woman as well as a tender, devoted mother. Pietro della Francesca's celebrated *Nativity*, now in London, which Simone de Beauvoir was too quick to see as a defeat for women because it depicts a mother kneeling before her new-born son, actually epitomizes the new cult of humanist sensibility. For the high spirituality that assimilated the Virgin to Christ, the painting substitutes an altogether human image of a mother of flesh and blood. Such maternal humility has inspired the most widespread of pious images and comes closer than early images to women's real-life experience.[70]

There is possibly an answer here to my earlier question. The answer is not the more obvious one that the young Simone de Beauvoir could not sustain a devotion to an icon of female submissiveness, but that an altogether human image of a flesh and blood mother might just have been *too human* for the young Simone. It would have had associations with her own mother, to whom she could not possibly have been devoted. Indeed, her relationship with her own mother was so distressful for her that, according to her sister Hélène, it was one of the reasons that neither sister had children of her own.

Kristeva's essay supplies yet a third possible explanation of Beauvoir's lack of devotion to Our Lady. It was not that Marian iconography depicted female submissiveness, nor that its associations with her own mother were so uncomfortably close as to make any strong attachment to Our Lady impossible. According to Kristeva:

> a woman rarely ... experiences passion – love or hate – for another woman, without at some point taking the place of her mother – without becoming a mother herself and, even more importantly, without undergoing the lengthy process of learning to differentiate herself from her own daughter, her simulacrum, whose presence she is forced to confront.[71]

It may seem far-fetched to claim that Beauvoir lacked a devotion to Our Lady because it would have meant confronting an image of *herself* as mother. Yet we know from her memoirs that she violently resisted this very image from a very early age. Recalling her childhod games at Meyrignac, she maintains that she accepted the role of mother on condition that she be allowed to disregard its nursing aspects. On such occasions she refused to allow a man, even an imagined man, to come between her and her imagined maternal responsibilities. Then she writes:

> In real life, I knew, things were quite different: the mother of a family is always flanked by her mate; she is overburdened by a thousand tiresome tasks. Whenever I thought of my own future, this servitude seemed to me so burdensome that I decided I wouldn't have any children; the important thing for me was to be able to form minds and mould characters: I shall be a writer, I thought.[72]

These words were published some forty years after she had the thoughts they contain. Yet it is a position from which she never wavered throughout her life. She did not want to be a mother. In these circumstances, devotion to the mother of all mothers, the mother of God, would have been a grotesque hypocrisy.

Notes

1   *Mémoires d'une jeune fille rangée*, p. 308. I have made my own translation here because, *pace* Kirkup, Catholics do not refer to themselves as Roman Catholics.
2   *Memoirs of a Dutiful Daughter*, p. 308.
3   By 'Catholicism', 'Catholic', etc., I mean the system of beliefs professed by the Catholic Church, and the system of practices, such as receipt of the sacraments, based on such beliefs. A Catholic is someone who holds such beliefs and engages in such practices, beginning with the sacrament of Baptism.
4   A situation which prevailed in Ireland during the inter-war, and post-war years until about the mid-60s.
5   *The Sunday Times*, 29 April 1990.
6   *The Barracks*, p. 7.
7   *The Country Girls*, p. 6.
8   *The Barracks*, p. 16.
9   *Ibid.*, p. 28.
10 *Ibid*, p. 31
11 *Ibid.*, p. 102.

12   *The Country Girls*, p. 92. See also p. 75.

13   *The Barracks*, p. 102.

14   *The Country Girls*, p. 77.

15   *The Dark*, pp. 41, 42.

16   *Girl With Green Eyes*, p. 100.

17   *The Barracks*, p. 178.

18   *Ibid.*, p. 161.

19   See Hans Küng, 'Christianity: A Drama Still Unfolding', *The Irish Times*, 31 January, 2000.

20   *Memoirs of a Dutiful Daughter*, p. 191.

21   *Ibid.*

22   *Ibid.*

23   *Ibid.*, p. 246.

24   *Ibid.*, p. 289.

25   *Ibid.*, p. 342.

26   *Ibid.*, p. 9.

27   *Ibid.*, p. 21.

28   *Ibid.*, p. 122.

29   *Ibid.*, p. 21.

30   *Ibid.*, pp. 21, 22.

31   *Ibid.*, p. 22.

32   *Ibid.*

33   *Ibid.*

34   *Ibid.*, p. 28.

35   *Mémoires*, p. 31. This is my own translation.

36   *Memoirs*, p. 28.

37   *Ibid.*, p. 29.

38   *Ibid.*

39   *Ibid.*

40   *Ibid.*

41   Ibid.

42   *Ibid. [Mémoires*, p. 33]

43   *Ibid.*

44   *Ibid.*

45   *Ibid.*

46   *Ibid.*, pp. 29, 30.

47   *Ibid.*, p. 73.

48   *Ibid.*

49   *Mémoires*, p. 75.

50   *Memoirs*, p. 75.

51   *Ibid.*, p. 57.

52   *Ibid.*, pp. 57, 58.

53   *Ibid.*, p. 58.

54   *When Things of the Spirit Come First*, p. 7.

55   *Ibid.*, p. 11.

56   *Memoirs of a Dutiful Daughter*, p, 135.

57   *Ibid.*, pp. 139, 140.
58   *When Things of the Spirit Come First*, p. 163.
59   *Memoirs*, p. 139.
60   *When Things of the Spirit Come First*, p. 7.
61   *Angela's Ashes*, p. 176.
62   *Catechism of the Catholic Church*, p. 294.
63   J. Keegan, 'Faith is the real miracle', *The Sunday Independent*, 24 August
      1997.
64   *Memoirs of a Dutiful Daughter*, p. 117.
65   *Ibid.*, p. 136.
66   *Ibid.*
67   *Ibid.*, p. 206.
68   *Ibid.*, pp. 206, 207.
69   *The Female Body in Western Culture*, p. 107.
70   *Ibid.*, pp. 107, 108.
71   *Ibid.*, p. 116.
72   *Memoirs*, p. 56.

Chapter Three

MEMORIES OF A CATHOLIC CHILDHOOD: SIMONE DE BEAUVOIR, KATE O'BRIEN AND MARY MCCARTHY

There are some strong parallels between Simone de Beauvoir's memories of a Catholic childhood and those of other female authors who had, and in some cases enjoyed, a similar experience.[1] But the most striking resonances are those which can be located in Kate O'Brien's autobiographical novel *The Land of Spices* (1941), and Mary McCarthy's *Memories of a Catholic Girlhood* (1957). In this chapter I propose to offer a comprehensive study of these three authors from the perspective mentioned, viz. their recollections of a Catholic girlhood. I shall first of all reconstruct Kate O'Brien's account of the formation received by a middle class girl in a boarding convent school in Limerick, and then summarise the account given by Mary McCarthy of her education at a Sacred Heart convent school in Seattle. In the third and final section I shall bring together the three sets of memoirs – those of Simone de Beauvoir, Kate O'Brien and Mary McCarthy – for the purposes of comparison and further comment. In doing so I will pay particular attention to the account of a 'crisis of faith' which is furnished by these authors, and to the different institutional responses to such a crisis.

Kate O'Brien, *The Land of Spices* (1941)

Literary critics are unanimous in regarding Kate O'Brien's *The Land of Spices* as the most autobiographical of all her works of prose fiction, and independent support for this perception can be found in the handful of printed pages that go under the title 'Memories of a Catholic Education: A Fragment from Kate O'Brien's Last Work', first published in *The Tablet*, 4 December 1976. The basic justification for the claim that *The Land of Spices* is O'Brien's most autobiographical work is the fact that its chronological narrative parallels in very close detail her own primary and secondary education with the nuns at Laurel Hill. Clare Boylan, another Irish novelist, gives the salient details as follows:

> Her own mother died of cancer in 1903 when she was six and her father thought that life would be less lonely for her if she joined her older sisters at Laurel Hill boarding school, a convent of a French order, The Faithful Companions of Jesus. This convent was the model for the order of the Compagnie de la Sainte Famille, even down to the English Reverend Mother, who was considered something of a cold fish, but who won Kate's immediate allegiance by telling her that they had to order a special small chair for her and had asked for three to be sent on approval so that she could choose one for herself. The school was viewed with suspicion locally because the children were taught languages other than Irish and both nuns and pupils drank real coffee. Like Anna, Kate O'Brien won a university scholarship and was pressured by her family into taking a 'decent' job in a bank instead. She went to college, got her degree, and was outraged when a waggish uncle sent a letter of congratulations which ended: 'I wonder what the next step will be – M.A. or Ma?[2]

The novel provides an abundance of information about the nuns at *Sainte Famille* (the fictional analogue of Laurel Hill). They were:

> dressed in black serge, the white coif and the leather girdle that, God willing, would be their fashion until death.[3]

There were two categories of nun, choir nuns and lay nuns. Kate O'Brien doesn't explain this division, but as it happens Edna O'Brien does, in her first novel *The Country Girls:*

> She was so small I thought she'd drop the teapot. She wore a white muslin apron over her black habit. The apron meant that she was a lay nun. The lay nuns did the cooking and cleaning and scrubbing; and they were lay nuns because they had no money or no education

when they entered the convent. The other nuns were called choir nuns.[4]

In additon to there being two classes of nuns at *Sainte Famille*, there was also a chain of command, a hierarchy comprising 'Reverend Mother, Mother Assistant, Mother Scholastic'.[5] Mother Assistant and Mother Scholastic were, in effect, vice-presidents, the lower echelon of senior management at the boarding school. The novel explains their functions as follows:

> The two, subject to Reverend Mother, were the school's intellectual directors, the younger being energetic in the busy general office of Mother Scholastic, and the old nun lecturing rather too well for her green audiences on Church and European history.[6]

The office of Mother Scholastic is further explained as follows:

> The office of Mother Scholastic in the schools of the Order of *Sainte Famille* is an onerous one. Its holder is responsible for time-tables, routine and discipline throughout the school; she is the meter-out of justice, the chief censor of behaviour, the arbitrator between pupil and teacher, the moral director and the gateway to the more detached and august authority of the Reverend Mother. She spends her entire day in active contact with her charges. Though she takes her share in teaching, she is usually elected to office because of qualifications of character and health rather than for intellectual ability.[7]

The novel defines a nun's vocation as 'the impersonal and active service of God'. The Reverend Mother, *Mère Marie-Hélène*, explains the concept of service to God in the following words:

> But vanity lay in exaggeration of surrender – vanity and a wider danger. Possible waste of service. She was a nun in order to serve God – not her capricious self. Such powers as she had were to be stretched and exhausted for His glory, and by no means so as to prove something odd and gratifying about her soul to her waiting vanity. She existed to work at full stretch for the *Compagnie de la Sainte Famille*, not to play a long-drawn game of skill with her own sensibilities.[8]

There is mention in the novel of nuns who were overheard singing at vespers, so we may presume that service to God also entailed observance of the canonical hours. The nuns also celebrated the forty-hours adoration – called *Quarante Ore* – the behind the scenes details of which are given as follows:

> *Quarante Ore* was usually celebrated at *Sainte Famille* during the last week of April, the tradition being that thus a particular blessing was laid on the work of the last term of the scholastic year; also at that

time the garden and greenhouses had fresh beauties to give to the Altar of Repose. The day preceding the forty–hour feast of the Blessed Sacrament was busy for Reverend Mother. Gardener, sacristan and choir mistress all particularly needed her attention, and the *dépense* and kitchen sisters had to be counselled, as the convent served lunch to the priests who celebrated and assisted at the Sung High Mass with which the exposition began and ended. Also, Mother Assistant required her to endorse the time–tables of the two all–night vigils sustained in the chapel by the community, and Mother Scholastic required a like endorsement for the names of the girls allowed to share this vigil. These two sets of arrangements involved debates on health and precedent; the latter also embraced argument as to whether a pupil's recent conduct merited the reward of rising in the night to keep guard for an hour before the Altar of Repose.[9]

The lives of the pupils at *Sainte Femille* were hardly less protocol–bound than those of their teachers and spiritual leaders. The pupils were broadly divided into Preparatory, Junior and Senior, with each of these categories further sub–divided; for example, there was First and Second Preparatory, and so on. They ate their meals in the refectory, and needless to say could not sit just anywhere they pleased. As Kate O'Brien explains:

> The room was lofty and lighted by four large windows; its four long tables were set in oblong, so that if a child came to school young enough to begin at Preparatory Table, she worked her way round the oblong – north to Junior, east to Latin, and finally south and up on to the dais to Foundress's Table, where she sat in honour during her last year under a copy of the portrait of Mère Marie-Félice de Gravons St. Roche.[10]

Behaviour at table, especially at the youngest end of the room, was also strictly supervised:

> Anna Murphy sat at the extreme south-west corner of Preparatory Table; a small hassock placed on her chair raised her to the level of the other children; Mother Josephine sat beside her, at the foot of the table, and peeled her fruit while also controlling the manners and conversation of the nine small girls who sat at the 'little ones' end of Preparatory Table. *La politesse* was a speciality of *Sainte Famille* education, and table manners were therefore tackled thoroughly at Preparatory Table, in particular at the 'little ones' end.[11]

The meal itself was preceded by Grace Before Meals, which by tradition was said in French:

> 'Au nom du Père et du Fils et du Sainte-Esprit, ainsi soit-il …' Grace was said in French, according to Sainte Famille tradition. Already

the strange sound fell familiarly on Anna's ears. Several times a day they danced like a bright, nonsense refrain, across this cavernous foreign life which was so resoundingly big and hard to apprehend, a life of giants. 'Ainsi soit-il' – there it was again – a very bright sound, like a bugle in a street.[12]

The school uniform comprised 'dresses of black cashmere' and 'black stockings'.[13] But on Foundress's Day, they wore:

white silk dresses and scratchy white gloves; the old girls watchful and shy of each other, in carefully chosen dinner-gowns.[14]

However, for Chaplain's Concert, for which the Foundress's Day concert was but a dress-rehearsal:

the white silk dresses were not worn. Instead the girls wore their Sunday black dresses, their prettiest white collars, white gloves – and, curious final touch, wide sashes, tied in great bows at the back, stiff silk sashes, uniformly of brilliant salmon pink ... There was a general feeling that they were diabolically ugly, and they were donned by the girls in a mood of hilarious ribaldry. But in truth their effect was miraculous. In the warmly lit *salle* with its dark red curtains and dark green potted palms, against the black garb of nuns and priests, and worn on black, these flashing, swishing sashes were urbane and gay. They made graceful girls into sylphs; they made the little ones look merry and surprised with themselves; and they lent a mild sophistication even to the plain and large.[15]

For the purposes of leisure-time, the pupils were divided into what were called three 'Recreations', described as follows in *The Land of Spices:*

Girls of the senior classes belonged to the First Recreation; those of Honours Junior, Second Junior and First Preparatory to Second Recreation; and Second Preparatories formed a small band with the courtesy title of Third Recreation. At midday these groups played, on their own playgrounds, the orthodox games: hockey, basket-ball, tennis. But after supper they danced or took whatever exercise they felt inclined for, in winter – and in summer they loafed at their ease, or sewed, or played desultory rounders, under the great trees. A nun took charge of each group or 'recreation', and kept its members within sight and loosely in order.[16]

Another 'institution' at *Sainte Famille* was 'Emulation Holiday'. This was 'a recurrent reward for good-class work, and it had to be earned by a not impossible series of trials'.[17] Rarely more than a quarter of the pupils, we are informed, earned the right to participate in Emulation Holiday, notwithstanding the fact that:

it was always the best of the school holidays, and it could be enjoyed at least once a term by the industrious or the fairly intelligent.

The examination – or should one say competition – for Emulation Holiday was:

> a short written examination on every Sunday morning of term. The subjects of these examinations were normally in rotation: Christian Doctrine, Scripture History, English Literature, History, Geography, and a mathematical subject. Class mistresses marked the papers, and the results were read aloud in the refectory and entered in a register. The maximum of marks was 100; 70 was Honours, 50 a pass. When in a series of six Sundays a girl had achieved 70 or more marks on three papers, and 50 or more on the remaining three, she was eligible to take the last fence for the Emulation Holiday. This fence was a special examination in French, in which 70 marks had to be scored. A surprising number of possibles fell out at this test.[18]

Emulation Holiday itself rewarded the successful examination candidates with an intoxicating mixture of freedom, adventure and luxurious foods:

> On Emulation Day the few who were, presumably, to be emulated, sat together and apart from the rest for their meals at Foundress's Table. These meals were of a very festive character, and were free of the everyday drawback, sustained at the other tables, of French conversation. For the rest, the pleasures of the day were planned with understanding. In summer there would be a picnic, or a steamboat expedition on the lake, with *Mère Martine* and her guitar for added grace; in winter, one of the smaller parlours, with fire and armchairs, was at the disposal of the elect. Toffee and caramels could be bought from the *dépense* Sister; story-books and even some magazines might be read, and there were bagatelle, chess and Happy Families to play. And always, winter or summer, after a supper of onion soup and tipsy cake and elderberry wine, the holiday-makers gathered again in their private parlour and – the fire piled high now, the lights turned out, and the curtains drawn to let moon, sky and lake shine inwards – Mother Eugenia came and took her place in the centre of the semi-circle and told ghost-stories.[19]

In addition to the Sunday morning academic examination, there was a Sunday evening report on the *conduct* of each pupil during the week. This event was held in the *salle d'études:*

> commonly called the *salle* and pronounced 'sal' by the school, [it was] a vast room on the first floor ... Every child had a desk in this room, which was the centre of the school's life. In the wide aisle between the desks the girls assembled many times a day in two graded lines; to be lectured by Mother Mary Andrew, to go to

chapel or the refectory, to sit in a demure 'hairpin' for Reverend Mother's 'deportment' class or for the chaplain's weekly lecture on Christian doctrine. This long, polished pool of space between the desks was the stage for much drama and tension.[20]

The conduct reports were called 'Marks'. Kate O'Brien reports that:

> Waiting for Marks on Sunday evening was a strain on everyone. What her own marks were was hidden from each girl until, her name called by Reverend Mother, she stood up in her place, bowed politely, heard the week's record of her behaviour read aloud, bowed again and sat down.[21]

Marks were awarded for Conduct, Silence, Politeness, Exactitude, Order and Application. Of these, conduct was the most important category, since:

> A mark lost for conduct was tantamount to expulsion; no one remembered it ever to have happened. The school sometimes liked to surmise how it might come about. Perhaps if you *kicked* Reverend Mother? or used some absolutely filthy word? or committed sacrilege?[22]

On such occasions the senior nuns also made public comments on the performance of pupils:

> The ritual went on. Reverend Mother made her customary comments on the bad, the good and the middling. Occasionally she suggested to a girl to stand more erect, or to bow with less contortion. Occasionally she foiled the savageries of Mother Mary Andrew, or softened the too forthright or too snobbish comments of Mother Eugenia on the idiosyncracies of this girl or that.[23]

A reward system also operated for those pupils who had very few marks deducted for failure to honour the school code:

> When the marks had been read silk sashes were distributed to those girls who had lost no more than a total of four marks in the week, and none against politeness. These sashes would be worn in chapel for seven days – across the shoulder, right to left, like secular honours. Anna watched their disposal with delight – and Reverend Mother's ceremonial kiss on the cheek to each recipient. She was glad to see Letitia Doyle arrayed in the broad blue sash of the Seniors. The Junior sash was purple, the Preparatories, scarlet. They were lovely stiff sashes.[24]

In *Sainte Famille* schools the duties of chaplaincy usually fell to 'an old and experienced priest'; but at this *Sainte Famille*, located in a rural parish, the duties of chaplaincy 'fell ex officio on the second curate of the village'. On the other hand, 'Jesuits usually directed the retreats alike of the school and of the community ...'[25]

As she approaches her seventh birthday, Anna is deemed by Reverend Mother to be ready to make her First Holy Communion:

> Well, since she shows understanding of her Catechism, we might let her make her first Confession before Lent. But that can be settled with Father Conroy a little later.[26]

First Communion is preceded by First Confession, and Anna will be given six tutorials on the Sacrament of Penance, to prepare her for her First Confession. She also gets extensive instruction on the Ten Commandments, and when her Christian Doctrine teacher, Mother Felicita, is unable to explain to her the meaning of 'adultery', the young chaplain steps into the breach in a way which:

> had shown perfect understanding of innocence and intelligence, and had spoken to them out of peace and humour, and without a shadow of evasiveness in word or implication.[27]

Sainte Famille provides its pupils with two kinds of education, an academic education where academic progress is tested at the end of each week, and a moral education, the fruits of which are continuously inspected, and also reported on at the end of each week. In *The Land of Spices* special emphasis is laid on the provision of a *moral education*. The school's ethos is summarised as follows by Reverend Mother:

> We educate our children in the Christian virtues and graces ... if the 'changing times' you are so sure of are to have no place for Christian discipline and common politeness, I can only say I'm glad I shall not see very much of them.[28]

Mother Scholastic is particularly severe on 'Insubordination *and* immodesty!' while Reverend Mother singles out cruelty and vulgarity for special condemation:

> For you are here at *Sainte Famille* to learn to live among your fellows as a Christian and a lady, and that cannot be learnt by any of us without tears and humiliations. You have learnt a little about that just now – by your own yielding to impulses of cruelty and vulgarity which far out-strip our usual temptations. But you have so deeply humiliated yourself before us all that I can for the moment imagine no further punishment. I shall speak to you in private for your own sake, of the details of your dreadful fit of self-indulgence. For the moment, since I am sure you could not bear to face your companions, I suggest that you return to the house and go to bed – but on your way upstairs perhaps you will go into the chapel and ask Our Lord to purify your heart and lips.[29]

When Anna is about to leave the school, destined for university, Reverend Mother reflects on her departure, and on what the years at *Sainte Famille* have accomplished, as follows:

> And now all was done that age may do for childhood. Anna's schooldays were closed, and there was no appeal against the advance of life and the flight of innocence. She had been taught to be good and to understand the law. Also, she had been set free to be herself. Her wings were grown and she was for the world. In poverty, in struggle, in indecisiveness – but for some these were good beginnings ... Prayer would follow her; prayer always could. It would have been happy to have been at hand a little longer, to have heard something of the first flights and first returns. But such a wish was nothing. All that could be done was done. Anna was for life now, to make what she could of it. Prayer could go with her, making no weight – and whether or not she remembered 'the days of the poems', an ageing nun would remember them.[30]

II

Mary McCarthy, *Memories of a Catholic Girlhood* (1957)

Mary McCarthy very deliberately calls her book *Memories*, rather than *Memoirs*, of a Catholic girlhood, in deference to the fact that her memory had not always recorded events as extensively, or even as accurately, as she would have wished. She is quick to advise, nonetheless, in the opening prefatory essay entitled 'To the Reader', that she is *not* writing fiction. She then continues:

> Many a time, in the course of doing these memoirs, I have wished that I *were* writing fiction. The temptation to invent has been very strong, particularly when recollection is hazy and I remember the substance of an event but not the details – the colour of a dress, the pattern of a carpet, the placing of a picture. Sometimes I have yielded, as in the case of the conversations. My memory is good, but obviously I cannot recall whole passages of dialogue that took place years ago. Only a few single sentences stand out: '*They'd* make you toe the chalk line', 'Perseverence wins the crown', 'My child, you must have faith'. The conversations, as given, are mostly fictional. Quotation marks indicate that a conversation to this general effect took place, but I do not vouch for the exact words or the exact order of the speeches.[31]

Having lost both her parents at a very young age, McCarthy experienced the extra difficulty, for the purposes of composing her 'memories', of not having available to her the recollections of the previous generation of her immediate family. As she herself very astutely observes:

> The chain of recollection – the collective memory of a family – has been broken. It is our parents, normally, who not only teach us our family history, but who set us straight on our own childhood recollections, telling us that *this* cannot have happened the way we think it did and that *that*, on the other hand, did occur, just as we remember it, in such and such a summer when So-and-So was our nurse.[32]

Because of these obstacles to total, accurate recall, McCarthy adopts a singular methodology in her presentation of her girlhood 'memories'. Having recalled a particular sequence of events, or formative period of her girlhood, one which will of necessity have some degree of invention in it, she then appends a commentary on the 'memory' in which she attempts to separate out the hard facts from the soft, less reliable, invented tissue which it also contains. This methodology carries its own dangers, of course: in particular, one might wonder why we should regard the commentary as always, or necessarily, more reliable than the memory? After all, isn't she falling back on her powers of recollection in both cases?

In the prefatory section addressed to the reader, McCarthy distinguishes broadly between two kinds of Catholicism: a Catholicism which extols an ideal of goodness and beauty, as opposed to the Catholicism of her grandmother's parlour – 'a sour, baleful doctrine in which old hates and rancours had been stewing for generations, with ignorance proudly stirring the pot'.[33] She associates the Catholicism of aesthetic and moral enlightenment with the parish priest who vigorously supported her against her grandmother when she had made known her wish to go to Vassar; and she associates it further with those priests and nuns who, unlike many lay Catholics who wrote angry and poisonous letters to her, assured her of their support, comforted and encouraged her, and gave her what extra assistance they could in the form of prayer and Masses. She remarks that:

> The idea that religion is supposed to teach you to be good, an idea that children have, seems to linger on, like a sweet treble, in their letters. Very few people appear to believe this any more, it is utterly out of style among fashionable neo-Protestants, and the average Catholic perceives no connexion between religion and morality, unless it is a question of someone *else's* morality, that is, of the supposed pernicious influences of books, films, ideas, on someone else's conduct.[34]

For this reason she concludes that religion is good only for people who are already good, and open to its refinements, unlike all those others in whom it is much more likely to foster the very vices it seeks to extirpate, such as pride, anger and sloth.

McCarthy attributes a number of positive features to the religious formation which she received. They are:

(i) the religious milieu in which she was raised provided her with the only *aesthetic* stimulus she received. She received this 'aesthetic outlet', she says:

> in the words of the Mass and the litanies, and the old Latin hymns, in the Easter lilies around the altar, rosaries, ornamented prayer books, votive lamps, holy cards stamped in gold and decorated with flower wreaths and a saint's picture. This side of Catholicism, much of it cheapened and debased by mass production, was for me, nevertheless, the equivalent of Gothic Cathedrals and illuminated manuscripts and mystery plays.[35]

(ii) The Catholic education system was intensely competitive. It gave the academically able the opportunity to excel, and it gave a rising, ambitious underclass the means of social advancement. As she explains:

> A desire to excel governed all my thoughts, and this was quickened, if possible, by the parochial-school methods of education, which were based on the competitive principle. Everything was a contest; our school-room was divided into teams, with captains, for spelling bees and other feats of learning, and on the playground we organized ourselves in the same fashion. To win, to skip a grade, to get ahead – the nun's methods were well adapted to the place and time, for most of the little Catholics of our neighbourhood were children of poor immigrants, bent on bettering themselves and also on surpassing the Protestants, whose children went to Whittier, the public school.[36]

(iii) A Catholic education, she also maintains, gives a certain intellectual advantage to an American student, by exploring the history of states which had Catholic sovereigns or Heads of State, and by getting pupils to care about political rejects and failed constitutional systems. In the latter case, she explains:

> To care for the quarrels of the past, to identify oneself passionately with a cause that became, politically speaking, a losing cause with the birth of the modern world, is to experience a kind of straining against reality, a rebellious nonconformity that, again, is rare in America, where children are instructed in the virtues of the system they live under, as though history had achieved a happy ending in American civics.[37]

She is not particularly bothered by the fact that Catholic history (teaching) is biased, since 'this can always be remedied later', and because its vice can also be turned to advantage: 'its virtue for the student, indeed, is that it has been made to come alive by the violent partisanship which inflames it'.[38]

Mary McCarthy did not receive her entire pre-university education within the Catholic system. Having first attended St. Stephen's (parochial) School in Minneapolis, she then went to a convent boarding-school run by the Ladies of the Sacred Heart at Forest Ridge in Seattle. Then she went to Garfield High, a public high school, but:

> After a year of public high school, my grandparents concluded that there was nothing to do but put me into a boarding-school, away from the distractions offered by the opposite sex. A convent, this time, was not considered; I was old enough now, my grandfather said, to choose for myself in religious matters. An Episcopal boarding-school in Tacoma, the Annie Wright Seminary, was selected ...[39]

McCarthy introduces Forest Ridge as:

> a strict convent school set on a wooded hill quite near a piece of worthless real estate he [her grandfather] had bought under the impression that Seattle was expanding in a northerly direction.[40]

Here the Mother Superior, Madame MacIllvra, appears to have made as big an impression on her as did the English Reverend Mother on Kate O'Brien at Laurel Hill. She recalls at great length two events in which the Mother Superior had played a crucial role:

A Jesuit had declared that all baptised Protestants went straight to Hell. In more elabrate detail:

> A good life did not count in their favour. The baptismal rite, by conferring on them God's grace, made them also liable to His organizational displeasure. That is, baptism turned them Catholic whether they liked it or not, and their persistence in the Protestant ritual was a kind of asseverated apostasy. Thus my poor grandfather, sixty years behind in his Easter duty, actually reduced his prospects of salvation every time he sat down in the Presbyterean church.[41]

Madame MacIllvra, reports McCarthy, 'understood; she was crying for my grandfather and the injustice of it too'. 'It was a measure of Madame MacIllvra's intelligence', she continues:

> or of her knowledge of the world, that she did not, even then, when my grandfather's soul hung, as it were, pleadingly between us, suggest the obvious, the orthodox solution. It would have been ridiculous for me to try to convert my grandfather.[42]

Instead, Madame MacIllvra summoned 'the learned prefect of studies ... the librarian and even the convent chaplain' to her study, and between them they produced the solution:

> The Benedictine view, it seemed, differed sharply from the Dominican, but a key passage in Saint Athanasius seemed to point to my grandfather's safety. The unbeliever, according to this generous authority, was not be to damned unless he rejected the true Church with sufficient knowledge and full consent of the will ... Clearly, he was saved. Sufficient knowledge he had not. The Church was foreign to him ...[43]

The second occasion on which Mother Superior made a very personal intervention – though not one to which the young McCarthy was in every respect receptive – came with the menarche. Having made the necessary sanitary arrangements, the dormitory duty nun arranged also for her to see the Mother Superior in private. McCarthy reports that:

> When I kept breaking in, she hushed me gently, and took me on her lap. Exactly like Mother Slattery, she attributed all my references to the cut to a blind fear of this new, unexpected reality that had supposedly entered my life. Many young girls, she reassured me, were frightened if they had not been prepared. 'And you, Mary, have lost your dear mother, who could have made this easier for you'. Rocked on Madame MacIllvra's lap, I felt paralysis overtake me and I lay, mutely listening, against her bosom, my face being tickled by her white, starched, fluted wimple, while she explained to me how babies were born, all of which I had heard before. There was no use fighting the convent. I had to pretend to have become a woman, just as, not long before, I had had to pretend to get my faith back – for the sake of peace.[44]

McCarthy was a five-day boarder at Forest Ridge, run by the Ladies of the Sacred Heart, who also had an association with the Jesuits. They were a French order founded in the nineteenth century, and their schools were run on the same centralised, protocol-bound lines as the schools of The Faithful Companions of Jesus. McCarthy supplies the following basic information:

> All Sacred Heart convent schools are the same – the same blue serge dresses, usually with white collars and cuffs, the same blue and pink moiré ribbons awarded for good conduct, the same books given as prizes on Prize Day, the same recitation of 'Lepanto' by an English actor in a piped waistcoat, the same congés, or holidays, announced by the *Mère Supérieure*, the same game of *cache-cache*, or hide-and-seek, played on these traditional feast days, the *goûter*, or tea, the same retreats and sermons, the same curtsies dipped in the hall, the same early morning chapel with processions of girls, like widowed queens, in sad black-net veils, the same prie-dieu, the same French hymns ('*Oui, je le crois*'), the same glorious white-net

veils and flowers and gold vessels on Easter and Holy Thursday
and on feasts peculiar to the order.[45]

The nuns at Forest Ridge did not adopt special religious names, but
retained their own:

> I could not get used to the idea that here were nuns who did not
> lose their surnames, as all normal nuns did, becoming Sister Mary
> Aloysia or Sister Josepha, but were called Madame Barclay or
> Madame Slattery, or *Ma Mère* or Mother for short.[46]

These nuns, she was informed, were no ordinary nuns:

> but women of good family, cloistered ladies of the world, just as
> Sacred Heart girls were not *ordinary* Catholics but daughters of the
> best families.[47]

Neither were their subjects ordinary subjects, such as spelling and
arithmetic, 'but rhetoric, French, literature, Christian doctrine, English
history'.[48] And finally, permeating and orchestrating all of convent life,
there was the code of conduct, which McCarthy likens to 'a branch of
civics and conformity'. She gives the following brief elaboration:

> The very austerities of our life had a mysterious aristocratic
> punctilio: the rule of silence so often clapped down on us at
> mealtimes, the pitcher of water and the bowl for washing at our
> bedsides, the supervised Saturday-night bath in the cold bathroom,
> with a red-faced nun sitting on a stool behind a drawn curtain with
> our bath towel on her lap. I felt as though I stood on the outskirts
> and observed the ritual of a cult, a cult of fashion and elegance in
> the sphere of religion.[49]

A little later she adds 'Though I often stood first in my studies, the
coveted pink ribbon for good conduct never came my way'. She
speculates that:

> this was because of my meanness, in particular the spiteful taunts I
> directed at a supercilious fat girl, the petted daughter of a rich meat
> packer, with heavy rings on her fingers and a real fur coat, who was
> my principal rival for honours in the classroom, but at the time I
> could not understand why the ribbon was denied me.[50]

Simone de Beauvoir, Kate O'Brien and Mary McCarthy:
Girlhood Memories Compared

While Simone de Beauvoir received a Catholic education at a private Catholic school for girls, she did not receive a *convent* education, unlike Mary McCarthy and Kate O'Brien. Three reasons are given by Deirdre Bair for her parents' decision to send the young Simone to 'a prestigious private school called the Cours Adeline Désir'.[51] First of all, her mother Françoise de Beauvoir had received a convent education, but one which she herself rated far inferior to the education received by her husband Georges at the Collège Stanislas. In the second place, 'convent schools in Paris required expensive uniforms completed by a fresh pair of white gloves every day, and all students were required to stay for elaborate lunches. These represented expenses much larger than Georges and Françoise could afford'.[52] Finally, the Cours Désir had been 'named after an aristocratic Catholic laywoman who had established it with the intention of making it a true educational institution and not just a finishing school for daughters of the upper classes'.[53] Bair observes that the Cours Désir did not live up to the expectations of its Foundress:

> the quality of teaching and the content of the courses guaranteed the pupils little more than a junior-high-school education, even though they attended for ten to twelve years.[54]

In my opinion, this evaluation of the academic standards at the Cours Désir is excessively harsh. While Simone's parents had later contemplated removing her to another school, and she herself was critical of the laboured, authoritarian style of teaching employed at the school, it did enter pupils for the baccalauréat, and in the final years the pupils had four hours a week of psychology, logic, ethics and metaphysics. At the same time it seems reasonable to infer, from the narratives supplied by McCarthy and O'Brien, that had Simone de Beauvoir attended a convent school for girls, she would have received a more rigorous education, in a more competitive academic environment, from teachers who were themselves of high academic calibre. Equally, it is highly unlikely that the *mothers* of the pupils would have been admitted to the classroom, to be actively involved in the grading of the pupils' conduct and academic progress.

But in other respects the similarities proliferate. Each of the schools that features in these three narratives had an association with the Jesuits.

Each of the schools engaged in the practice of formally preparing, and formally presenting, each week, conduct and academic reports on the pupils. In all cases a reward system operated to the advantage of the ablest students. The prizes varied from books (which were carefully selected) to special holidays and privileges, to medals and the honour of wearing special garments, especially sashes. Each of the schools had its own private chapel, its own chaplain, and annual retreats. However, while the Catholic education received by Simone de Beauvoir was longer in duration that that recounted by Kate O'Brien and Mary McCarthy – since quite apart from the eleven years spent at the Cours Désir, she afterwards attended the Institut Catholique at Neuilly – it was not as intensive an exposure to the Catholic experience as that recalled by the other two authors. For one thing, she had not been a boarder, and as such did not experience all the formalities associated with meals, evening recreation, bath-time and bed-time in convent boarding schools. In the second place, she did not have the experience of being taught, supervised and counselled by nuns. Kate O'Brien and Mary McCarthy explain, in different ways, the kind of difference such an experience can make. From McCarthy we learn that it was possible for nuns, particularly at senior levels in the Order, to be adept at evading some of the more unfortunate and unforseen consequences of doctrinal orthodoxy, such as by searching out alternative readings of the canon. Another major feature of convent life was the extent to which these were *self-governing* establishments, i.e. schools run by and for women. The kind of tension which such independent enclaves could generate in a rigidly hierarchical male institution such as the Catholic Church is exquisitely explained by Kate O'Brien:

> She realised wearily that he was circling, as usual, round the Irish hierarchy's distrust of an independent religious order. It was a patent exasperation to the authoritarian Bishop that, short of grave scandal, he had no power to counsel or direct the *Compagnie de la Sainte Famille*. And this exceptional privilege of the Order increased the offence of its foreigners; in fact, Reverend Mother knew very well that, as far as his Lordship was to be reckoned with, the independence of this house was the sole safeguard of its peculiar tradition, which the Bishop called 'exotic' and *démodé*, and which he would have overthrown without hesitation had he the power.[55]

But the main difference, I would say, between these narratives of a Catholic education is that Simone de Beauvoir did not come under the influence of a Mother Superior (McCarthy), or a Reverend Mother (O'Brien). These were formidable women, chosen by their Order with great deliberation and great care, at least as much for their management skills as for their intellectual calibre. In Kate O'Brien's barely fictive narrative *The Land of Spices*, young Anna is more or less taken under her wing by Mère Marie-Hélène. This woman intervenes powerfully in the girl's life on a number of occasions, but principally following her brother's death by drowning – when she consoles her at length about the meaning of death, including premature death – and later by persuading the girl's wealthy grandmother, by devious means, to allow her grandaughter to go to university. The impact made by this nun is such that if Anna has a vocation, it will undoubtedly be the example set by this nun that has nurtured it. As she prepares to leave the school, Anna reflects: 'I shall never hear that again ... I shall never know anything about her'. The following exchange then ensues:

> 'It is a very hard thing, I suppose', she said impulsively. 'It is a very hard thing to be a nun'.
> 'I think so', Reverend Mother said.
> 'I – I thought of it sometimes this year – but not properly. Not for holy reasons. Only because I was frightened'.
> 'I know. Holy reasons are the only ones – and they are hard to be sure about, and hard to sustain'.
> 'I don't think I could possibly be a nun!'
> 'You are young, Anna'.[56]

IV

Crises of Faith

It is instructive, finally, to examine the way in which a 'crisis of faith' is handled in each of the schools that feature in these three narratives. In *The Land of Spices*, Anna confides in Reverend Mother about a recurrent dream that troubles her immensely, a dream featuring her brother Charlie who had recently died by drowning. Reverend Mother consoles her in various ways, and suggests she discuss the matter with the priest, in particular that he might help in lessening her resistance to God's Will. Anna replies that she hasn't been resisting God's Will, but the nun reminds her that she had 'acknowledged God's ordinance in that fact of his death ...' In that case, Reverend Mother continued, Anna would also have to recognise God's ordinance in the fact of Charlie's birth, for 'If God took away his human life, God also gave it'.[57] She then builds on this argument as follows:

> And if you say that you don't know why God took his life away, you must equally admit that you don't know why He bestowed it. Of course, as a Catholic you should, and you do, know both these 'whys' – the only point I'm stressing is that you either know both or

neither. You cannot accept the mystery of life and refuse that of death.[58]

Anna retorts that she is not refusing the mystery of death, but Reverend Mother insists that she refuses Christian acceptance 'by making it into an abnormal, unnatural horror which contradicts everything else you know of Charlie'. The nun then reflects that:

> she was being trite, but that only two things, both vague, should be attempted at present against Anna's confused desolation – to appear non-inquisitive, and simultaneously to ensure that the ice of reserve did not harden again.[59]

She offers the following philosophical meditation.

(i) Long and short lives are equally 'tiny in eternity';

(ii) Charlie's life had been taken from her, but it was *his* life, 'an absolutely private thing, marked off by itself in eternity, as yours is, and mine';

(iii) That it had been given its particular shape:

> as it happens, a lovely, untarnishable, poetic shape, unlike the outward shapes of most lives – is a part of this privacy, on which your love actually has no claim, Anna[60];

(iv) She was *in* this life, but as the possessor of an immortal soul needed to take 'the longer view';

(v) Ending on a consolatory note, she observes that Anna's brother cannot have known for more than a fraction of a second that he would drown, so that there was no need to suffer for him on that score. He had suffered a single, sudden blow to his head when he hit a submerged rock, and had been rendered immediately unconscious. Finally, she commends Anna for her bravery.

This was not a full-blown crisis of faith, but – to employ Kate O'Brien's own felicitous phrasing of it – a state of 'confused desolation'. For the present I merely want to draw attention to the following features of the episode:

(i) The Reverend Mother uses a combination of analytic theological argument and psychological counselling in her handling of the situation.

(ii) She reflects throughout on the effect her words are having.

(iii) She reassures Anna that she can stay at the convent over Christmas, so that she can avoid the ordeal of going home, and

(iv) Anna ends up profusely *thanking* the Reverend Mother for her kindly disposition towards her: 'Oh thank you!' she said. And then, in tones of deeper wonder: 'You are extraordinarily good to me'.[61]

In her commentary on her own essay *C'est le Premier Pas Qui Coute*, Mary McCarthy remarks that:

> the whole drama of my loss of faith took place during a very short space of time, and I believe it was during a retreat. The conversations, as I have warned the reader, are mostly fictional, but their tone and tenor are right. That was the way the priests talked, and those, in general, were the arguments they brought to bear on me.[62]

As she recalls it in the main narrative, she had *decided* to lose her faith in order to become a school celebrity, confidant also that a faith which had been lost on a Sunday morning could always be recovered 'in time for Wednesday confessions'. As such there would be only a period of four days during which her soul would be in mortal danger should she happen to die suddenly. The main problem would be foregoing Communion on Sunday, since she had always been 'an ostentatious communicant'.

When she informs Mother Superior of her recent loss of faith, she is first of all exhorted to pray, and when she professed an inability to pray, she was ordered to go to her room to await the arrival of an elderly Jesuit who would speak to her. Alone in her cubicle, she reflects that she knew nothing of atheism, though she had learned about scepticism from Madame MacIllvra. She had been taught how to defeat the argument that God could not exist since He was incapabe of being perceived, by replying that the wind, too, could not be perceived, and yet 'its touch was everywhere, like God's invisible grace blowing on our souls'.[63] Heaven and Hell, she had also been instructed, did not belong to the spatio-temporal order investigated by science, but that did not entail their non-existence unless one tacitly *assumed* that the only possible world was the spatio-temporal world, an assumption not shared by the great religions.

When she meets the priest in 'the dark parlour, he addresses her with the words 'You have your doubts, Mother says', to which she replies 'Yes, Father', adding 'I doubt the divinity of Christ and the Resurrection of the Body and the real existence of Heaven and Hell'. When the priest inquires whether she had been reading 'atheistic literature', she replies in the negative, adding that the doubts were entirely her own. He then asks her for a detailed statement of her doubts, and half way through her disquisition interrupts her as follows: 'These are scholastic questions ... Beyond the reach of your years. Believe me, the Church has an answer for them'.[64] Next he questions her on the divinity of Christ, and when she expresses further doubts about that – mainly on the basis that it could not be proven that He had risen from the dead – the priest accuses her of 'calling Our Blessed Saviour a liar and a cheat'.[65] The priest tries to bring the session to a close by telling her that she 'must have faith', but his use of the word 'faith' serves only to remind her that perhaps she *had*, in reality, lost her faith, and that, perhaps, there was suddenly 'a gulf between us, a gulf that could not be bridged by words'.[66] They continue arguing, and he concludes another round of argument by advising her that she must accept his words since she is too young to understand these things. Then they explore 'the five *a priori* proofs of God's existence, at the end of which the priest implores her to 'give up reading that atheistic filth. Pray to God for faith and make a good confession'.[67] These events predictably, and calculatedly, ensured that the author became a school celebrity, becoming known as 'the girl a Jesuit had failed to convince'.[68] Mother Superior felt she had failed in her obligations to the girl's dead mother, and because of all the accumulating fuss and bother the young Mary McCarthy concluded that she would *have* to regain her faith, if only to bring all the commotion to an end. Yet the more she tapped and tested herself, she confesses:

> the more I was forced to recogize that there was no belief inside me. My very soul had fled, as far as I could make out.[69]

She resolved then to *pretend* she had recovered her faith, and her second encounter with a priest, the younger Jesuit conducting the retreat, served only to strenghten her in this resolve. Having traversed the same theological and philosophical areas of disputation, he had pointed out that:

> Natural reason ... will not take you the whole way today. There's a little gap that we have to fill with faith.[70]

She herself takes this to mean, not that faith precedes reason, but that faith constitutes a black hole at the core of religious belief, rendering it fundamentally unacceptable. Convinced now that she will never intellectually regain a respect for religious belief, she realises that she will have to *pretend* she has regained her faith for the sake of peace and harmony. The younger priest had simply made a bad situation even worse by calling her Thomasina, 'in a would-be funny reference to doubting Thomas'. This sobriquet merely succeeded in:

> driving me straight into fraud. Thanks to his incompetence, the only thing left for me to do was to enact a simulated conversion.[71]

We have, then, two very different outcomes to a 'crisis of faith' occurring in two convent schools run by French Order nuns on two different continents. In Kate O'Brien's narrative Reverend Mother deals with the matter herself, and due mainly to the trust, respect, and even affection which over the years she had cultivated in the doubting pupil, she counsels her to an acceptance of her brother's death and the will of God. The pupil leaves with an enhanced respect for the Reverend Mother, and thanks her profusely.[72] The very opposite happens in Mary McCarthy's memoir. Here a pupil who *contrives* to lose her faith ends up actually losing it. Two priests are summoned to prevent this occurring, but they succeed only in making a bad situation worse. Their tone is often accusatory, and patronising, and one of them tries to undermine her with psychological subterfuge. Above all, there is no attempt to understand the girl, to investigate what had driven her into a situation necessitating an urgent institutional response. There was very little respect for her *personally*, only a fear of, and profound antipathy towards what she represented.

Simone de Beauvoir's 'crisis of faith' went through a number of stages. First of all, she disowned her spiritual director Abbé Martin, for exchanging confidential information about her with her mother. She recalls that following this discovery, the sound:

> of his black skirts swishing along a school corridor ... made me feel physically sick, as if the Abbé's deceit had made me his accomplice in some obscene act.[73]

At the same time, on account, she suspects, of the rule of absolute secrecy attaching to the confessional, the Abbé never confronted her about her 'defection'.

She distinguishes immediately between disowning her spiritual director and disowning God. She had not disowned God, at least not yet. She concentrated all of her 'revulsion' on this occasion:

> on the traitor who had usurped the role of divine intermediary. When I left the chapel, God had been restored to His position of omniscient majesty; I had patched up heaven again.[74]

She searched for a new confessor 'who would not alter the messages from on high by the use of impure human words'.[75] She tried two different priests, the second of whom 'suggested a few themes for meditation and lent me a *Handbook of Ascetic and Mystical Theology*'.[76] But she found it difficult to take to these new confessors 'who had not been given to me when I was a small girl'.[77]

Then one evening at Meyrignac, as she dipped her hands 'into the freshness of the cherry laurel leaves', and 'listened to the gurgling of the water', she knew, she reports:

> 'that nothing would make me give up earthly joys. 'I no longer believe in God', I told myself, with no great surprise. That was proof: if I had believed in Him, I should not have allowed myself to offend Him so light-heartedly ... I was not denying Him in order to rid myself of a troublesome person: on the contrary, I realized that He was playing no further part in my life and so I concluded that He had ceased to exist for me.[78]

For the present, I am concerned solely with the institutional response to this loss of faith. She describes it as follows:

> I had to return the *Handbook of Ascetic and Mystical Theology* to the Abbé Roulin. I went back to Saint-Sulpice, kneeled down in his confessional, and told him that I had not partaken of the sacraments for several months because I had lost my faith. Seeing the *Handbook* and measuring the height from which I had fallen, the Abbé was astounded, and with a disconcerting brutality asked me: 'What mortal sin have you committed?' I protested that I had not committed any sin. He did not believe me and advised me to pray hard. I resigned myself to the life of an outcast.[79]

What is noteworthy about this train of events is that she did not turn to anyone in the school for guidance. This is hardly surprising since there was no one there of whom she had a high enough opinion. Second, she met both priests in the confessional, a location not in the least conducive to balanced, equal, extended dialogue. Third, the priest made no effort to engage her in argument or discussion, still less to inquire into the provenance of her loss of faith. Since he had listened to her in the confessional, it is perhaps not surprising that his immediate instinct was to situate her admission in the context of grievous sin. He then exhorted her to pray, but did not express any intention on his own part of praying for her. The impression one eventually gets is of someone being left to her own devices, and since she also reports that 'I still went to Mass and took Holy Communion ...',[80] they may well have thought that nothing was too seriously amiss.

What is most striking, I find, about these three narratives of a crisis of faith – two of them resulting in an actual loss of faith – is the role which can be played by a mentor. In the Kate O'Brien narrative, a powerful, articulate and sympathetic institutional figure does not shirk delivering the institutional theological line relating to the will of God. But her overriding concern is to comfort and protect the student rather than the institution. This mentor, it is also worth noting, did not seek the assistance of the priests. Mary McCarthy's Mother Superior was more concerned about her obligations to the girl's deceased mother, and did call in the priests. She became more and more concerned about the loss of faith as such, and correspondingly less and less concerned about *who* was losing her faith, and what might have brought such a situation about. Simone de Beauvoir, too, lacked a mentor. Her father had rejected and humiliated her during adolescesnce; her mother oppressed her, and there was no teacher she sufficiently admired. The school chaplain had betrayed her, and Abbé Roulin had proved a poor substitute. One can but speculate on what difference a strong female mentor might have made, in this and other matters, had such an individual been available to her.

Notes

1   I have in mind the accounts of a Catholic education found in Edna O'Brien's *The Country Girls* (1960), and in Mary Lavin's short story *Lemonade.*

2   Introduction to 2000 Virago edition of *The Land of Spices,* pp. ix, x.

3   *The Land of Spices,* p. 6.

4   *The Country Girls,* p. 75. For more detailed information about nuns in Ireland, see C. Clear, 'Walls Within Walls: Nuns in Nineteenth-Century Ireland', in C. Curtin *et al.* (eds) *Gender in Irish Society,* pp 134–151, and M. MacCurtain, 'Godly Burden: Catholic Sisterhoods in Twentieth-Century Ireland', in A. Bradley and M.G. Valiulis (eds), *Gender and Sexuality in Modern Ireland,* pp. 245–256. Edited versions of both these articles are reprinted in A. Hayes and D. Urquhart (eds), *The Irish Women's History Reader,* Routledge, 2001.

5   *The Land of Spices,* p. 7.

6   *Ibid.,* p. 17.

7   *Ibid.,* p. 24.

8   *Ibid.,* p. 53.

9   *Ibid.,* p. 134.

10   *Ibid.,* p. 31.

11   *Ibid.*

12   *Ibid.,* p. 34.

13   *Ibid.,* p. 36.

14   *Ibid.,* pp. 165, 166.

15   *Ibid.,* p. 175.

16   *Ibid.,* p. 117.

17   *Ibid.,* p. 98.

18   *Ibid.,* p. 100.

19   *Ibid.,* p. 99.

20   *Ibid.,* pp. 65, 66.

21   *Ibid.*, p. 66.
22   *Ibid.*, pp. 72, 73. [The heroines of Edna O'Brien's *The Country Girls* deliberately contrive to get themselves expelled, by circulating a holy picture on which they had written, on the reverse side, the details of a sexual encounter between a priest and a nun].
23   *Ibid.*, p. 73.
24   *Ibid.*, p. 79.
25   *Ibid.*, p. 186.
26   *Ibid.*, p. 44.
27   *Ibid.*, p. 96.
28   *Ibid.*, pp. 92, 93.
29   *Ibid.*, p. 132.
30   *Ibid.*, p. 281.
31   *Memories of a Catholic Girlhood*, p. 9. For further background information on Mary McCarthy's childhood, and on the *Memories*, see F. Kiernan, *Seeing Mary Plain: A Life of Mary McCarthy*, pp. 15–60
32   *Ibid.*, p. 10.
33   *Ibid.*, p. 22.
34   *Ibid.*, p. 24.
35   *Ibid.*, p. 20.
36   *Ibid.*
37   *Ibid.*, p. 25.
38   *Ibid.*
39   *Ibid.*, pp. 119, 120.
40   *Ibid.*, p. 77.
41   *Ibid.*, p. 78.
42   *Ibid.*, p. 80.
43   *Ibid.*
44   *Ibid.*, p. 116.
45   *Ibid.*, p. 89.
46   *Ibid.*, p. 90.
47   *Ibid.*
48   *Ibid.*
49   *Ibid.*
50   *Ibid.*, p. 94.
51   *Simone de Beauvoir, A Biography*, p. 42.
52   *Ibid.*
53   *Ibid.*
54   *Ibid.*, pp. 42, 43.
55   *The Land of Spices*, p. 92.
56   *Ibid.*, p. 284.
57   *Ibid.*, p. 235.
58   *Ibid.*
59   *Ibid.*, p. 236.
60   *Ibid.*
61   *Ibid.*, p. 238.

62   *Memories of a Catholic Girlhood,* p. 108.

63   *Ibid.,* p. 99.

64   Ibid., p. 102.

65   Ibid.

66   Ibid., p. 103.

67   Ibid., p. 105.

68   Ibid., p. 106.

69   Ibid.

70   Ibid., p. 107.

71   Ibid.

72   In the autobiographical fragment *Memories of a Catholic Education,* Kate O'Brien writes about Reverend Mother as follows: 'I think she was remarkably wise and considerate, as a passive authority, in a climate of thought which she could not enter. But then, she did not enter the climate of thought. From outside them, I think she watched with an attention of sensibility which only those could measure whose confidence, in distress, she would force. She forced mine, as I suppose she knew she could, after twelve years of love. And she forgave me then for all this after-life, which has been an insult to her simple ideals', *The Limerick Compendium,* p. 28.

73   *Memoirs of a Dutiful Daughter,* p. 135.

74   *Ibid.*

75   *Ibid.*

76   *Ibid.*

77   *Ibid.*

78   *Ibid.,* p. 137.

79   *Ibid.,* pp. 139, 140.

80   *Ibid.,* p. 139.

Chapter Four

THE BODY

'Human beings have bodies and their bodies were full of suffering'
  — Memoirs of a Dutiful Daughter, p. 206

'In our universe, the flesh had no right to exist'
  — Memoirs, p. 58

There are two fundamentally differing theoretical perspectives on the body, which following current academic practices I shall call *essentialism* and *constructivism*. For essentialism the body is basically anatomy, biology, and destiny. You are born with a body, you enter and encounter the world by means of a body [*à travers un corps*, as Merleau-Ponty has it], wherever you go your body goes with you, and when your body ceases to function and rots, you too cease to exist. Charged with the task of repairing the body when it malfunctions, and arresting the effects of its decline when it ages, medicine is pre-eminently the science of the body. The various medical disciplines, from anatomy and physiology on the one hand, to cardiology and oncology on the other, give some indication of how specialised this area of science has actually become.

Essentialism distinguishes between two kinds of bodies, male and female bodies respectively, and it does so on the basis of the distinctive kind of contribution of each kind of body to human reproduction. Both of these concepts, that of body binarism (also called gender binarism) and that of reproductive binarism, are acknowledged by Simone de Beauvoir in the opening pages of *The Second Sex*. On the second and third pages of the Introduction she writes that:

> In truth, to go for a walk with one's eyes open is enough to demonstrate that humanity is divided into two classes of individuals whose clothes, faces, bodies, smiles, gaits, interests and occupations are manifestly different. Perhaps these differences are superficial, perhaps they are destined to disappear. What is certain is that they do most obviously exist.[1]

And further on down she writes:

> Woman has ovaries, a uterus: these peculiarities imprison her in her subjectivity, circumscribe her within the limits of her own nature.[2]

On page nineteen she writes, using the alternative phraseology of 'the sexes', that:

> The division of the sexes is a biological fact, not an event in human history. Male and female stand opposed within a primordial *Mitsein*, and woman has not broken it.[3]

Finally, the terms 'male' and 'female', synonyms when combined for the expression 'the sexes', are defined as follows on the opening page of the first chapter, 'The Data of Biology': 'Male and female are two types of individuals which are differentiated within a species for the function of reproduction'.[4] So far as reading Beauvoir correctly is concerned, then, the first claim I wish to make is that, *whatever else it may be*, Beauvoir's feminism is an essentialism. She acknowledges body binarism (there are two fundamentally differing kinds of bodies) and reproductive binarism (there are two fundamentally differing kinds of contribution to human reproduction, without which it cannot occur), and does so without any equivocation or hesitation.

Beauvoir is an essentialist in the stronger, more primary sense that she repeatedly acknowledges the immensity of the body in human existence. In her work on old age she gives the following sobering insight among others:

> It is usual to put forward wearing-out and fatigue as an explanation for the way some old people resign themselves to death; but if all a man needed was to vegetate he could put up with his life in slow motion. But for man living means self-transcendence. A

consequence of biological decay is the impossibility of surpassing oneself and of becoming passionately concerned with anything; it kills all projects, and it is by this expedient that it renders death acceptable.[5]

This sombre tone is, perhaps, to be expected from a woman author in her sixties writing on the topic of old age. The balance is struck the other way, in favour of self-transcendence and against the constraints of the body, in the much earlier work, her feminist classic *The Second Sex*. There, again, the centrality of the body is underscored:

> These biological considerations are extremely important. In the history of woman they play a part of the first rank and constitute an essential element in her situation. Throughout our further discussion we shall always bear them in mind. For, the body being the instrument of our grasp upon the world, the world is bound to seem a very different thing when apprehended in one manner or another. This acounts for our lengthy study of the biological facts; they are one of the keys to the understanding of woman.[6]

But she immediately adds that there is much more to woman than possessing a woman's body:

> But I deny that they [the biological data] establish for her a fixed and inevitable destiny. They are insufficient for setting up a hierarchy of the sexes; they fail to explain why woman is the Other; they do not condemn her to remain in this subordinate role for ever.[7]

Possession of a body is a necessary, but not a sufficient condition of leading, and accounting for, a *human* existence because human beings are historical beings. Taking her cue from Merleau-Ponty, Simone de Beauvoir develops this idea – of the body's limitations, on this occasion – as follows:

> But man is defined as a being who is not fixed, who makes himself what he is. As Merleau-Ponty very justly puts it, man is not a natural species: he is a historical idea. Woman is not a completed reality, but rather a becoming, and it is in her becoming that she should be compared with man; that is to say, her *possibilities* should be defined. What gives rise to much of the debate is the tendency to reduce her to what she has been, to what she is today, in raising the question of her capabilities; for the fact is that capabilities are clearly manifested only when they have been realized – but the fact is also that when we have to do with a being whose nature is transcendent action, we can never close the books.[8]

The true nature of a human being – be it female or male – is transcendent action, and not its bodily nature: this is the up-beat tone of a sinecured woman in her late thirties who still retains a sense of life's adventure. She gives the following vivid description of this situation in the second volume of her memoirs:

> Like every bourgeois, we were sheltered from want; like every civil servant, we were guaranteed against insecurity. Furthermore, we had no children, no families, no responsiblities: we were elves. There was no intelligible connexion between the work we did ... and the money we got for it, which seemed to lack all proper substance ... we flourished, in fact, like the lilies of the field, and circumstances fostered our illusions. We were bursting with good health, and our bodies objected to no demands we made on them unless we pushed things to extremes.[9]

But elsewhere in the same volume of the memoirs she assumes a more measured attitude towards the struggle between the body and history, between, if you like, the body as constraint and the body as instrument of liberation. 'Today', she writes:

> I believe that, under the specially privileged conditions in which I exist, life contains two main truths which we must face simultaneously, and between which there is no choice – the joy of being, the horror of being no more. At the time I vacillated between one and the other. It was only for brief moments that the second triumphed, but I had a suspicion that it might be the more valuable of the two.[10]

Writing on another occasion about the war between 'our rational and physical selves',[11] she explains that they [herself and Sartre] were always trying to distinguish, both in their own lives and those of others:

> between the built-in physical characteristic and the freely willed act. I criticized Sartre for regarding his body as a mere bundle of striated muscles, and for having cut it out of his emotional world. If you gave way to tears or nerves or seasickness, he said, you were simply being weak. I, on the other hand, claimed that stomach and tear ducts, indeed the head itself, were all subject to irresistible forces on occasion.[12]

If the body not only constrains us, but sometimes defeats our projects altogether, then not only is our freedom curtailed, but women have even less freedom than men. This is because women are more constrained and put upon by their bodies, and by their social and historical circumstances. To be free, on this view of freedom, is to be able actively to transcend any given situation, and this, ventured Sartre in his early writings, was a power that every human being always retained. Beauvoir replied to him that if you are sick, decrepid or suffering from dementia you perforce lack the energy and/or the mental resources to do much, if indeed anything at all. She presses home the point by asking 'what sort of transcendence could a woman shut up in a harem achieve?'[13] Sartre was wont to reply, she confides:

> that even such a cloistered existence could be lived in several quite different ways. I stuck to my point for a long time, and in the end made only a token submission. Basically I was right. But to defend my attitude I should have had to abandon the plain of the individual, and therefore idealistic, morality on which we had set ourselves.[14]

Women are still further constrained by their bodies, of course, in that it is women who carry the reproductive burden. Beauvoir writes at length about this unique responsibility in the chapter on biology, a narrative whose salient features I have documented in my 1997 book, *Existentialism, Feminism and Simone de Beauvoir*. For the present, I wish to conclude this section on Beauvoir's essentialist feminism by directing the reader's attention to her remarks on the possibility of resisting, and overcoming, the constraints of the body. In the second volume of her memoirs she refers to an International Congress for Sexual Reform which had met at Brno, and had 'discussed such problems as birth control, voluntary sterilization, and general eugenics'.[15] 'We approved', she notes:

> of this effort to free man from social conformity and emancipate him from Nature's dominion by giving him mastery over his own body. Procreation in particular was not something to be endured, but deliberately chosen.[16]

So reproductive control, or reproductive freedom, she believes, is both possible and desirable. Moreover, when a woman does opt to become pregnant the burden of pregnancy and childbirth will also vary in accordance with economic and cultural circumstances. As she writes in *The Second Sex*:

> As with her grasp on the world, it is again impossible to measure in the abstract the burden imposed on woman by her reproductive function. The bearing of maternity on the individual life, regulated naturally in animals by the oestrus cycle and the seasons, is not definitely prescribed in woman – society alone is the arbiter. The bondage of woman to the species is more or less rigorous according to the number of births demanded by society and the degree of hygienic care provided for pregnancy and childbirth. Thus, while it is true that in the higher animals the individual existence is asserted more imperiously by the male than by the female, in the human species individual 'possibilities' depend upon the economic and social situation.[17]

I have defined 'essentialism' at the outset as the claim that the body is anatomy, biology and destiny. You enter the world with an assemblage of limbs, a torso and vital organs, and when these same organs are injured or atrophy beyond repair you die. In the meantime you possess either a male or a female body, and live the life of a man or a woman. Either way, the body both constrains and liberates, but the female body constrains more than the male. As Beauvoir most memorably put it, 'The female is the victim of the species'.[18] Essentially this is because 'The female organism is wholly adapted for and subservient to maternity'.[19] However, where human females are concerned, reproductive freedom is both feasible and desirable. What is more:

> The bondage of woman to the species is more or less rigorous according to the number of births demanded by society and the degree of hygienic care provided for pregnancy and childbirth.[20]

Finally:

> Woman is not a completed reality, but rather a becoming, and it is in her becoming that she should be compared with man; that is to say, her *possibilities* should be defined.[21]

This is the essentialist existentialism of Simone de Beauvoir.

However, a stronger and more controversial meaning can be assigned to the claim that the body is destiny. I have taken it simply to mean that sooner or later the body perishes and corrupts, and that bodily death is also to be understood as personal extinction. But there is a stronger and more pugnacious meaning to the claim that the body is destiny; on this stronger essentialist view, the body is epistemically primary, while the self (the person you become/the person you have been) is epiphenomenal. In plainer English, innate body difference marks you all the way down, from top to bottom, so to speak. It affects not just physical appearance and reproductive roles, but also intelligence, personality and moral sense, and does so in a way that cannot be evaded. Phil Baty puts it as follows in an article on transsexuals and the difficulties they are wont to encounter in the workplace:

> There is a remaining essentialist strand in some theoretical feminism, which argues that women are innately different from men. As well as the obvious biological differences between men and women, essentialists argue, women are born with inherent, recognizably female characteristics; sympathy, a different moral sense, a willingness to nurture and work co-operatively, for instance. It follows that someone who is born male can never become truly female, or vice versa.[22]

All such claims are encapsulated in the aphorism *My body, my self*, or *My body, myself*. But the basic idea is that the self is supervenient on the body. This is sometimes known as 'difference feminism'.

Julia Kristeva gave her approval to difference feminism in an interview with *Tel Quel* in 1974:

> Because of the decisive role that women play in the reproduction of the species, and because of the privileged relationship between father and daughter, a woman takes social constraints even more seriously, has fewer tendencies towards anarchism, and is more mindful of ethics.[23]

And Hélène Cixous writes that:

> it is at the level of sexual pleasure, in my opinion, that the difference makes itself most clearly apparent in as far as woman's libidinal economy is neither identifiable by a man nor referable to the masculine economy.[24]

Luce Irigaray develops this idea of sexual difference at the level of sexual pleasure (*jouissance*) by reminding her readers of the unique characteristics of female autoeroticism:

> Thus, for example, woman's autoeroticism is very different from man's. He needs an instrument in order to touch himself: his hand, woman's genitals, language – And this self-stimulation requires a minimum of activity. But a woman touches herself by and within herself directly, without mediation; and before any distinction between activity and passivity is possible. A woman 'touches herself' constantly without anyone being able to forbid her to do so, for her sex is composed of two lips which embrace continually. Thus, within herself she is already two – but not divisible into ones – who stimulate each other.[25]

Simone de Beauvoir did not embrace this stronger essentialism; that is to say, she is not a difference feminist. In her memoirs, she explains her position as follows:

> I know that when certain critics read this autobiography they will point out, triumphantly, that it flatly contradicts my thesis in *The Second Sex*, a suggestion they have already made with regard to *Memoirs of a Dutiful Daughter*. The fact is that they have failed to grasp the point of *The Second Sex*, and probably even refer to it without having read it. Have I ever written that women were the same as men? Have I ever claimed that I, personally, was not a woman? On the contrary, my main purpose has been to isolate and identify my own particular brand of femininity. I received a young lady's education, and when my studies were finished, my position was still that of any woman in a society where the sexes are divided into two embattled castes. In a great many ways I reacted like the woman I was: what distinguishes my thesis from the traditional one is that, as far as I am concerned, femininity is neither a natural nor an innate entity, but rather a condition brought about by society, on the basis of certain physiological characteistics.[26]

She does not, then, hold the 'traditional' position that women and men are different *through and through*. They differ physically, and that much is 'innately' given, but they also differ in many other ways which are not innately bestowed but are socially constructed ('brought about by society'). Such differences as these (relating, for example, to clothes, posture, names, hairstyle, schooling, and so on) are historical and therefore mutable. The feminine self is not supervenient on the female body; in Judith Butler's way of putting it:

> Not only is gender no longer dictated by anatomy, but anatomy does not seem to pose any necessary limits to the possibilities of gender.[27]

These points are captured by the distinction between *sex* and *gender*. 'Sex' describes what you are born with, while 'gender' describes what becomes of you in the society into which you are inserted.

In her 1976 interview with Alice Schwarzer of *Marie-Claire*, Beauvoir returns to the theme of 'the eternal feminine'. She makes two points very forcibly:

> (i) 'feminine' qualities, such as patience and irony, are capable of being acquired by men as well, and men ought to acquire them;

> (ii) feminine qualities are not supervient on the female body.

These are her own words:

> I think that today certain masculine shortcomings are absent in women. For example, a masculine manner of being grotesque, of taking oneself seriously, of thinking oneself important. Note that women who have a masculine career can also adopt these shortcomings. But all the same, women always retain a little nook of humour, a little distance between themselves and the hierarchy. And that way of squelching competitors: in general, women do not act that way. And patience which is, up to a certain point, a quality (later it becomes a shortcoming), is also a characteristic of women. And irony, a sense of the concrete, because women are more strongly rooted in every day life. These 'feminine' qualities have their origin in our oppression, but they should be preserved after our liberation. And men, too, should acquire them.[28]

She turns her critical gaze on the more extreme, New Age forms of difference feminism as follows:

> But we must not exaggerate in the other direction. To say that woman has special ties to the earth, the rhythm of the moon, the tides, etc., that she has more soul, that she is less destructive by nature, etc. No, if there is something true in all that, it is not in terms of our nature, but of the conditions of our life. 'Feminine' little girls

are also made and not born that way. Numerous studies prove this. A priori, a woman has no special value because she is a woman. That would be the most retrograde 'biologism', in total contradiction with everything I think.[29]

II

In her article on transsexuals, Baty goes on to say:

> Most feminist theory, however, adheres to the 'constructionist' Simone de Beauvoir view that 'one is not born a woman, one becomes one' through immersion in and adherence to social expectations.[30]

This reading of Beauvoir is correct as far as it goes, but conceals as much of the truth as it reveals. As I have been arguing, Beauvoir is, in part, a constructivist, and in part an esssentialist. Femininity, she holds, is constructed, and it is constructed 'on the basis of certain physiological characteristics'. But there is no suggestion that these characteristics are themselves socially constructed. In this sense, then, Beauvoir is a shallow as opposed to a deep constructivist. As I observed in the closing chapter of my 1997 book on Beauvoir, she opens the second volume of *The Second Sex* with the words 'One is not born, but rather becomes, a woman'. She does not write 'One is not born, but rather becomes, a female'. This, once again, is the distinction between sex and gender, between femaleness and femininity, to which I have previously alluded.

Constructivism is the claim that gender is socially created and socially sustained; more narrowly, it is the claim that femininity is socially created and socially sustained. The intended implication is that gender (the division into masculine and feminine, into men and women) can be altered if that is what is required, and indeed re-created in such a way that long-standing social practices and stereotypes would, or could, disappear altogether. In keeping with this intention we could then witness, as to an increasing extent we are witnessing, the emergence of a wide range of social persons: traditional men and women, new men and new husbands, singles or live-alones, spouses, partners, women childless by choice, lone parents, career women, androgynes, transsexuals, gays, lesbians, bisexuals, preference lesbians and gays, lesbians who are butch (display a masculinized female body) and lesbians who are femme (display a feminized lesbian body), celibates, and so on and so forth.

67

It is, I think, important to notice that terms whose original purpose was to denote sexual orientation (e.g. 'lesbian' and 'gay') have come to acquire many additional associations having nothing in particular to do with sex, but having a great deal to do with lifestyle. Increasingly there is an emphasis on such gay and lesbian signifiers as hairstyle, clothes, preference in music, and so on. There is also a transference or swapping of images and cultural paraphernalia between the various sexual subcultures. These developments are captured in the following overview of lesbian subculture in the 1980s:

> Just as femininity in mainstream cultural images has been inflected by butch, producing a 'dykey het' image, so in lesbian subculture lesbian sexual identities have been re-eroticized by a reappropriation of femininity, producing the 'femme dyke' and the 'lipstick lesbian'. A recent article in *The Guardian* Women's Page identified this trend, contrasting the stereotypical images of political and desexualized 'rad les fems' of the 1970s with the new femme fatales and 'nubile nude vixens' of the late 1980s. The comeback of the femme and the reincorporation of gender differences into lesbian identities suggests a rejection of 1970s feminist androgyny and certain of its feminist orthodoxies around the body and self-presentation: the injunction against feminine adornment and its oppressive signifiers – makeup, high heels, skirts, long hair and so on – became oppressive and trapping in itself.[31]

The intermingling of culture with subculture is documented at length in the anthology *The Good, the Bad and the Gorgeous,* subtitled 'Popular Culture's Romance with Lesbianism'. The following paragraph gives a useful illustration of what I mean by the intermingling of culture and subculture:

> While there had been, at least since the early 1970s, women in popular music who defied conventions of femininity – Patti Smith, Pat Banatar, Janis Joplin, Annie Lennox were among the most central figures – what was new about the 1980s wave of androgyny was that its proponents, though not always lesbian – identified with, tended to be rooted, at least partially, in lesbian subcultures. Tracy Chapman made the rounds in women's music festivals in 1986 and 1987, while Melissa Etheridge, k.d. lang, Michelle Shocked and others knocked around lesbian and 'alternative' clubs in Austin, Atlanta, San Fransisco and New York City.[32]

The famous opening sentence of Book II of *The Second Sex* ['One is not born, but rather becomes, a woman' ; *On ne naît pas femme, on le devient*] is, taken in isolation, liable to be misleading. It strongly suggests that females become women *by choice*. But it is clear from the sentences which immediately follow the opening one that it is a much stronger meaning that Beauvoir has in mind. She writes:

No biological, psychological, or economic fate determines the figure that the human female presents in society; it is civilisation as a whole that *produces* [my emphasis] this creature, intermediate between male and eunuch, which is described as feminine. Only the intervention of someone else can establish an individual as an *Other*.[33]

Book II then sets out to document, at very great length, the process by which infant females are transformed into 'women', into adult females whose whole destiny is marriage and the rearing of children.

The social production of 'women' and 'men' begins from a very early age. Though they are raised (or 'reared', as we say in Ireland) in the same family, by the same parents, females quickly become little girls, their brothers little boys, i.e. they are turned into little girls and little boys. The differentiation and streaming which these designators ('girl', 'boy') connote is beautifully conveyed by the following passage from Beauvoir's classic:

This is just where the little girls first appear as privileged beings. A second weaning, less brutal and more gradual than the first, withdraws the mother's body from the child's embraces; but the boys especially are little by little denied the kisses and caresses they have been used to. As for the little girl, she continues to be cajoled, she is allowed to cling to her mother's skirts, her father takes her on his knee and strokes her hair. She wears sweet little dresses, her tears and caprices are viewed indulgently, her hair is carefully done, older people are amused at her expressions and coquetries – bodily contacts and agreeable glances protect her against the anguish of solitude. The little boy, in contrast, will be denied even coquetry; his efforts at enticement, his play-acting, are irritating. He is told that 'a man doesn't ask to be kissed ... A man doesn't look at himself in mirrors ... A man doesn't cry'. He is urged to be 'a little man'; he will obtain adult approval by becoming independent of adults. He will please them by not appearing to please them.[34]

Constructivism has two other meanings, each of them relating not to the body, but to cultural representations of the body. The emphasis here is on the body as text or narrative, not on the body as possession, nor as instrument, nor even as cultural construct, where to be a cultural construct is to be socialised into becoming someone who occupies an assigned place in a social economy. We are, instead, talking of the body as symbolic construct, and of the implications of this kind of construction. Susan Suleiman puts it as follows in her Introduction to the anthology *The Female Body in Western Culture*:

The cultural significance of the female body is not only (not even first and foremost) that of a flesh-and-blood entity, but that of a *symbolic construct*. Everything we know about the body – certainly as regards the past, and even, it could be argued, as regards the present – exists for us in some form of discourse; and discourse, whether verbal or visual, fictive or historical or speculative, is never unmediated, never free of interpretation, never innocent.[35]

The claim that the body is socially constructed decodes, then, into the claim that our *awareness* of the body is socially constructed. This awareness is theory-laden and historically situated. Two consequences are attendant on this meaning:

(i) We need to engage in meticulous research to ensure that we do not rush to conclusions about the cultural products of other peoples and past civilisations;

(ii) The more sceptical, nihilistic inference that we cannot claim any *knowledge* of cultural constructs. Suleiman gives vent to this scepticism when she writes:

To be aware of the specificity or the limits of one's views is to realize that unchanging truths, even about something as concrete, as biologically 'fixed' as the human body, are impossible to arrive at.[36]

Julia Kristeva also becomes this sceptical when she writes as follows about the difficulties involved in furnishing an adequate representation of 'woman':

The belief that 'one is a woman' is almost as absurd and obscurantist as the belief that 'one is a man'. I say 'almost' because there are still many goals which women can achieve: freedom of abortion and contraception, day-care centres for children, equality on the job, etc. Therefore, we must use 'we are women' as an advertisement or slogan for our demands. On a deeper level, however, a woman cannot 'be'; it is something which does not even belong in the order of *being*. It follows that a feminist practice can only be negative, at odds with what already exists so that we may say 'that's not it and 'that's still not it'. In 'woman' I see something that cannot be represented, something that is not said, something above and beyond nomenclature and ideologies.[37]

In fact, Kristeva says at least two distinguishable things here:

(1) Women do not constitute a natural kind, a class of objects having its characteristics necessarily, and

(2) It is not possible to have a discourse concerning women.

As I see it, Beauvoir would agree with (1), but not with (2). Women (as distinct from females) are not natural kinds, but social constructs. 'When I use the words *woman* or *feminine* I obviously refer to no archetype', she writes in her Introduction to Book II of *The Second Sex*, no changeless essence whatever'.[38] Then she adds:

It is not our concern here to proclaim eternal verities, but rather to describe the common basis that underlies every individual feminine existence.[39]

Clearly, this is no radical philosophical scepticism, but an honest appraisal of what is measurably feasible. It is meant to express epistemic optimism rather than theoretical certainty or arrogance.

III

I wish, finally, to address some points made by Judith Butler in her essay 'Sex and Gender in Simone de Beauvoir's *Second Sex*'.[40] Both in this essay and in her later writing Butler is widely taken to have attacked, and undermined, the distinction between sex and gender, essentially by arguing that sex, too, is socially constructed, and not just gender. This is the way she is read by Peggy Pascoe, for instance, in the following piece on 'Gender' for the volume *A Companion to American Thought*:

> The argument that sex is socially constructed is a very recent development. While it is both logically consistent and theoretically ingenious, it is not yet widely accepted. Like the arguments that race, sexuality, and gender are socially constructed, it goes against many people's 'common sense'. In some respects, the emergence of this argument reflects the coming of age of a new generation of feminist theorists. In her book *Gender Trouble*, postmodern feminist Judith Butler makes the case for the social construction of sex in language saturated with the terminology of poststructuralism. 'Perhaps', she writes, 'this construct called 'sex' is as culturally constructed as gender; indeed, perhaps it was always already gender, with the consequence that the distinction between sex and gender turns out to be no distinction at all'.[41]

Margaret A. Simons also takes Butler to have dispensed with the sex/gender distinction, especially when Butler writes, in her essay on Beauvoir, that 'The body is, in effect, never a natural phenomenon'. Simons takes these words to mean that 'Biology and sex differences become social constructs whose meaning is shaped through the actions of individuals'.[42] Seemingly we are left, then, with the conclusion that there is no such thing as the body, a conclusion which anyone who has spent a few days in hospital cannot regard as anything other than a bizarre kind of intellectual madness.

There is no support for the conclusion that there is no such thing as the body, or that the body is not identifiable as a natural phenomenon, in the opening paragraphs of Butler's essay on sex and gender in Beauvoir's writing. Quite the contrary, in fact, is the case. She begins by explaining the distinction between sex and gender:

> sex is understood to be the invariant, anatomically distinct, and factic aspect of the female body, whereas *gender* is the cultural meaning and form that that body acquires, the variable modes of that body's acculturation.[43]

and noting its importance for feminist theory:

> With the distinction intact, it is no longer possible to attribute the values or social functions of women to biological necessity, and neither can we refer meaningfully to natural or unnatural gendered behaviour: all gender is, by definition, unnatural.[44]

Butler concludes the opening paragraph of her essay by noting that Beauvoir, too, had drawn the distinction between sex and gender, between being a female and being a woman, and that her initiative in doing so may rightly be considered a landmark in Western thought. In Butler's own more technical prose:

> At its limit, the sex/gender distinction implies a radical heteronomy of natural bodies and constructed genders with the consequence that 'being' female and 'being' a woman are two very different sorts of being. This last insight, I would suggest, is the distinguished contribution of Simone de Beauvoir's formulation, 'one is not born, but rather becomes, a woman.[45]

So far as I can see, this is the proposition for which I have argued throughout this chapter, namely, that Beauvoir was an essentialist about sex, and a constructivist about gender.

In the penultimate section of her essay, Butler focusses on Beauvoir's concept of the body as 'situation', arguing that 'In clarifying the notion of the body as 'situation', she suggests an alternative to the gender polarity of masculine disembodiment and feminine enslavement to the body'.[46] The idea of the body as situation has two meanings:

> (a) It is an object, 'a material reality', which is always already saturated with meaning and symbolic associations. [In post-war Catholicism, for example, it used to be the Temple of the Holy Ghost, while in Beauvoir's own account of first-menstruation – an account not unconnected, surely, to her Catholic formation and Catholicism's relentless strictures on body exposure – it becomes the location of a 'flat and stagnant odour ... an odour of the swamp, of wilted violets', occasioning 'disgust at this blood, less red, more dubious, than that which flowed from her childish abrasions'[47]].

(b) The body is the vantage point from which we negotiate these received meanings and associations. In Butler's words, it is 'a field of interpretative possibilities'. The thesis that there is no natural body, that 'the notion of a natural body and, indeed, a natural 'sex' seems increasingly suspect',[48] is, then, a thesis to the effect, not that there is no such thing as the body [bodies don't exist], but the claim that there are no bodies about which we lack information and insights, with whose meanings and associations we are entirely unfamiliar. References to the 'body' are, in effect, shortened references to the body as it presents itself to the medical profession, as it is represented in the history of Western art, as it functions in Plato's substance dualism, and so on.

Context makes clear which set of meanings and associations are appropriate. What Butler calls the 'ontological' body doesn't exist, i.e. the body devoid of all meaning and associations; but this is not reducible to the claim that there are no bodies. What Butler means is that there are no bodies about which we know nothing, something which, of course, is patently true.

Notes

1   *The Second Sex*, pp. 14, 15.
2   *Ibid.*, p. 15.
3   *Ibid.*, p. 19.
4   *Ibid.*, p. 35.
5   *Old Age*, pp. 493, 494.
6   *The Second Sex*, p. 65.
7   *Ibid.*
8   *Ibid.*, p. 66.
9   *The Prime of Life*, pp. 362, 363.
10   *Ibid.*, p. 208.
11   *Ibid.*, p. 128.
12   *Ibid.*, pp. 128, 129.
13   *Ibid.*, p. 434.
14   *Ibid.*
15   *Ibid.*, p. 132.
16   *Ibid.*, pp. 132, 133.
17   *The Second Sex*, p. 67.
18   *Ibid.*, p. 52.
19   *Ibid.*
20   *Ibid.*, p. 67.
21   *Ibid.*, p. 66.
22   *THES*, 18 July 1997.
23   *New French Feminisms*, p. 138.

24   *Ibid.*, p. 93. This despite writing, on the very same page, that 'We must guard against falling complacently or blindly into the essentialist ideological *interpretation ...*'

25   *Ibid.*, p. 100.

26   *The Prime of Life*, p. 367.

27   In E. Fallaize (ed.), *Simone de Beauvoir: A Critical Reader*, p. 39.

28   *New French Feminisms*, pp. 152, 153.

29   *Ibid.*, p. 153.

30   *THES*, 18 July, 1997.

31   *The Good, the Bad and the Gorgeous*, pp. 34, 35.

32   *Ibid.*, pp. 20, 21.

33   *The Second Sex*, p. 295.

34   *Ibid.*, p. 298.

35   *The Female Body in Western Culture*, p. 2.

36   *Ibid.*

37   *New French Feminisms*, p. 137.

38   *The Second Sex*, p. 31.

39   *Ibid.*

40   *Yale French Studies*, 1972. Reprinted in E. Fallaize (ed.), *Simone de Beauvoir: A Critical Reader*, pp. 30–42.

41   *A Companion to American Thought*, p. 275.

42   *Beauvoir and the Second Sex*, p. 141.

43   *Simone de Beauvoir: A Critical Reader*, p. 30.

44   *Ibid.*

45   *Ibid.*, p. 31.

46   *Ibid.*, p. 38.

47   *The Second Sex*, p. 338.

48   Butler, *op. cit.*

Chapter Five

THE MODEST BODY

She found her nightdress under the pillow, and keeping an arm around her, kissing the hot, wet face, but silent as death, she undressed her. As she pulled the nightdress over Anna's head, Mother Mary Andrew entered the cubicle and gripped her by the shoulders. 'How dare you leave your bed and enter another. Insubordination *and* immodesty! I suppose you know that I could give you a mark for conduct now, or have you expelled!'

– Kate O'Brien, *The Land of Spices*, 1941

The new girls won't know this, but our convent has always been proud of its modesty. Our girls, above anything else, are good and wholesome and modest. One expression of modesty is the way a girl dresses and undresses. She should do so with decorum and modesty. In an open dormitory like this, girls are requested to dress and undress under the shelter of their dressing-gowns. Girls should face the foot of the bed, doing this, as they might surprise each other if they face the side of the bed.

– Edna O'Brien, *The Country Girls*, 1960

At that period of my life I associated indecency with the baser bodily functions; then I learnt that the body as a whole was vulgar and offensive: it must be concealed; to allow one's underclothes to be seen, or one's naked flesh – except in certain well-defined zones – was a gross impropriety.

– Simone de Beauvoir, *Memoirs of a Dutiful Daughter*, 1958

Modesty is not a uniquely Catholic virtue, but it is a characteristic Catholic obsession. It is linked in Catholic teaching to an elaborate virtue ethics, which itself belongs to an even more extensive moral theology. In this chapter I will first of all provide an outline account of the concept of modesty such as it is understood and presented in orthodox Catholic teaching. Then I will document the accounts of the modest body, and of modest feelings, which feature extensively in Simone de Beauvoir's writings, but especially in the memoirs and in the prose fiction. Beauvoir's disquisition on modesty satisfies all three criteria for the application of the predicate 'Catholic' to an author: it concerns a Catholic obsession, it employs the Catholic vernacular, and in it she continues to see the world through Catholic eyes. In her memoirs Beauvoir gives detailed information about the Catholic way of regulating sexual behaviour, on this occasion by getting Catholics to internalise the virtue of modesty. It is considerably more interesting, however, to discover that she *adopts* the Catholic attitude towards modesty, as well as towards sexual intimacy, in her prose fiction.

I

The Virtue of Modesty in Catholic Teaching

The Catholic concept of modesty finds its eventual place in its theory of the virtues. Catholicism distinguishes very broadly, first of all, between the *human* and the *theological* virtues. The human virtues are understood as stable dispositions of the intellect and will, conducing to the morally good life. To quote the New *Catechism*, 'Human virtues are firm attitudes, stable dispositions, habitual perfections of intellect and will that govern our actions, order our passions and guide our conduct according to reason and faith. They make possible ease, self-mastery and joy in leading a morally good life'.[1] There are two things to be noted about the human virtues thus understood:

(i) they lead to the morally good life;

(ii) leading to the morally good life they *ipso facto* make possible the feelings and accomplishments which accompany the morally good life, namely, ease, self-mastery and joy.

This is an extremely optimistic view of the rewards of virtue, in marked contrast to the views of non-naturalist moral philosophers such as D.Z. Phillips and H.O. Mounce, who hold that morality can never be justified heteronomously, and differing also, *prima facie*, from the views of naturalist philosophers such as Philippa Foot and P.T. Geach who tend to emphasise not what morality can do for us, but what we are likely to *suffer* if we fail to exercise moral virtue. As Geach puts it, 'to choose to lack a virtue would be to choose a maimed life, ill-adapted to this difficult and dangerous world'.[2]

Among these human virtues, pre-eminence is given to 'the cardinal virtues', so-called because 'all the others are grouped around them'. The cardinal virtues are four in number, and they are prudence, justice, fortitude, and temperance. *Prudence* is defined as 'the virtue that disposes practical reason to discern our true good in every circumstance and to choose the right means of achieving it'.[3] *Justice* is defined as 'the moral virtue that consists in the constant and firm will to give their due to God and neighbour'.[4] Giving to God what God is due is called 'the virtue of religion', while justice towards other human beings 'disposes one to respect the rights of each and to establish in human relationships the harmony that promotes equity with regard to persons and to the common good'.[5] There are, once again, several emphases in this definition. They are:

(i) respect for human rights;

(ii) establishing harmony in human relationships;

(iii) promoting impartiality or fairness in our dealings with others, and

(iv) promoting an egalitarian sense of community.

Fortitude is defined as 'the moral virtue that ensures firmness in difficulties and constancy in the pursuit of the good'.[6] The explanation of this definition shows that the common tendency to treat 'fortitude' and 'courage' as synonyms, or at any rate as synonymous in the Catholic lexicon, is mistaken. The *Catechism* distinguishes between *resolve* and *courage* in its disquisition on fortitude. Thus, on the one hand, fortitude 'strengthens the resolve to resist temptations and to overcome obstacles in the moral life'.[7] But, in addition, fortitude 'enables one to conquer fear, even fear of death, and to face trials and persecutions. It disposes one even to renounce and sacrifice one's life in defence of a just cause'.[8] Finally, *temperance* is defined as 'the moral virtue that moderates the attraction of pleasures and provides balance in the use of created goods'.[9] Again, this is a much richer concept of temperance than that which is conventionally provided. Conventionally, temperance is said to stiffen resistance to desire. The Catholic definition varies and augments this concept in various ways:

(i) temperance is the virtue that makes pleasures seem less pleasurable than they are, and

(ii) it disposes us to strike a balance between created goods. This is a more intellectualised concept of temperance than that which has gained the most currency.

The *theological* virtues are three in number; they are faith, hope, and charity. These theological virtues are considered more fundamental in Catholic virtue ethics because the human virtues are said to be 'rooted in the theological virtues'.[10] They are said to be rooted in the theological virtues because these latter 'adapt man's faculties for participation in the divine nature: for the theological virtues relate directly to God'.[11]

The theological virtues are designed to conduce to the leading of a *Christian* life. As the *Catechism* explains, 'The theological virtues are the foundation of Christian moral activity; they animate it and give it its special character'.[12] They are designed to conduce to the leading of a Christian life because:

> They are infused by God into the souls of the faithful to make them capable of acting as his children and of meriting eternal life. They are the pledge of the presence and action of the Holy Spirit in the faculties of the human being.[13]

Faith is defined as:

> the theological virtue by which we believe in God and believe all that he has said and revealed to us, and that Holy Church proposes for our belief, because he is truth itself.

The concept of *belief* which is identified here is much stronger than that standardly used by philosophers. It requires, of those who believe:

(i) that they believe that God exists,

(ii) that they believe *everything* that the Catholic Church proposes they believe, and

(iii) that they believe *everything* that God has said and revealed.

What is more, belief is not merely a matter of acceptance, it is also a matter of *commitment*, of following through on one's beliefs, matching one's deeds to one's beliefs. To quote the *Catechism*:

> By faith man freely commits his entire self to God. For this reason the believer seeks to know and do God's will.[14]

Hope is defined as:

> the theological virtue by which we desire the Kingdom of heaven and eternal life as our happiness, placing our trust in Christ's

promises and relying not on our strength, but on the help of the grace of the Holy Spirit.[15]

It is clear from this definition of 'hope' just why it is classified as a *theological* virtue: it is because its object is theological. It directs the aspiration to happiness in a heavenly direction, towards 'the kingdom of heaven and eternal life'. Nothing less would constitute happiness. But the *Catechism* also introduces the more mundane concept of hope as well, when it adds that this virtue also:

> keeps man from discouragement; it sustains him during times of abandonment; it opens up his heart in expectation of eternal beatitude.[16]

Finally, *charity* is defined as:

> the theological virtue by which we love God above all things for his own sake, and our neighbour as ourselves for the love of God.[17]

Charity disposes us to do the following, then:

(i) to love God above all things;

(ii) to love God for his own sake;

(iii) to love our neighbour just as – to the same extent that – we love ourselves, and

(iv) to love our neighbour because we love God and to enhance that same love.

The virtue of charity is the supreme Catholic virtue. It is pre-eminent or supreme for the following reasons:

(i) by loving others, we imitate the love of Jesus for his disciples.

(ii) Charity conduces to keeping God's commandments, and charity disposes us to love God. The *Catechism* quotes John, Matthew and *Romans*: 'Abide in my love. If you keep my commandments, you will abide in my love'.[18]

(iii) Charity was made a completely new commandment by Jesus: 'This is my commandment, that you love one another as I have loved you'.[19]

(iv) Christ asked for forgiveness, even for those who had tortured and crucified him. Christ's example shows how far charity must extend: we are to love not just known and anonymous others, but *even* those who hurt and persecute us.

According to the *Catechism*, the fruits of charity are joy, peace and mercy. It does not make clear whether these benefits flow continuously to the charitable person, or whether they flow to such a person to a greater extent that they do to someone who is not charitable. The point has been made, by philosophers such as Philippa Foot and P.T. Geach, that people need to be virtuous, notwithstanding the fact that the practice of the virtues may sometimes bring disappointment. Indeed, Foot is prepared to acknowledge that the practice of justice may even bring disaster, namely, death itself; yet the just man still had cause to be just. He had cause to be just because we are better off for being just.[19a]

It is at this stage that the Catholic insistence on *modesty* makes its appearance. A distinction is drawn between the *gifts* and the *fruits* of the Holy Spirit. The gifts of the Holy Spirit are 'permanent dispositions which make man docile in following the promptings of the Holy Spirit'.[20] These gifts, we are told, complete and perfect the virtues of those who receive them. The gifts are seven in number: they are wisdom, understanding, counsel, fortitude, knowledge, piety and the fear of the Lord. Presumably these gifts complete and perfect the *theological* virtues of those who receive them, for fortitude is one of the cardinal virtues, and the gift of fortitude is hardly intended to perfect and complete the virtue of fortitude.

In addition to the gifts of the Holy Spirit, Christians receive what are called the *fruits* of the Spirit, defined as 'perfections that the Holy Spirit forms in us as the first fruits of eternal glory'.[21] The tradition of the Church lists twelve such fruits: they are charity, joy, peace, patience, kindness, goodness, generosity, gentleness, faithfulness, modesty, self-control, and chastity. Modesty and chastity, it may be noted, are distinguished from each other.

Modesty makes its fullest appearance in Catholic virtue ethics in its teaching on *purity*. Two concepts of purity are utilised:

(a) freedom or purification from all sin, a condition first conferred on those who receive the sacrament of Baptism;

(b) freedom or purification from all *sexual sin*, from what the Catechism calls 'concupiscence of the flesh and disordered desires'.[22]

The virtue of purity is designed to protect the Christian from all such sexual sin. To this end it draws on the following further disciplines and virtues:

(i) chastity, 'which lets us love with upright and undivided heart'.[23]

(ii) purity of intention, 'which consists in seeking the true end of man'.[24]

(iii) purity of vision, which disciplines the feelings and imagination, and refuses 'all complicity in impure thoughts that incline us to turn aside from the path of God's commandments ...'. [25]

(iv) prayer.

To achieve purity, i.e. freedom from sin, and in particular from sexual sin, *modesty* is required. Modesty is an integral part of temperance, first of all, i.e. of that virtue which moderates the attractiveness of pleasures and provides a balance in the use of created goods. The function of modesty is to protect 'the intimate centre of the person', to protect 'the mystery of persons and their love'.[26] The mystery of persons is protected, on this view, by 'refusing to unveil what should remain hidden',[27] by encouraging 'patience and moderation in loving relationships',[28] by ensuring that 'the conditions for the definitive giving and commitment of man and woman to one another be fulfilled',[29] by remaining decent,[30] by remaining discreet,[31] and by maintaining 'silence or reserve where there is evident risk of unhealthy curiosity'.[32] Modesty involves all of the following, therefore:

(i) keeping hidden from view what should not be seen;

(ii) patience and moderation in loving relationships;

(iii) decency;

(iv) discretion, and

(v) silence or reserve where there is a danger of unhealthy curiosity.

The *Catechism* then relates the virtue or practice of modesty, as follows, to the contemporary world:

> There is a modesty of the feelings as well as of the body. It protests, for example, against the voyeuristic explorations of the human body in certain advertisements, or against the solicitations of certain media that go too far in the exhibition of intimate things. Modesty inspires a way of life which makes it possible to resist the allurements of fashion and the pressures of prevailing ideologies.[33]

II

In the remainder of this chapter I propose to offer one detailed proof of my thesis that Simone de Beauvoir was, among other things, a Catholic writer. I hope to accomplish this by documenting the accounts of the modest body, and of modest feelings, which feature extensively in her writings, but especially in the memoirs and in the early prose fiction. In her memoirs, Beauvoir gives detailed information about the Catholic way of regulating sexual behaviour, on this occasion by getting Catholics to internalise the virtue of modesty. It is considerably more interesting, however, to discover that she *adopts* the Catholic attitude towards modesty, and also towards sexual intimacy, in her prose fiction.

The object of modesty, in Catholic virtue ethics, is to protect the mystery of persons and of their love. On this view, modesty involves keeping hidden what should remain hidden. It also involves patience, moderation in loving relationships, decency, discretion, silence and reserve, as the occasion demands. What should remain hidden is the body, and in particular those parts of the body which are uniquely capable of stimulating 'concupiscence of the flesh and disordered desires'. Simone de Beauvoir gives many illustrations, in her memoirs, of what the virtue of modesty involves *in practice,* such as in the following extract:

> I had never seen grown-ups other than hermetically clad from top to toe; during my bath-time, Louise scrubbed me with such vehemence that self-appraisal was impossible; besides, I had been taught never to look at my naked body, and I had to contrive to change my underwear without uncovering myself completely. In our universe, the flesh had no right to exist.[34]

And yet the 'flesh' was soft to the touch, and beautiful to gaze at:

> And yet I had known the softness of my mother's arms; in the neck of certain ladies' dresses I could see the beginning of a darkening cleft which both embarrassed and attracted me. I was not ingenious enough to be able to re-create those pleasurable sensations I had accidentally discovered during my gymnastic lessons; but from time to time the soft touch of downy flesh against my own, or a hand stroking my neck, made me shiver with tender anticipation.[35]

'I had been taught never to look at my naked body ...' It was her mother, above all, who had taught her never to do so, her mother who 'preserved, in her heart of hearts, a rigorously inflexible personal morality'.[36] Beauvoir elaborates as follows:

> Although she had been without doubt happy in her marriage, she was apt to confuse sexuality with vice; she always associated fleshly desires with sin. Convention obliged her to excuse certain indiscretions in men; she concentrated her disapproval on women; she divided women into those who were 'respectable' and those who were 'loose'. There could be no intermediate grades. 'Physical' questions sickened her so much that she never attempted to discuss

them with me; she did not even warn me about the surprises awaiting me on the threshold of puberty.[37]

And yet this same woman was, to quote her daughter once more:

> profoundly conscious of her responsibilities, and took to heart the duties of mother and counsellor. She sought guidance from the Union of Christian Mothers, and often attended their meetings. She took me to school, attended my classes and kept a strict eye on my homework and my lessons; she learnt English and began to study Latin in order to be able to follow my progress. She supervised my reading, and accompanied me to mass and compline; my mother, my sister, and I performed our devotions together, morning and evening. At every instant of the day she was present, even in the most secret recesses of my soul, and I made no distinction between her all-seeing wisdom and the eye of God himself.[38]

She recalls one phrase which the grown-ups were constantly using in their efforts to inculcate the virtue of modesty: 'It's not proper!' [*c'est inconvenant*]. At one stage Beauvoir took this statement to have a scatalogical meaning, explaining that in:

> Madame de Segur's *Les Vacances,* one of the characters told a story about a ghost, a nightmare ending in soiled sheets which shocked me as much as it did my parents. It was not proper. At that period of my life I associated indecency with the baser bodily functions; then I learnt that the body as a whole was vulgar and offensive: it must be concealed; to allow one's underclothes to be seen, or one's naked flesh – except in certain well-defined zones – was a gross impropriety. Certain vestimentary details and certain attitudes were as reprehensible as exhibitionist indiscretions. These prohibitions were aimed particularly at the female species; a real 'lady' ought not to show too much bosom, or wear short skirts, or dye her hair, or have it bobbed, or make up, or sprawl on a divan, or kiss her husband in the underground passages of the Metro: if she transgressed these rules, she was not a 'lady'. Impropriety was not altogether the same as sin, but it drew down upon the offender public obloquy that was infinitely worse than ridicule.[39]

The severity of these censures on bodily exposure, as well as the rigid refusal to entertain discussion of 'physical' matters, served only to heighten curiosity concerning such secret matters. As Beauvoir explains, what bits and pieces of information she had managed to pick up left many mysteries unexplained. For instance, 'What relationship was there between this serious affair, the birth of a child, and things that were 'not nice' or 'not proper'? If there were none, then why did Madeleine's tone of voice and Mama's own reticence force us to suppose there was one? ... Physiological facts are as much a part of common knowledge as the rotation of the earth: what was it prevented her from telling us about them as about anything else? ... I did not actually ask myself these questions, but they tormented me all the same. It must be that the body was by reason of its own nature a dangerous object when every allusion to its existence, whether serious or frivolous, seemed fraught with peril'.[40]

As she entered adolescence, one of the first things which Beauvoir was to discover about the body's 'own nature' was that it has a life of its own, and is capable of being completely indifferent to its owner's desires. She spells this out as follows:

> During the day, I had dizzy spells; I became anaemic. Mama and the doctor would say: 'It's her development'; I grew to detest that word and the silent upheaval that was going on in my body. I envied 'big girls' their freedom; but I was disgusted at the thought of my chest swelling out; I had sometimes heard grown-up women urinating with the noise of a cataract; when I thought of the bladders swollen with water in their bellies, I felt the same terror as Gulliver did when the young giantesses displayed their breasts to him.[41]

In view of her Catholic formation, and in particular the wisdom that the body is vulgar and offensive and must, therefore, be concealed, it is hardly surprising that the young Simone de Beauvoir's reaction to bodily change and development would be a negative one. She reacted with detestation, disgust, terror, embarrassment, humiliation, horror, a fleeting pride, but, above all, shame. Most, if not all, these emotions were provoked by the menarche, while some were provoked by her father's deplorably puerile reaction to this same event. As she recalls, 'I didn't mind too much when I heard my mother whispering about it to her friends. But that evening when we joined my father in the rue de Rennes, he jokingly made reference to my condition: I was consumed with shame. I had imagined that the monstrous regiment of women kept its blemish a secret from the male fraternity. I thought of myself in relationship to my father as a purely spiritual being: I was horrified at the thought that he suddenly considered me to be a mere organism. I felt as if I could never hold up my head again'.[42]

As she progressed into her late teens Beauvoir's 'virtuous revulsion' of the body became, on her own admission, more intellectually refined. She remained, nonetheless, firmly locked within the negative sexual ethics of Catholicism, especially in its unrelenting denigration of the body. Now the body could be valued, but only because it housed the soul. This concept of the body, which at this juncture she finds admirable, she claims to have located in the Catholic writer Paul Claudel:

I loved Claudel above all because he celebrates in the body the miraculously sensitive presence of the soul. I refused to read the end of Jules Romain's *Le Dieu des corps* because in it physical pleasure was not described as the expression of the spirit. I was exasperated by Mauriac's *Souffrances du chrétien* which the NRF was publishing just then. In the former triumphant, in the latter humiliated, I found that in both of them the flesh was given too much importance.[43]

III

Intimacy, Agony and Allure

Simone de Beauvoir's collection of short stories *When Things of the Spirit Come First* features a selection of young heroines trying to claw their way out of Catholicism, and sometimes succeeding. Their attempted escape from Catholicism involves, among other things, a growing discomfort with the inhibitions of modesty. One of these stories, *Marcelle*, charts the movement away from modesty towards frankness and intimacy; another, *Anne*, charts the movement from modesty to luxury, elegance and allure. Beauvoir herself put the following spin on these short stories:

> A few years before this I had discovered the harm done by the religiosity that was in the air I breathed during my childhood and early youth. Several of my friends had never broken away from it: willingly or unwillingly they had undergone the dangerous influence of that kind of spiritual life. I decided to tell their stories and also to deal with my own conversion to the real world.[44]

In this section I will argue that these stories accomplish other things as well; in particular, they show us a Catholic imagination still actively at work. Doubtless, these are narratives of suffering and escape; but they are not always the rebukes to Catholicism that Beauvoir would have us suppose them to be.

The modesty instilled in Catholic households and society is depicted as follows: 'in the Vignon's circle, women did not make up apart from the barely tolerated powder'. Mme Vignon was on constant alert for signs of immodesty, as the following passage illustrates:

> The meal came to an end: conversation began to die away. Mme Vignon turned a severe eye upon the sleepy bodies half-lying under the poplars: the Rungis girl's hair was almost touching Pierre

d'Alaissai's shoulder; Nicole Duflos had linked her hands behind her neck; and Suzanne's skirt showed her legs as far as the knee.[45]

She then rebukes her daughter Anne for her choice of reading material, as well as her choice of friends, in the following stinging words: 'I do not judge anyone', said Mme Vignon sharply:

> Every night I pray for souls who have lost their way; but first and foremost we must preserve ourselves from sin and not allow scabbed sheep to contaminate us. Believe me, it wounds me to feel that you are soiled by unclean books, by associating with young men who have no scruples, and with puffed-up immodest women.[46]

'Anne, my poor child', she counsels her daughter:

> you don't know anything about life ... Listen: I shall never allow one of my daughters to have a friendship with a man who is not intended to be her husband. I know what men are: they talk about ideals, but they are full of base desires. The fine theories of Chantal and her friends are only good for justifying the lowest instincts. I am sorry to be forced to tell you these harsh truths, but that is how things are.[47]

As you would expect, the exact same message is drummed into the girls at school, where the headmistresss fulminates against immodesty as follows: 'Before giving you your rolls of honour', she said:

> I wish to tell you that at present I am thoroughly displeased with your behaviour and the way you dress'. There was a great silence. 'You know that you are not to come to school in short sleeves', she went on, 'and that you are not merely to throw your coats over your shoulders: I wish them to be put on properly, with your arms in the sleeves – offences against this rule are reported to me from all over the town. There are even some among you who take their hats off the moment they turn the corner of the street. And there are some, whom I choose not to name but who will know they are meant, who have been caught bare-headed and bare-armed on cafe terraces. This unrestrained conduct is deeply improper: it reveals both a want of self-discipline and of dignity. How can you hope to be respected if you do not respect yourselves?[48]

While the heroines, almost without exception, tend to rebel against the regime of modesty, it still leaves its marks on them. Lisa, a boarder at the Institut Saint-Ange, undresses as follows:

> with a modesty learnt in her childhood she put on her pyjama trousers before she took off her slip, and when she put on the flowered jacket she averted her eyes from her breasts.[49]

When the *ingénue*, Marguerite, is taken in hand by the twice-divorced patron of the arts Marie-Ange, she, too, experiences feelings related to 'a modesty learnt in her childhood'. These are mainly feelings of embarrassment, and astonishment, occasioned by having to dress and undress in front of Marie-Ange and hear her appraise her body. The following passage captures the situation exquisitely: 'I scarcely knew her before she took me into her bedroom and said, with gentle authority, 'Take off that hideous frock: I'm going to try one of my dresses on you ... I took my frock off: it embarrassed me because my underclothes were often rather dubious ... I was more and more embarrassed; I was not very prudish, but I had never undressed in front of anyone. I turned my back as I took off my petticoat and I could not prevent myself from blushing when she came and stood in front of me with a critical look. 'You have a lovely body', she said. 'You are quite right not to wear a suspender belt'. She smiled archly. 'I don't wear one either', she added. 'Feel'. She grasped my hand and pressed it to her belly. It was indeed all soft'.[50] Marie-Ange, she reports:

> had no modesty; she often walked about the apartment in a brassiere and panties, and she often obliged me to feel her breasts and her belly to see how young they had remained.[51]

But Marguerite remained unimpressed, reporting that Marie-Ange 'had a red, granular flesh that disgusted me'. This tension, or struggle, between modesty and immodesty grows when Marie-Ange tries to teach her young protégée the rumba. According to Marguerite, Marie-Ange was incapable of explaining or teaching anything:

> 'Follow', she said. 'All you have to do is follow'. I tried; but the smell of opium and *chypre* that permeated her went to my head; I swam in a kind of insipid sweetness and I blundered at every step.[52]

The struggle between modesty and immodesty reaches boiling point when Marguerite decides to stay the night with Marie-Ange, and finds herself the reluctant object of the older woman's sexual advances. As the attempted seduction intensifies, Marguerite reacts and resists with mounting determination. She confesses to not:

> knowing how far friendship and gratitude required me to put up with it: I did not want to make an unnecessary fuss, yet I did not want to encourage her either.[53]

Moreover, in keeping with a Catholic formation in which mothers and teachers displayed a profound reluctance to discuss 'physical' matters with their daughters and pupils, it is only slowly that it comes to dawn on Marguerite what is actually occurring:

> She put out the last light, and suddenly I felt her arms around my body and her breath on my cheek ... I decided to lie there as if I were a corpse. Her hand moved all over my body, sliding under my

jacket and down my belly: I clamped my legs together, making no movement at all. I think it must have been half an hour that she silently caressed me; but it was only when I felt her thick lips on mine that these manipulations took on a clear meaning for me. 'She wants to make love to me', I thought, turning my head away and trying to disentangle myself.[54]

When Marie-Ange clasps her tighter, Marguerite confides that she was 'on the rack'.[55] She clenched her teeth, we are told, and struggled for a while in the darkness. When the older woman releases her grip, 'I was', says Marguerite, 'furious with her and myself: I thought the whole scene odious'.[56] It is worth remarking, I believe, that what we have here is more than a clash between two perceptions of the female body, the one describing itself as 'nudist', and claiming incomprehension at the idea of people who are 'ashamed of showing themselves naked',[57] the other rooted in a belief that the body should remain hidden, and that same-sex desire is analogous to torture for the object of that desire. Undoubtedly there is much in the way of comic excitement and suspense in this narrative of the encounter between naturism (transmuting into lesbianism) and Catholicism, but this same narrative, I further submit, is designed to solicit the reader's sympathies for the younger woman. She is portrayed as the victim of an extended, often clumsy, often hilarious seduction, but a victim nonetheless. 'I reflected that modesty was just another old Catholic prejudice', says Marguerite, 'and I tried to smile naturally'.[58] But she finds it impossible to maintain the smile, and eventually has to flee the older woman's apartment. Beauvoir is not neutral in her presentation of the sexual ethics of these two warring vernaculars of the female body, and it is instructive to note that she reserves her most condemnatory tone, not for the 'old prejudices', but for the new sexual morality.

In the memoirs, when modesty is confronted by first-menstruation and other bodily developments, the consequence is disgust, terror, guilt, embarrassment, humiliation, horror, a short-lived pride and, above all, shame. In the short stories, modesty is associated with a closed suffocating world, with constant surveillance, with frequent rebukes from those in positions of authority, and with a deep-rooted reluctance to acknowledge the presence of the body. On the other hand, those who *extol* the virtue of modesty associate it with self-discipline, social propriety, self-respect, winning the respect of others, and with sanctity. So modesty appears as a very mixed blessing.

If modesty is a mixed blessing, what happens as a consequence of the loss of modesty? The answer to this question can be found in the story *Marcelle.* The eponymous heroine and her boyfriend Desroches agree on the necessity for modesty in their courtship. Desroches is of the view that:

> their engagement had to be long: and so that their wedding night might retain all its touching solemnity they should take care that their bodies did not grow used to each other, even through the most chaste of caresses.[59]

Marcelle, we are informed:

> thought it admirable that an engaged couple should be able to talk about such things with no false shame, and she told Desroches how much she appreciated his delicacy.[60]

But privately, she was bothered, for:

> it grieved her to see how easily he obeyed the rules he set himself. His was neither a passionate nor a troubled nature.[61]

On this account, modesty produces a dull and conformist type of person.

At this juncture the narrative introduces an explosive catalyst in the person of Denis Charval, a poet 'whose green eyes gave one the impression of an artless, capricious spirit, given to extremes'.[62] Indeed, so given to extremes was he that 'Marcelle felt that in speaking of Rimbaud he would present a picture of himself'.[63] The reader is not surprised when not long afterwards Marcelle has a bitter row with her fiancé:

> she had accused him of being timid, obtuse, insensitive; she told him that she was sick of his tender care and his unfailing good humour, and since then their relationship had been strained ...[64]

Marcelle and modesty part company when she dines with Charval at a restaurant on the banks of the Marne. First of all, she dresses for the occasion: 'It was a beautiful summer evening and Marcelle was wearing a wide-brimmed straw hat and a green print dress with puffed sleeves'.[65] Following the meal, during which she has drunk nearly half a bottle of wine, though she 'was not very fond of wine', Marcelle relaxes her attitude towards modesty, and succumbs to love's inflammation:

> After the meal they lay on the grass, side by side, on the river-bank. Paris was a great way off; the rue de Ménilmontant, 'Social Contract' and Desroches had ceased to exist; it seemed to Marcelle that she was being carried along like an obedient toy by a fate that was quite out of her control. She was no longer aware of anything but the beating of her heart and the warm breath close, very close to her face. Something was going to happen, and she would not do

anything to prevent it: motionless and passive she acquiesced. For years she had filled the role of a strong, affectionate, anxious woman and now she yearned to give it all up, if only for a moment, and think of nothing, wish for nothing.[66]

The 'moment' is described as follows:

At first it was a shower of urgent kisses on her eyes, the corner of her mouth, and then the warmth of a body against her own and a long deep kiss full on her mouth: she let herself go – there was nothing in her but well-being and weakness, and lying there in Denis' arms she discovered the sweet exerience of communicating with the void.[67]

Modesty, we were advised earlier, is something of a mixed blessing; now we are led to believe that the movement away from modesty brings with it similar consequences for the agent. On the positive side, Marcelle experiences warmth, well-being, and the sweetness of communicating with the void; but in the process she becomes 'passive', 'like an obedient toy', needing to 'acquiesce' and, in addition to well-being she also experiences 'weakness'. This understanding of what sexual intimacy involves for the female partner in a heterosexual relationship is a long-standing one in Catholic circles, even in liberal Catholic circles. For example, in a pastoral letter on married love, published in 1964, Emile-Joseph de Smedt, Bishop of Bruges, quotes with abundant enthusiasm the following extract from a parishioner's correspondence concerning sexual intimacy within marriage: 'The initiative must come from the man; the relative passivity of his wife is not without spiritual and moral significance; all through her married life, the woman makes use of her special innate gifts and wins the mysterious victories of femininity in a kind of general submissiveness'.[68]

These 'mysterious victories of femininity' are graphically described by Beauvoir in her account of Marcelle's wedding night. To begin with, 'the idea that a man's eyes were delighting in her nakedness made her whole being quiver with a shame whose stab was sweeter than the sweetest caress'.[69] Further on in their love-making she experiences both tyranny and pleasure, passivity and desire, slavery and ecstasy, fear and joy, violation and gratitude. The following is the crucial passage:

She opened her eyes: Denis' face appeared before her, charged with desire, intensely eager, almost unrecognizable: he looked capable of beating her, torturing her, and the sight filled Marcelle with so piercing a pleasure that she began to groan. 'I'm at his mercy', she said to herself and she was engulfed by an ecstasy in which shame and fear and joy were all inter-mingled ... she would have liked to call out to Denis that she was his thing, his slave: and tears ran down her cheeks. All at once he penetrated her: she did not exactly feel pleasure, but this violation of her most secret flesh made her gasp with gratitude and humility. She took every one of Denis' piercing thrusts with passionate submission, and to make his possession of her the more complete she let her consciousness glide away into the night.[70]

There are, of course, overtones of the Latin sadism that Beauvoir always associated with Catholicism to be found in this passage, as well as touches of the sado-masochism that features even more graphically in the accounts of her religious reveries to be found in the memoirs. In the present fictive narrative she endorses the Catholic refrain that sexual gratification *per se*, no matter how ecstatically felt, must always carry the stigmas of violation, objectifiction and shame; indeed, the greater the ecstasy, the greater the shame. But this approach to sexual gratification is more than recognizably Catholic: it retains the uniqueness, the very special flavour, of the Catholic imagination.

This can be proven by comparing Beauvoir's narrative of first-sex (for the wife, in her example) with that provided, from a Lutheran perspective, by the American novelist John Updike. In his epic novel *In the Beauty of the Lilies,* Updike gives the following description of a wedding night during the 1940s:

> Shyly keeping the bathroom door closed, first Emily, then he, took a bath in the vast tub. Water pounded from the long-nosed faucet with the force of a geyser and the heat of a volcano. The cabinet mirror steamed; vapour turned to frost-ferns on the bathroom window, at whose edges Teddy's hand felt the whisper of January wind. Dry spatterings of snow appeared in the windowlight and fell away, down into the dirty city. On the big brass bed the hotel provided, with fringed pillows and a quilted coverlet smelling of crushed lavender, Teddy and Emily, fumbling and wincing, devirginated each other, and then fell asleep with odd speed, hardly giving themselves a minute in which to discuss the events of a day so momentous and active.[71]

Both Emily and Teddy have a sense of modesty, but it is the modesty of inexperience and hesitation, of shyness and embarrassment, of sophistication and delicacy. Their sexual intimacy is not saturated with fear, or shame, or slavery, or passivity. When their modesty acquiesces to the inflammations of the flesh it does so exhaustively, with both of them falling quickly, indeed with 'odd speed', into a post-coital slumber. Months later Teddy – unlike Emily, to some extent, who quickly develops a very strong appetite for sex – confesses that:

in his mind lurked the Protestant suspicion that there must be a hook to it, and that there was something corrupt and punishable about enjoying your flesh so much.[72]

But compared to the masochistic ecstasy of Beauvoir's Marcelle, this admission is like water to urine. Beauvoir's narrative of the encounter between modesty and intimacy issues from a potent Catholic imagination in which it luxuriates, even if Updike is much more accomplished as a prose fiction writer.

Notes

1   *Catechism of the Catholic Church*, p. 400.
2   *God and the Soul*, pp. 122, 123.
3   *Catechism*, p. 400.
4   *Ibid.*, pp. 400, 401.
5   *Ibid.*, p. 401.
6   *Ibid.*
7   *Ibid.*
8   *Ibid.*
9   *Ibid.*
10   *Ibid.*, p. 402.
11   *Ibid.*
12   *Ibid.*
13   *Ibid.*
14   *Ibid.*
15   *Ibid.*, p. 403.
16   *Ibid.*
17   *Ibid.*, p. 404.
18   *Ibid.*, p. 405.
19   The quotation is from *John*, 15: 9: 12.
19a See Geach, *God and the Soul* (1969), and Foot, 'Moral Beliefs', in J.J. Thomson and G. Dworkin (eds.), *Ethics*, pp. 239–260.
20   *Catechism.*, p. 406.
21   *Ibid.*
22   *Ibid.*, p. 536.
23   *Ibid.*
24   *Ibid.*
25   *Ibid.*
26   *Ibid.*
27   *Ibid.*
28   *Ibid.*
29   *Ibid.*, pp. 536, 537.
30   'Modesty is decency'., *ibid.*, p. 537.

31   'It is discreet', *ibid.*
32   *Ibid.*
33   *Ibid.*
34   *Memoirs of a Dutiful Daughter*, p. 58.
35   *Ibid.*, pp. 58, 59.
36   *Ibid.*, p. 38.
37   *Ibid.*
38   *Ibid.*
39   *Ibid.*, p. 82.
40   *Ibid.*, pp. 87, 88.
41   *Ibid.*, p. 100.
42   *Ibid.*, p. 101.
43   *Ibid.*, p. 290.
44   *When Things of the Spirit Come First*, p. 124.
45   *Ibid.*, p. 118.
46   *Ibid.*, p. 119.
47   *Ibid.*, p. 120.
48   *Ibid.*, p. 77.
49   *Ibid.*, p. 109.
50   *Ibid.*, p. 187.
51   *Ibid.*, p. 194.
52   *Ibid.*, pp. 194, 195.
53   *Ibid.*, p. 195.
54   *Ibid.*
55   *Ibid.*, p. 196.
56   *Ibid.*
57   *Ibid.*, p. 194.
58   *Ibid.*, p. 188.
59   *Ibid.*, p. 24.
60   *Ibid.*
61   *Ibid.*
62   *Ibid.*, p. 35. Since Beauvoir applies one of her favourite words of moral
     condemnation – 'capricious' – to this poet, we immediately expect the
     new relationship to end disastrously, which it does.
63   *Ibid.*
64   *Ibid.*, p. 27.
65   *Ibid.*
66   *Ibid.*, p. 28.
67   *Ifbid.*
68   *Married Love*, p. 74.
69   *When Things of the Spirit Come First*, p. 30.
70   *Ibid.*, pp. 30, 31.
71   *In the Beauty of the Lilies*, p. 207.
72   *Ibid.*

Chapter Six

THE PREGNANT BODY

There is an abundance of anecdotal evidence to the effect that the Catholic Church has always had a special predilection for fecundity as the natural end of marital love. 'You have them, and God will provide for them', the Redemptorists are reported to have shrieked at female parishioners in Limerick.[1] Whether the message was always heeded is a moot point: if the Irish-American author Frank McCourt is to be believed, a Limerick woman's favourite word, at that time, was 'No!' Moreover, in the Catholic Ireland of my boyhood (the 1950s) there was a surprising number of Catholic couples who, contrary to the legend of the large Catholic family, had no children at all – a legacy, I suspect, of the twin ravages of tuberculosis (affecting the fallopian tubes) and the intensity of Catholic strictures on pre-marital sex (creating a morbid fear of, or distaste for, sex in female minds especially). But if the message was lost on some Irish parishioners, it apparently settled down quite comfortably in Catholic Belgium where women had a saying 'Rather ten on your hands than one on your conscience'.[2] The benign Bishop of Bruges, Emile-Joseph de Smedt, advised that:

> Married people for whom physical fecundity is possible will come to full self-realisation only if they freely take upon themselves the mission God has entrusted to them.[3]

Warming to his theme – in a pastoral which was democratic even by today's standards[4] – he further advised that:

> To be happy, a couple must fall in with the wishes of Nature who constantly urges generosity and fecundity. Love is essentially

creative. 'Increase and multiply and fill the earth'. That was the mission God entrusted to men on the day of their creation.[5]

'My dear people', he went on:

> don't misunderstand me. I am not telling you not to be sensible, or recommending you to throw prudence to the winds. But I am asking you to be *generous*. Don't be content with the minimum. Behave like dedicated collaborators with God. You won't repent of it, either in this world, or in eternity. Duty and courage are within the grasp of each of us. But I add for your reassurance: not everyone is called upon to found a *very* large family. Having said that and without in any way belittling the esteem and love we owe to our smaller families, I think it my duty to ask the Christian community to be fairer in its judgments and to give more respect to parents who have accepted a great number of children from the hands of God.[6]

These sentiments find ample expression in the revised *Catechism of the Catholic Church*. 'Sacred Scripture and the Church's traditional practice', it says, 'see in *large families* a sign of God's blesssing and the parents' generosity'.[7] The theological underpinning of this sentence is provided a few sentences further back, where we are told that:

> Fecundity is a gift, an *end of marriage*, for conjugal love naturally tends to be fruitful. A child does not come from outside as something added on to the mutual love of the spouses, but springs from the very heart of that mutual giving as its fruit and fulfilment. So the Church, which is 'on the side of life' teaches that 'each and every marriage act must remain open to the transmission of life'.[8]

It is well known that Simone de Beauvoir had no interest in *becoming* pregnant, but her horror of maternity did not in the least diminish her *interest* in maternity and motherhood as conditions which a great many women either voluntarily adopt or have forced upon them. Her Catholic formation, and exposure to the large families favoured in the Catholic circles to which she belonged, gave her many insights into the social and domestic features of fecundity, while the writing of *The Second Sex* forced her to research the more biological and evolutionary dimensions of reproduction among humans and non-humans alike. Her writing on the subject of fertility and large families is typically provocative, but much of the science and the philosophy built on that science, is outdated and literally dangerous so far as the expectant mother is concerned. In this chapter on the pregnant body I propose to substantiate all of these statements comprehensively.

In volume I of her memoirs, *Memoirs of a Dutiful Daughter,* Simone de Beauvoir recalls the distaste which she harboured for pregnancy and offspring even when she was a child:

> I don't know why, but organic phenomena very soon ceased to interest me. When we were in the country, I helped Madeleine feed her rabbits and her hens, but these tasks soon bored me and I cared very little for the softness of fur or feather. I have never liked animals. I found red-faced, wrinkled, milky-eyed babies a great nuisance. Whenever I dressed up as a nurse, it was to go and bring in the wounded from a battlefield; but I never nursed them ... When we played games, I accepted the role of mother only if I were allowed to disregard its nursing aspects ... I accepted the discreet collaboration of my sister whom I high-handedly assisted in the bringing up of her own children. But I refused to allow a man to come between me and my maternal responsibiities: our husbands were always abroad. In real life, I knew, things were quite different: the mother of a family is always flanked by her mate; she is overburdened by a thousand tiresome tasks. Whenever I thought of my own future, this servitude seemed to me so burdensome that I decided that I wouldn't have any children; the important thing for me was to be able to form minds and mould characters[9]: I shall be a teacher, I thought.[10]

When she abandoned her plan of becoming a Carmelite, Beauvoir's thoughts turned to love and marriage. She says that she could easily envisage the prospect of being married without having any feelings of repugnance; but she could not envisage *maternity* without repugnance:

> Maternity was something I couldn't entertain, and I was astounded whenever Zaza started cooing over new-born infants with crumpled red faces.[11]

In the second volume of her memoirs, *The Prime of Life,* Beauvoir offers a long series of personal observations on maternity and motherhood in response to the numerous questions she had been posed on this whole topic. First, she had no antipathy towards motherhood as such: while babies held no interest for her, older children were far more tolerable, sometimes even 'charming'. Moreover, when she had contemplated marrying her cousin Jacques, she had envisaged herself having children in that context. Now, in later life, a child did not enter the equation for the following reasons:

> (a) 'my happiness was too complete for any new element to attract me'.[12]

> (b) 'A Child would not have strengthened the bonds that united Sartre and me'.[13]

(c) 'nor did I want Sartre's existence reflected and extended in some other being'.[14]

(d) 'I was too self-sufficient: I never once dreamed of rediscovering myself in the child I might bear'.[15]

(e) her relationship with her own parents had been so bad that she expected the same difficulties to arise between herself and any children she might have.

(f) finally:

> maternity itself seemed incompatible with the way of life upon which I was embarking. I knew that in order to become a writer I needed a great measure of time and freedom. I had no rooted objection to playing at long odds, but this was not a game: the whole value and direction of my life lay at stake. The risk of compromising it could only have been justified had I regarded a child as no less vital a creative task than a work of art, which I did not.[16]

Since she could perceive little creative achievement in childbearing, she was not prepared to make *any* of the sacrifices childbearing demands of expectant mothers:

> I have recounted elsewhere how shocked I was by Zaza's declaration – we were both fifteen at the time – that having babies was just as important as writing books: I still failed to see how any common ground could be found between two such objects in life. Literature, I thought, was a way of justifying the world by fashioning it anew in the pure context of imagination – and, at the same time, of preserving its own existence from oblivion. Childbearing, on the other hand, seemed no more than a purposeless and unjustifiable increase of the world's population. It is hardly surprising that a Carmelite, having undertaken to pray for all mankind, also renounces the engendering of individual human beings.[17]

Beauvoir returns with a vengeance to the topic of pregnancy in her collection of short stories *When Things of the Spirit Come First*. She does so in the second of these stories, that called *Chantal*. Chantal teaches at a private Catholic school for girls, where one of her pupils, Monique, confides to another student Andrée, that she is pregnant. There were two authorised Catholic solutions to this 'crisis': adoption or fast-track marriage (the latter colloquially called 'shotgun marriage'). The latter solution is the one which has been mooted, though Monique herself wants neither the baby nor the wedding: 'Andrée, I don't want to have a baby. I don't want to marry Serge. 'It is left to Andrée, however, to conceptualize the state of pregnancy. She does so in unremittingly negative terms. Gazing at Monique, she finds it impossible to imagine that 'a mysterious rot should be spreading in that slim, graceful body'.[18] A little later, when she looked at Monique's familiar face she finds herself overcome by 'an immense disgust'. ['un immense écoeurement'[19]] This nauseous feeling is occasioned, not by Monique's face, but by the fact that it was the face of a woman under whose 'belly's satiny skin there was something shapeless, something living, that grew and swelled with every minute'.[20] Andrée imagines the entire period of gestation as follows:

> In seven months! Monique's waist was going to thicken: her belly would grow drum-tight: already her features were drawn and her eyes had rings under them. Caresses had made her body faint with pleasure: soon it would be torn by the pangs of childbirth. Andrée looked away. A train crossed the iron bridge, making a great din; then everything felt silent again. It was a warm, calm evening. Sometimes a woman's voice or the cry of a child floated up from the barges with their painted sides. The cathedral spire could be seen, far away and slightly misty.[21]

II

In *The Second Sex*, the section on pregnancy is part of a more extensive section on the biology of mammals. The story of the male mammal is relatively short and simple: the male basically breezes through life. His sex life synchronises with the remainder of his life. He is so at home in his body that one can even say that he *is* his body. As Beauvoir herself phrases it:

> the male sex life is normally integrated with his individual existence: in desire and in coition his transcendence towards the species is at one with his subjectivity – he is his body.[22]

In marked contrast to the comfortable biological odyssey of the male subject, that of the female is one of unremitting struggle with the body, and through the body with the species. Beauvoir has three connected points to make here:

(i) The species imposes itself on woman.

(ii) The species controls woman from puberty to menopause.

(iii) The mechanism of control is the female body. As a consequence, a woman experiences her body as an alien, evil thing. She is not one with her body.

The enslavement of the woman by the species occurs in four separate stages: during embryonic development, at birth, at puberty, and during pregnancy. 'In embryonic life', first of all:

> the supply of oocytes is already built up, the ovary containing about 4,000 immature eggs, each in a follicle, of which perhaps 400 will ultimately reach maturation.[23]

Then:

> From birth, the species has taken possession of woman and tends to tighten its grasp. In coming into the world woman experiences a kind of first puberty,as the oocytes enlarge suddenly; then the ovary is reduced to about a fifth of its former size – one might say that the child is granted a respite. While her body develops, her genital system remains almost stationary; some of the follicles enlarge, but they fail to mature. The growth of the little girl is similar to that of the boy.[24]

However:

> At puberty the species reasserts its claim. Under the influence of the ovarian secretions the number of developing follicles increases, the ovary receives more blood and grows larger, one of the follicles matures, ovulation occurs, and the menstrual cycle is initiated; the genital system assumes its definitive size and form, the body takes on feminine contours, and the endocrine balance is established.[25]

As Beauvoir sees it, the menstrual cycle 'is a burden, and a useless one from the point of view of the individual'.[26] 'Almost all women', she claims:

> more than 85%, show more or less distressing symptoms during the menstrual period. Blood pressure rises before the beginning of the flow and falls afterwards; the pulse rate and often the temperature are increased, so that fever is frequent; pains in the abdomen are felt ... perspiration is increased and accompanied at the beginning of the menses by an odour *sui generis*, which may be very strong and may persist throughout the period ... The central nervous system is affected, with frequent headache, and the sympathetic system is overactive ... The woman is more emotional, more nervous, more irritable than usual, and may manifest serious psychic disturbance.[27]

Beauvoir concludes her account of the menstrual cycle with the claim that:

> It is during her periods that she feels her body most painfully as an obscure, alien thing; it is, indeed, the prey of stubborn and foreign life that each month constructs and then tears down a cradle within it; each month all things are made ready for a child and then aborted in the crimson flow.[28]

So, like a man, a woman 'is her body', but unlike a man 'her body is something other than herself'. It is something other than herself in that she is put upon continuously by it, and feels it like an obscure, alien presence. It is a pain, not just in the neck, but all over.

But worse, much worse, is to come:

> Woman experiences a more profound alienation when fertilization has occurred and the dividing egg passes down into the uterus and proceeds to develop there.[29]

Beauvoir then documents 'the profound alienation' of pregnancy in the following stages.

(1) Under normal conditions, pregnancy is not harmful, i.e. does not cause serious health problems for the mother; indeed, 'certain interactions between her and the foetus become established which are even beneficial to her'.[30]

(2) Beauvoir adds in a footnote that she is taking 'an exclusively physiological point of view' here, adding 'It is evident that maternity can be very advantageous psychologically for a woman, just as it can also be a disaster'.[31]

(3) While pregnancy is not, under normal conditions, physically harmful for the woman, she gains nothing from it, and it exacts great sacrifices of her.

Beauvoir gives the following depressing account of pregnancy:

> In spite of an optimistic view having all too obvious social utility, however, gestation is a fatiguing task of no individual benefit to the woman, but on the contrary demanding heavy sacrifices. It is often associated in the first months with loss of appetite and vomiting, which are not observed in any female domesticated animal and which signalize the revolt of the organism against the invading species. There is a loss of phosphorous, calcium, and iron – the last difficult to make good later; metabolic overactivity excites the endocrine system; the sympathetic nervous system is in a state of increased excitement; and the blood shows a lowered specific gravity, it is lacking in iron, and in general it is similar to 'that of persons fasting, of victims of famine, of those who have been bled frequently, of convalescents'. All that a healthy and well-nourished woman can hope for is to recoup these losses without too much difficulty after childbirth; but frequently serious accidents or at least dangerous disorders mark the course of pregnancy; and if the woman is not strong, if hygienic precautions are not taken, repeated childbearing will make her prematurely old and misshapen, as often among the rural poor.[32]

(4) Childbirth itself, she continues:

> is painful and dangerous. In this crisis it is most clearly evident that the body does not always work to the advantage of both species and individual at once; the infant may die, and, again, in being born, it may kill its mother or leave her with a chronic ailment.[33]

This is Beauvoir's account of pregnancy. Whether, and how often, women get pregnant is – as she soon points out – another matter, and one for which society has the primary responsibility. Indeed, the extent to which a woman will experience pregnancy as burdensome will also depend on the extent of the social supports she has available to her. Still, 'The enslavement of the female to the species and the limitations of her various powers are extremely important facts ...'[34]

III

In this closing section I shall offer some critical comments on Beauvoir's narrative of the pregnant body in her memoirs, in her prose fiction (short stories), and in *The Second Sex*. She reacted with revulsion to pregnancy and infant offspring during her childhood, but that is not altogether unusual; apart altogether from sibling rivalry, it is well known that youngsters sometimes act with revulsion, and even extreme cruelty, in the presence of new-born creatures, especially when the fledglings do not look in the least attractive (e.g. pidgeons), or bear little resemblance to their later, fully-grown selves.

Her reasons for rejecting children when she was an adult are much more interesting, not least for the insight they give us into her *concept* of children. For instance, she neither wanted nor needed a child, she says, because her happiness was already complete. Neither would a child have strengthened the bonds which already united herself and Sartre. She expected that the relationship she would have with any children of her own would be determined by a rigid law of genetics: her own disastrous relationship with her parents was *bound* to be replicated in a later generation. Finally, work and children could not be combined; the care of children would make it impossible to pursue the career of writer.

Several of these reasons combine realism with self-serving argument. She clearly, and wisely, felt that there was too much of her own mother in herself to make it possible for her to be an accomodating parent; at the same time, she is uncharacteristically quiescent and fatalistic in her acceptance of an iron law of genetics controlling human relationships. To say the least, it is an odd stance for an existentialist. Undoubtedly it *is* extremely difficult to combine a career with the care and rearing of children. But it has been done. More to the point, the assistance of a supportive partner, and/or the availability of other social support systems can, as Beauvoir herself so often argues, mitigate dramatically the burdens of childcare. I note, finally, in this connection, that Beauvoir evinces no interest in *family history*, in the succession of generations, in the inheritance of some characteristics and not others, in the long-term view. I can see two reasons for this: her massive alienation from her own family and relations, and her profound, ultra-bourgeois detestation of the (bourgeois) family as a social institution and social milieu. Sometimes, this kind of alienation does not last a lifetime, and bridges can be mended; but sometimes also they are not.

In the short stories anthologised in the collection *When Things of the Spirit Come First*, we are presented with the following statements about pregnancy:

(i) During pregnancy, a 'mysterious rot' spreads through the otherwise 'slim, graceful body';

(ii) under 'the belly's satiny skin there was something shapeless, something living, that grew and swelled with every minute';

(iii) during the final trimester the pregnant woman's waist thickens and her belly grows drum-tight;

(iv) labour itself is unavoidably painful.

Some of these statements are banal truths; others have been made less and less true by medical advances, and others still are seriously misleading. Thus the size, shape and weight of the foetus can now be measured with considerable accuracy, from as early as the eighth week of pregnancy.[35] But it is the master metaphor of pregnancy as a mysterious rot which is most at odds with the medical facts. A rot is a condition in plants characterised by breakdown and decay of tissues, caused by parasitic bacteria, fungi and so on. Pregnancy, by contrast, is characterized by development and growth, corresponding to the two stages of pre-natal development. As Margie Profet explains:

> During the formation stage, the embryo's cells multiply very rapidly and differentiate into the various organs and tissues that make up a human body. During the growth stage, the fetus grows from a tiny entity that could easily fit into the palm of the mother's hand to a seven-or-so pound baby ready for birth. The formation stage spans the period from about two weeks to fourteen weeks

after conception. The growth stage spans the period from about fourteen weeks after conception until birth.[36]

Beauvoir writes at some length about pregnancy in *The Second Sex*, in the section on biology. In keeping with the worst traditions of chauvinistic French 'scholarship', however, she rarely cites her sources. In the footnotes she gives the following five references, without an accompanying page reference: 'Hegel, *Philosophy of Nature*'; 'Louis Gallien, *La Sexualité*'; 'Merleau-Ponty, *Phénoménologie de la perception*'; 'H. Vignes', contribution to Roger and Binet (eds.), *Traité de physiologie, Vol. XI*' and 'Zuckermann, *The Social Life of Monkeys (1932)*'. There is an interesting, but not altogether surprising, anecdote in Deirdre Bair's biography to the effect that at an early stage in the correspondence between Howard Parshley (the much-maligned translator of the English-language edition of *The Second Sex*) and Beauvoir, Parshley had requested her to supply him with a list of the sources she had consulted in researching *The Second Sex*. Months later, Bair reports, Beauvoir had replied as follows:

> I am sorry, but it is impossible to recover the references to the English books which I consulted. There are too many of them, and some I had only in translation. In any case, I would not know how to find the passages I cited without a tremendous amount of work.[37]

According to Bair, Parshley – 'a professor emeritus of zoology at Smith College' – was a gentle, tactful man, virtues which were, I surmise, taxed to the full when he set about translating the section on biology. He says himself that:

> At the publisher's request I have, as editor, occasionally added an explanatory word or two (especially in connection with existentialist terminology) and provided a few additional footnotes and biographic data which I thought might be to the reader's interest.[38]

This is disingenuous, however, since by far the most extensive of these interventions occurs in the section on biology where it is clear that, as a zoologist, Parshley had difficulty containing his embarrassment at some of the material he had to edit and translate. He furnishes eight lengthy explanatory notes, where he evidently feels Beauvoir's narrative has serious shortcomings. These notes refer to the mixing of genes brought about by sexual reproduction; isogamy; the soma in humans and animals; the ratio between ova and children in women and animals; hermaphroditism; mortality rates for women and men; the sex physiology of the larger apes, and pregnancy sickness in women. In relation to this last, Beauvoir had written:

In spite of an optimistic view having all too obvious social utility, however, gestation is a fatiguing task of no individual benefit to the woman but on the contrary demanding heavy sacrifices. It is often associated in the first months with loss of appetite and vomiting, which are not observed in any female domesticated animal and which signalise the revolt of the organism against the invading species. Parshley politely advises the reader that 'It may be said that these symptoms also signalize a faulty diet, according to some modern gynaecologists'.[39]

Beauvoir's views on pregnancy sickness – that vomiting and nausea represent the revolt of organism against the invading species – are violently contradicted by the 'adaptationist' Margie Profet in her book *Protecting your baby-to-be*, as well as by even more recent research findings published in the *Quarterly Review of Biology*. Profet does not mention Beauvoir by name, but she includes such views as are found on this topic in *The Second Sex* in the following catalogue of 'the most harmful attitudes about pregnancy sickness (which were) developed during the twentieth century'[40]:

After the advent of psychoanalysis, some physicians and psychologists began to blame women for their pregnancy sickness, attributing it to female neuroses. Many pregnant women were told that their severe nausea and vomiting represented a subconscious rejection of pregnancy, an ambivalence about motherhood, a loathing of coitus, an unrelieved frustration at failing to find gratification in pregnancy, a rejection of femininity, or an oral attempt at abortion. The root of their pregnancy sickness was variously viewed as hysteria, an immature personality, or an undue attachment to their own mothers. Hurtful, punitive 'treatments' were inflicted on women who were vomiting so severely that they required hospitalization ... The misconception that pregnancy sickness was psychosomatic undoubtedly increased pregnant women's emotional distress because it made them feel guilty about feeling sick.[41]

In her rejection of this whole line of thought – pregnancy sickness represents a rejection by the pregnant woman, or by her body, of the foetus – Profet defines pregnancy sickness as 'a collection of symptoms, which invariably include food and odour aversions, and often includes nausea and vomiting as well'.[42] Her general thesis concerning pregnancy sickness – explained and defended with great plausibility – is that it:

protects the embryo from naturally occurring plant and bacterial toxins in the mother's diet that can cause birth defects or miscarriage. It does this by causing the mother to become repulsed by smells and tastes that indicate toxicity.[43]

The philosophical principle underlying Profet's medical arguments – one which also underpins her account of menstruation, which again is violently at odds with Beauvoir's account of it[44] – is that every mechanism in the body was designed to solve some problem in the ancestral environment (hence the epithets 'adaptationist' and 'Darwinian' which have often been applied to her). The problem, then, that pregnancy sickness was designed to solve was 'the vulnerability of the developing embryo to the natural toxins in the human diet'.[45] She explains that 'Humans, like other animals, have evolved many defenses against toxins, which is why we can eat so many of the toxins in foods without being harmed by them. Such mechanisms include ways to detect and avoid dangerous levels of toxins as well as ways to detoxify and eliminate toxins that have been eaten. Many toxins that in low doses are easily tolerated by adults, however, can harm or even kill an embryo by disrupting the process of organ formation and causing permanent malformations ... Because the human body cannot possibly know inherently which *particular* toxins, of the vast spectrum that exist in nature, would cause defects in the embryo's organ formation, pregnancy sickness is designed to recognize *general* cues of toxicity, thereby preventing the embryo from being exposed to high doses of potentially devastating toxins'.[46]

While Profet's thesis has in the past been unceremoniously rejected by some of her medical colleagues,[47] it has received impressive support from recent research which shows that expectant mothers who do *not* experience pregnancy sickness are more than twice as likely to suffer a miscarriage than those who do. An article by Amanda Kelly in *The Independent on Sunday* (11 June, 2000), based on recently published research in the *Quarterly Review of Biology*, reports as follows:

> A study of 80,000 pregnancies by American academics has concluded that even natural remedies such as ginger, which have been favoured by doctors since the Thalidomide disaster of 40 years ago, could put mother and child at greater risk. Professor Paul Sherman and Samuel Flaxman, evolutionary biologists at Cornell University in New York looked at pregnancies documented in 56 studies from 16 different countries and found that while approximately 10 per cent of women who did not suffer vomiting in pregancy lost their baby, this was true of only 4 per cent of those who did. They are convinced that far from being a negative side-effect of having a baby, morning sickness is actually good for the two-thirds of pregnant women who experience it. They claim it is an evolutionary mechanism that protects mother and child from harmful organisms in food. They believe their findings help explain why many pregnant women develop an aversion to the same kinds of foods. The most common aversions were to meats, fish, poultry and eggs – foods more likely to carry harmful micro-organisms and

parasites before the advent of modern refrigeration and food-handling processes. Writing in the latest issue of the *Quarterly Review of Biology*, Professor Sherman said:

'Our study is the first to gather compelling evidence that morning sickness is nature's way of protecting mothers and foetuses from food-borne illnesses and of shielding the baby from chemicals that can deform foetal organs at the most critical time in development. Morning sickness is therefore a complete misnomer. It does not just occur in the morning and it is not a sickness in the pathological sense. Morning sickness and the aversion to potentially harmful foods is the body's way of preserving the mother's health at a time when her immune system is naturally suppressed to prevent rejection of the child that is developing in her uterus and has reduced defences against food-borne pathogens. Alleviating the symptoms through the use of drugs or natural remedies could therefore have harmful effects if doing so interferes with the expulsion and subsequent avoidance of dangerous foods'.[48]

Profet's thesis is diametrically at odds with Beauvoir's account of pregnancy sickness, and with all representations of such 'sickness' as a conscious or subconscious rejection of the womb's new occupant. On the contrary, pregnancy sickness is designed to protect the developing embryo from dangerous toxins. Profet plausibly argues that pregnant women in all cultures experience pregnancy sickness, regardless of whether their pregnancy is voluntary or otherwise. Profet's thesis also synchronises with the single most dominant feature of all voluntary pregnancies: their intended and desired effect. Beauvoir writes that gestation is a fatiguing task of no individual benefit to the woman. One can easily see what she means. But the fatigue and other burdens of pregnancy, including pregnancy sickness, are a price that many women are prepared to pay for what pregnancy literally delivers: in the vast majority of cases, a healthy baby.

Notes

1   These exhortations were directed at *married women*, of course. A dreadful fate lay in store for unmarried women who had the misfortune to become pregnant. See M. Milotte, *Banished Babies* (1997), for a comprehensive documentation of the details, in so far as Catholic Ireland was concerned.
2   See E.J. de Smedt, *Married Love*, p. 58.
3   *Ibid.*, p. 58.
4   Instead of simply preaching at, or to, the faithful, he prints huge chunks of their correspondence to him.

5   *Married Love*, pp. 55, 56.

6   *Ibid.*, pp. 57, 58.

7   *Catecism of the Catholic Church*, p. 508.

8   *Ibid.*, p. 507.

9   This is a *very* Catholic mission, it should be noted. The words of the novelist Jenny Newman, herself an ex-nun, are apposite: 'Catholicism is a religion that encourages you as a child to pay a lot of attention to what is going on inside and to assess why you do things ... In general religious life you have to examine your conscience a couple of times a day, which is something that is useful for a novelist', *The Times Higher Education Supplement*, 2 June 2000.

10   *Memoirs*, p. 56.

11   *Ibid.*, p. 143.

12   *The Prime of Life*, p. 77.

13   *Ibid.*

14   *Ibid.*

15   *Ibid.*

16   *Ibid.*, p. 78.

17   *Ibid.*

18   *When Things of the Spirit Come First*, p. 81.

19   *Quand prime le spirituel*, p. 94.

20   *When Things of the Spirit Come First*, pp. 81, 82.

21   *Ibid*, p. 82.

22   *The Second Sex*, p. 58.

23   *Ibid.*

24   *Ibid.*

25   *Ibid.*, pp. 58, 59.

26   *Ibid.*, p. 60.

27   *Ibid.*, p. 61.

28   *Ibid.*

29   *Ibid.*, p. 62.

30   *Ibid.*

31   *Ibid.*

32   *Ibid.*

33   *Ibid.*

34   *Ibid.*, p. 69.

35   See *She* magazine, 'Having a Baby', Autumn/Winter 1997, pp. 9–12.

36   *Protecting your baby-to-be*, p.1.

37   *Simone de Beauvoir, A Biography*, p.434.

38   *The Second Sex*, Translator's Preface, p.11.

39   *Ibid.*, p.62.

40   *Protecting your baby-to-be*, p.11.

41   *Ibid.*, pp.11,12.

42   *Ibid.*, p.5.

43   *Ibid.*

44 See Deborah Hutton, 'Blessing in Disguise', *Vogue*, May 1994, pp. 170, 209.
45 *Protecting your baby-to-be*, p. 5.
46 *Ibid.*, p. 6.
47 See Hutton, *op. cit.*
48 A. Kelly, 'Morning sickness halves the risk of miscarriage', *The Independent on Sunday*, 11 June 2000.

Chapter Seven

SIMONE DE BEAUVOIR ON ABORTION

The central thesis of this book is that while Simone de Beauvoir ceased to be a practising Catholic relatively early in life, and wrote openly in her memoirs of having abandoned God mid-way through adolescence,[1] she nonetheless continued to see the world through Catholic eyes. In more detail, this thesis will mean that she draws extensively from the Catholic lexicon in her writings, that the major themes of her writings – such as death, morality, the virtues and vices, God, human sexuate nature, reproduction and motherhood – are *all* quintesssentially Catholic obsessions, and, more controversially, that the positions she adopts on such subjects and issues are far less anti-Catholic than she herself, and a host of commentators, would have us believe. In this chapter I propose to concentrate on her views on abortion. To present her views, I will first of all distinguish between two different questions about abortion:

(1) Is it morally permissible to procure, or to assist in the procurement, of an abortion?

(2) How should the law, and the Health Services, respond to the demand for abortion?

Question (1) treats abortion as an issue in *personal morality,* while question (2) treats it as an issue in *social morality.*[2] As I see it, Beauvoir's answer to question (1) is: Yes, abortion is morally permissible, even though there are serious moral reasons against it. However, the reasons against it are not those standardly adduced in Catholic moral theology, but reasons drawn from the feminist ethics which she herself adumbrates in *The Second Sex*. Beauvoir's answer to question (2), with which people are vastly more familiar, is that abortion should be fully legalised, and at this end of things she remains, of course, stridently and comprehensively anti-Catholic.

The plan of the present chapter is as follows. In the first place, I will provide a short history of Catholic teaching on the morality of abortion, particularly in the post-war period. In the second section, I will summarise the account of Beauvoir's views on abortion which is furnished by the secondary literature. In the third section, I will document, at considerable length, Beauvoir's views on abortion as found in *The Second Sex*. In the fourth and final section, I will do these three things:

> (i) summarise her views on abortion as found in her later writings for the pro-choice organization *Choisir*;

> (ii) draw what salient conclusions there are to be drawn from all this material; in effect, amplify and defend the claims with which I have just opened this chapter;

> (iii) finally, I will make some tentative remarks on the feminist ethics which is adumbrated in *The Second Sex*, and explore the question of whether there are any ecoes here of a Catholic viewoint still beckoning from the past.

I

Catholic Teaching on Abortion

Catholic teaching on abortion has remained rigidly absolutist during the post-war period. It depicts abortion as the killing of the unborn, and such killing, it holds, is wrong in all circumstances. It is the duty of the law to protect unborn human beings, and any legislation which withdraws such protection is variously condemned as 'grossly unjust', 'an act of violence', and 'a corruption of law'.[3]

There are small, but fascinating, variations in the thinking behind, and in the presentation of, this moral teaching. In 1952, the Jesuit theologian Henry Davis summarised decades of Catholic teaching on abortion with the following words:

> So soon as life is present and as long as it is present, no one has the disposal of it. It is therefore never permissible to adopt any means

> which have the intentional and direct physical result of removing the product of conception from the mother's womb. To do so would be to take a living being from the environment in which alone it can continue to live, and to put it into one in which it cannot possibly survive ... Consequently Catholic teaching condemns all direct abortions under every circumstance.[4]

In other words, it condemns all procedures where the intention of the procedure is to kill the foetus.

In January 1980 Britain's seven Catholic archbishops issued a joint statement in which they called for a renewed national campaign against abortion, in defence of what they called the nation's 'weakest, totally silent minority group', the unborn. The archbishops invoked the principle of the sanctity of human life when they argued that the vast majority of abortions carried out in Britain represented 'a massive and growing trivialisation of human life, and increasing acceptance of the practice of killing on demand'.[5] The archbishops declared that 'These developing human lives may be unborn and silent, but they are already part of our human family. They need to be defended'.[6] They stressed that the law ought to respect and embody the principles that are basic to civilisation and to existing law in every other domain, namely, that innocent life is to be protected by the criminal law and public policy, and that no law should countenance discrimination by the strong against the weak. They condemned the 1967 Abortion Act as 'grossly unjust'. It permitted the killing of the unborn because of their 'handicap' or even because of some 'substantial risk' that they may suffer some 'serious handicap'. It wrongly presumed that such individuals could be treated as if they were 'better off dead'. The Act, they assserted, treated the very life and existence of a new human being as outweighed in value by another human being's perhaps slight or passing problems of physical or mental well being. At least two principles, then, were invoked in this statement:

(1) The principle of the sanctity of innocent human life, and

(2) the principle of the equal value of all human beings.

The human race is seen as a family, and unborn human beings are seen as members of this family, albeit silent ones.

The metaphor of the family was localised by Pope John Paul II during the summer of 1979, when he preached to a vast crowd on a return visit to Krakow: 'I desire that the Polish family should give life', he intoned:

> that it should be faithful to the sacred right to life. If the right of man to live is transgressed at the very moment when he starts to

become a human being, in his mother's womb, then the entire moral order – which indirectly serves to protect the inalienable welfare of man – is jeopardised.[7]

Here John Paul II reaffirms the principle of the sanctity of human life in the guise of 'the sacred right to life', and adds, implicitly at least, a third principle, that of non-exclusion from the human family.

In May 1992 the Irish Catholic Bishops' Conference issued a statement on 'the constitutional amendment whereby Ireland would adhere to the Maastricht Treaty of European Unity', an amendment which was submitted to the vote of the people in a referendum on 18 June of that same year. This constitutional amendment, they declared, 'raises many issues of the greatest importance for the future of our country'. The referendum on the Maastricht Treaty, the statement allowed, was primarily concerned with matters of a political and economic nature. But in paragraph 5 of their statement, the Bishops went on to say that 'The substantive and fundamental issue is the right to life of the unborn child'.[8] 'The Catholic Church', it declared:

> in common with many Christians in other Churches and many of the great religious and moral traditions of humanity, teaches that the direct and intentional killing of innocent human life, at any stage from conception to natural death, is gravely morally wrong.[9]

This teaching, it advised:

> should not be labelled an 'extremist' or 'fundamentalist' view held by some Catholics; it is the clear and universal teaching of the Catholic Church. Human life is at its most defenceless in the womb, and has a right to receive the protection of the law. Care for all human life is the foundation of our responsibilities to one another and to the earth which is entrusted to men and women by the Creator. It contributes to the emergence of the new creation for which Christians are eagerly longing and of which we are all called to be instruments.[10]

Here we are offered another variation on the principle of the sanctity of human life, on this occasion in the guise of the principle 'It is gravely morally wrong to directly and intentionally kill innocent human beings'. What is forbidden is the *direct and intentional* taking of innocent human life. This principle does not forbid – and this is formally acknowledged – the provision of:

> urgent medical treatment ... (to) An expectant mother with a life-threatening illness ... even when the treatment puts the life of the child at risk.[11]

The Bishops explain that:

> Obstetrical practice in Ireland has an outstanding record of success
> in preserving the lives both of the mother and the baby. This in itself
> indicates that recourse to abortion is not necessary to save the life of
> the mother, and that the absence of abortion does not endanger the
> lives of women. Abortions carried out in other countries are very
> seldom even claimed to be necessary to save the mother's life.[12]

In November 1992 the Irish Bishops' Conference issued a detailed
statement on abortion and the law in its contribution to the debate
surrounding the second Irish referendum on the issue. The moral
principle governing the practice of abortion 'is not open to question', it
declared. It then formally declared this principle to be: 'The intentional
destruction of innocent human life, at any stage from conception to
natural death, is gravely wrong'.[13] The Bishops then amplified their
view of this moral principle as follows:

> This principle admits of no exceptions. It does not depend on a
> particular religious conviction. The unborn child's right to life 'is a
> primary, natural, inalienable right that springs from the very
> dignity of every human being' (Pope John Paul II to the Irish
> Bishops, September 25, 1992). This is the principle which ought to
> guide conscience and behaviour, whatever the Constitution or law
> might say.[14]

The moral principle governing the practice of abortion, from the
Catholic perspective, re-emerges, then, as the principle of the right to
life, enjoyed inalienably by all human beings from conception to natural
death. This principle, in turn, has its roots in the idea of the dignity of
the human being, in the idea that human beings are deserving of a
special recognition. Humans are considered to be deserving of a special
recognition for the following three reasons:

(1) 'This life comes from God'[15];

(2) Human beings enjoy a life which is immortal: 'Conception marks the
beginning of a life which will never end, because each human being is
called to live with God forever.[16]

(3) Each human being is a member of the human family and, as such,
entitled to special respect:

> The new human being, by the very fact of existing, belongs to the
> human family and must not be denied the respect and protection of
> every other member of the human family, of society and of the
> law.[17]

The Catechism of the Catholic Church [1994], in the section on abortion, opens with the declaration that 'Human life must be respected and protected absolutely from the moment of conception'.[18] It immediately adds that:

> From the first moment of his existence, a human being must be recognized as having the rights of a person – among which is the inviolable right of every innocent being to life.[19]

The *Catechism* affirms that this absolutist teaching has, in addition, the weight of tradition behind it:

> Since the first century the Church has affirmed the moral evil of every procured abortion. This teaching has not changed and remains unchangeable. Direct abortion, that is to say, abortion willed either as an end or a means, is gravely contrary to the moral law.[20]

The penalty for what it terms 'formal co-operation in an abortion' is excommunication, quoting the Code of Canon Law, canon 1398, which declares 'A person who procures a completed abortion incurs excommunication *latae sententiae*, by the very commission of the offence'.[21]

In 1995 the Irish Bishops' Conference issued a 22-paragraph statement on a Bill before the Oireachtas (Irish Parliament) which proposed to deal with the provision of information on abortion. The Bishops opposed this Bill on the basis that it would facilitate women in procuring an abortion. The Bishops then addressed the basic question raised by the proposed piece of legislation, which was, as they saw it, 'the attitude which we adopt as individuals and as society towards the child in the womb'.[22] The view which they opposed they identified as the view that 'the life of the child may be sacrificed to the interests or well-being of his or her mother',[23] which belief, they reasoned, implied 'that the child need not be treated as a human being'.[24] The Bishops then proceeded to reply to these propositions as follows:

> Once a child has been conceived, a human life has begun. God has formed that life and called the new human being by name. There is already present an individual with unique characteristics who is an unrepeatable instance of the richness and variety of the human family. It can never be right to choose to destroy his or her life.[25]

Abortion is always wrong, on this restatement of Catholic teaching, because:

(1) it involves the destruction of a human life;

(2) because it involves killing a member of the human family;

(3) because it involves the destruction of a unique individual, 'an unrepeatable instance of the richness and variety of the human family';

(4) because it involves killing someone created by God, and

(5) because it involves killing someone who has already been *named* by God.

Finally, in July 1995, the Irish Bishops' Conference issued a lengthy statement on civil law and the right to life. In its opening paragraph this statement declared that:

> Society and the law exist in order to serve the human person. A law which purports to authorise the direct and intentional killing of an innocent human being withdraws the protection to which every innocent life is entitled and denies the equality of everyone before the law.[26]

It went on to argue, *inter alia,* that:

> The declaration that it is legal, at least under certain conditions, deliberately to kill an unborn child authorises the violation of a defenceless human being's most basic right.[27]

Abortion is wrong, then, on this restatement of the orthodoxy, because it is a violation of a defenceless human being's right to life and, as such, a violation of the most basic right such an individual possesses.

To summarise: Catholic teaching on abortion, especially in the post-war period, has remained unwaveringly opposed to abortion. But the reasons adduced for opposing abortion have varied to some extent. Abortion is held to be wrong because it violates all of the following principles: the principle of the sanctity of life, the principle of the equal value of all human beings, the principle of the right to life, and the principle of the inalienable dignity of the human being. It is also condemned on the basis that it deprives the human family of one of its members (each time it is carried out), that it destroys part of God's creation, and withdraws the protection to which every innocent, and every defenceless, human being is entitled.

Simone de Beauvoir's views on abortion:
the secondary literature

There isn't an extensive secondary literature on Beauvoir's views on abortion; indeed, some secondary works do not consider it worth mentioning at all. Mary Evans remarks that Beauvoir's stance on abortion, coupled with her opposition to the politics of the French government in Algeria during the decolonising period of the 1950s:

> should be sufficient to clear de Beauvoir of the charge that she failed either to take a stand on issues of conscience or to lend her prestige and fame to causes that involve the decrease of privilege.[28]

This, too, is the way that Evans views Beauvoir's stance on abortion *per se:* Beauvoir, as she sees her, not only was not opposed to abortion, but campaigned for a widening of access to abortion clinics for those who did not belong to a sophisticated social elite:

> When she, and other women, signed the *Manifeste de 343* (a manifesto signed by 343 women who had themselves had abortions), it was apparent that what was at stake was not simply the possibility of the termination of pregnancy, but the extension of that possibility to those outside the cosmopolitan and well-connected circle of women who made up the group of '343'.[29]

Judith Okely presents Beauvoir's stance on abortion in the context of an extensive post-war embargo on pre-marital sex, as well as the many obstacles to reproductive freedom which women had to face. She writes:

> This catalogue of constraints on the sexuality and experience of women in higher education before the women's liberation movement reveals a very different picture from what might have been presumed to be in the centre of enlightened privileged circles. The restrictions were often no less severe on middle-class women outside higher education. The ideal of pre-marital sexuality among working-class women may have been less rigid, but birth control and abortion both before and after marriage were even more difficult to obtain ... Thus de Beauvoir's demand for women's sexual autonomy and control over reproduction had dramatic impact in those early years and again in the 1960s.[30]

In chapter 3, 'The Impact of *The Second Sex*', Okely writes that:

> De Beauvoir presents what are seen today as familiar arguments for the legalisation of abortion. For example, she argues that it is illegal

abortion, not the operation as such, which is the major health risk. De Beauvoir argues that contraception and legal abortion would allow women freedom of choice in maternity: meanwhile women are often obliged to reproduce against their will. In the majority of cases, the mother requires the economic support of a man.[31]

Claude Francis and Fernande Gontier, in their 1985 biography *Simone de Beauvoir*, give more attention than most other commentators to their subject's stance on abortion. At the age of eighteen, they report:

> She was already of the opinion that abortion should not be a crime, that her body was her's alone, and that what she chose to do with it was nobody's business but hers.[32]

Francis and Gontier comment that:

> It was inconceivably bold for a young woman of Catholic upbringing to talk that way about something one did simply not discuss. If ever there was a taboo, this was it. That Simone was capable of even uttering the word 'abortion' demonstrated the force of her provocation.[33]

Francis and Gontier resume their account of Simone de Beauvoir's stance on abortion with their account of the support she gave to the crusading Dr. Weill-Hallié, for whose publication *Family Planning* Beauvoir had written the Preface in 1956. Weill-Hallié, they report, had resolved to shake the medical establishment out of its inertia concerning the abortion issue. Thus in 1955 she had presented a report on 'voluntary maternity' to the Academy of Ethical and Political Sciences. Attacked by most of her male medical colleagues, she decided to establish the French Family Planning Movement in 1958, and called on Simone de Beauvoir for support. Francis and Gontier document Beauvoir's response as follows: 'The author of *The Second Sex* shared Weill-Hallié's ideas. She considered it only proper that women have the right to choose maternity freely, and she approved of the French Family Planning Movement's efforts to spread the use of contraceptives. She saw the law prohibiting abortion as a surefire means of oppressing women and was surprised by the reaction of the communists, who denounced the campaign for contraception as a conspiracy to weaken the proletariat by depriving it of children'.[34]

Francis and Gontier conclude their account of Beauvoir's stance on abortion with a detailed report of her participation in the campaign to legalise abortion in France. Spearheaded by the *Mouvement de Liberation des Femmes* (MLF), this campaign gathered momentum with the publication, in the Spring of 1971, in *Le Nouvel Observateur* and in *Le Monde*, of the *Manifeste de 343*, a manifesto signed by 343 women, each declaring that she had had an abortion, and calling for the introduction of medically supervised abortion in French hospitals. When approached by Anne Zelinski and two others, Beauvoir had immediately agreed to sign the Manifesto, which said:

> One million women have abortions each year in France. They do this in dangerous conditions because of the clandestine nature of the operation when, performed under proper medical supervision, this procedure is among the most simple. Everyone remains silent about these million women. I declare that I am one of them. I declare that I have had an abortion.[35]

Francis and Gontier remind their readers that some twenty years earlier, in *The Second Sex:*

> de Beauvoir had protested the repression of abortion and its tragic consequences. She had never failed to point out that contraception was always preferable, but in the meantime, according to her the majority of French women had no alternative. On November 20th the Women's Liberation Movement (MLF) marched through Paris. De Beauvoir marched along from the Place de la République to the Place de la Nation, under placards and banners demanding the freedom to choose maternity, birth control, and abortion. Four thousand militant women brandished lengths of wire decked with dust rags, laundry, and paper dolls and handed out parsley, the symbol of clandestine abortion.[36]

Finally, in June 1972, Simone de Beauvoir was elected President of *Choisir,* an association which she had co-founded with Gisselle Halimi, Christiane Rochefort, Delphine Seyrig, and Jean Rostand of the Académie Française. 'The association', report Francis and Gontier, 'counted two Nobel Prize winners, in physiology and medicine, among its members: Professor Jacques Monod and Professor François Jacob'. The association had three objectives:

> to make contraception readily available free of charge, to see to it that all legislation pertaining to the illegality of abortion was repealed, and to assume the costs of defending any person accused of having or performing an abortion.[37]

That their association would not be allowed to degenerate into an intellectuals' talking shop is confirmed by the fact, noted by Francis and Gontier, that on 15 June:

> before two thousand people assembled in the 'Maison de la Culture' in Grenoble, de Beauvoir and Halimi announced that *Choisir* had developed a proposition for authorizing legal abortion, and would take it upon itself to publish, despite a law forbidding such publication, the court proceedings of these trials.[38]

Choisir published its first transcript of an abortion trial in November 1972, and in:

> a vigorous preface, Simone de Beauvoir wrote that it was not the accused but the law in whose name they were charged that was on trial ...[39]

The law on abortion, she argued, was 'a law radically divorced from the collective conscience'.[40] She meant that the law gave protection to the foetus, when it was the daily practice all over France to dispose of the remains of miscarriage without ceremony, and without Church blessing. To legalize abortion, she added, 'would be to spare useless suffering, humiliation, fear, and occasionally mutilation and death'.[41]

Finally, in her mammoth personal (as distinct from intellectual) biography of Beauvoir, *Simone de Beauvoir, A Biography*, Deirdre Bair, like other biographers, retraces Beauvoir's involvement with the 1970s women's movement and its campaign to have abortion legalised. But she also delves a little into Beauvoir's views on abortion understood as an issue in *personal* morality, and even more so, understood as a personal *experience* for a woman. Considered first of all as an issue in *social morality*, Bair attributes all of the following views on abortion to Simone de Beauvoir:

(1) Abortion should be legalized.

(2) Contraception should also be legalised.

(3) Contraception is always preferable to abortion.

(4) When contraception is legalised and made easily available, the need for abortion will diminish.

(5) It is sometimes necessary to campaign for *extreme* measures, as a matter of practical politics, so to speak, since such a campaign usually results in achieving more moderate goals.

(6) Quoting Beauvoir:

> Women who must find the courage for this most drastic of measures frequently are crippled for life and many are even killed. How much more humane for everyone if the unwanted life is prevented from occurring in the first place.[42]

Bair reports that while Beauvoir had been one of the most prominent signatories of the 'Manifesto of the 343', she had never had an abortion herself. The truth – known only to close friends 'and a few trusted feminists' – was that:

> Simone de Beauvoir had never had an abortion; however, she frequently allowed illegal abortions to be performed in her

apartment when women had no other choice, and she often paid for them, whether they were carried out in her apartment or somewhere else. 'I was never pregnant, so how could I have an abortion?' Beauvoir said in 1982.[43]

So why had she signed the Manifesto, declaring that she, too, had had an abortion? She did so for the usual strategic reasons, she explained, namely, that as the spiritual mother of the young generation, her physical presence or written support guaranteed a forum, and often brought in converts to the cause. She also believed that she had a duty to a venerable tradition of French intellectuals, not least Victor Hugo and Emile Zola, to be the conscience of her generation, and to lend her voice to unpopular causes. And she was honest enough to admit that as an eminent public figure – owing in no small measure to the status of the writer in French public life – she had less to lose than other women who were less well known, and for that reason, she felt, she had a duty of protection towards them as well. As she put it herself:

> By the time I signed 'The Manifesto of the 343', I was no longer a stranger to the threat of arrest or imprisonment ... *La Cause du Peuple* prepared me for that. I believed that it was up to women like me to take the risk on behalf of those who could not, because we could afford to do it. We had the money and the position and we were not likely to be punished for our actions. Like Sartre, I was now a sacred cow to the authorities and no one would dare arrest me, so don't give me too much credit for bravery because I was untouchable. Save your sympathy for the ordinary women who really suffered by their admission.[44]

III

Simone de Beauvoir on abortion in The Second Sex

Simone de Beauvoir focusses twice over on the topic of abortion in *The Second Sex*: in chapter 5, Part II of Book 1, entitled 'Since the French Revolution: The Job and the Vote', and in chapter 2, Part V of Book II. In Book 1 she traces the history of attidudes towards abortion from Roman law ('which accorded no especial protection to embryonic life ... it regarded the *nasciturum* (to be born) as part of the maternal body, not as a human being'[45]), to Christianity (which 'revolutionized moral ideas in this matter by endowing the embryo with a soul; for then abortion became a crime against the foetus itself'[46]) to the Code of 1791 (which 'excused the woman but punished her accomplices'[47]). Speaking of

Ecclesiastical law during the Middle Ages, she reports that it developed gradually:

> with interminable discussions on such questions as when the soul actually enters the body of the foetus. St. Thomas and others set the time of animation at about the fortieth day for males, and the eightieth for females.[48]

She adds that different degrees of guilt were attached to abortion in the Middle Ages according to when it was performed and why:

> There is a great difference between the poor woman who destroys her infant on account of the difficulty of supporting it, and her who has no aim other than hiding the crime of fornication', said the book of penitence.[49]

In the nineteenth century, she continues, the claim that abortion is murder is replaced by the idea that abortion is a crime against the State. Yet while the French law of 1810 forbade it absolutely, with heavy penalties:

> physicians always practised it whenever it was a question of saving the mother's life. The law was too strict and at the end of the century few arrests were made and still fewer convictions reached. New laws were passed in 1923 and 1939, with some variation in the penalties; and in 1941 abortion was decreed a crime against the safety of the State.[50]

Next, she returns to the task of chronicling developments in Catholic teaching. It did not in any way soften its opposition to the practice of abortion, she reports, observing that 'in 1917 the code of canon law called for the excommunication of all concerned in an abortion'.[51] The Pope, she continues:

> has again quite recently declared that as between the life of the mother and that of the infant, the former must be sacrificed: of course the mother, being baptised, can gain entrance to heaven – oddly enough, hell never enters the calculations – whereas the foetus is doomed to limbo for eternity.[52]

Then in a lengthy footnote, she remarks that:

> the Catholics are far from keeping to the letter of St. Augustine's doctrine. The confessor whispers to the young fiancee the day before the wedding that she can behave in no matter what fashion with her husband from the moment that intercourse is properly completed; positive methods of birth control, including *coitus interruptus*, are forbidden, but one has the right to make use of the calendar established by the Viennese sexologists (the 'rhythm') and commit the act of which the sole recognized end is reproduction on days when conception is supposed to be impossible for the woman.

There are spiritual advisers who even give this calendar to their flock. As a matter of fact, there are plenty of Christian mothers who have only two or three children even though they did not completely sever marital relations after the last accouchement.[53]

There exists, she maintains, a considerable leeway between official attitudes towards abortion and the actual behaviour of citizens. Thus, on the one hand:

> Abortion has been officially recognized during a brief period only: in Germany before Nazism, and in Russia before 1936. But in spite of religion and the law, it holds a place of considerable importance in all countries. In France abortions number each year from 800,000 to 1,000,000 – about as many as there are births – two thirds of those aborted being married, many already having one or two children.[54]

By means of contraception, abortion, and progress in obstetrical science, she concludes, the whole area of reproduction has become one of freedom, one more domain over which women can now take control:

> These changes are of tremendous importance for woman in particular; she can reduce the number of her pregnancies and make them a rationally integral part of her life, instead of being their slave. During the nineteenth century woman in her turn emancipated herself from nature; she gained mastery of her own body. Now protected in large part from the slavery of reproduction, she is in a position to assume the economic role that is offered her and will assure her of complete independence.[55]

This has been 'in spite of prejudices, opposition and the survival of an outdated morality'.[56]

Beauvoir returns to the topic of abortion in Book II, in the chapter on motherhood. She takes up where she left off, with the fact that the reproductive function in human beings has, for about a century, no longer been at the mercy of biological fate, but 'has come under the voluntary control of human beings'.[57] With this observation she then proceeds to a discussion of contraception and abortion.

In countries subject to what she calls (the) Catholic influence, contraception, she reports, is practised in a clandestine manner: 'either the man uses *coitus interruptus* or the woman rids her body of the sperm after intercourse'.[58] But neither form of contraception is satisfactory:

> the man dislikes having to be on his guard at the moment of enjoyment; the woman dislikes the disagreeable task of douching; he is resentful of the woman's too fertile body; she dreads the germs of life that he risks placing within her.[59]

When, despite all such precautions, she finds herself pregnant:

> Then resort is had to an especially desperate remedy: that is, abortion. No less illegal in countries that permit contraception, it is far less often needed. But in France it is an operation to which many women are forced to resort and which haunts the love-life of most of them.[60]

In the remaining pages on abortion Beauvoir discusses, at length, the attitudes of the legal and medical professions towards abortion in France; the fate of unwanted children; Catholic teaching on abortion; the class character of abortion, and the ways in which abortion is personally experienced by women.

Despite the persistence of abortion as a very widespread practice in France – she estimates that there are as many abortion per annum as there are births – 'The law persists ... in making it a misdemeanor and so requires that this delicate operation be performed in secret'.[61] She dismisses arguments against the legalisation of abortion as 'absurd', in particular the argument that it is dangerous for women:

> honest physicians recognize with Magnus Hirschfield that 'abortion performed by a competent specialist in a hospital, and with proper precautions, does not involve the grave dangers asserted by the penal code'. On the contrary, what makes it a serious risk for women is the way in which it is actually done under present conditions. The lack of skill on the part of abortionists and the bad conditions under which they operate cause many accidents, some of them fatal.[62]

The *moral* considerations advanced against abortion amount 'in the end to the old Catholic argument'.[63] The old Catholic argument, as she reads it, is an argument to the effect that 'the unborn child has a soul, which is denied access to paradise if its life is interrupted without baptism'.[64] In other words, abortion is wrong because it denies the grace of baptism to the unborn child, for without such grace it cannot enter the kingdom of heaven.

Simone de Beauvoir attacks this moral theology with the following three arguments:

> (a) The Church permits killing adult human beings during war or when the criminal justice system deems it necessary; yet 'it reserves an uncompromising humanitarianism for man in the foetal condition'.[65] In other words, the Church places an absolute ban on the taking of *unborn* human life, but under specifiable conditions it permits the taking of *born* human life. This is inconsistent; or, it has one moral law for the born, and

another for the unborn, and to reason in this manner is to deny the equal moral value of all human beings.

(b) Abortion is condemned by the Catholic Church because it makes it impossible for the unborn child to obtain redemption by baptism; 'but in the times of the Holy Wars the infidels were equally unbaptized, and yet their slaughter was heartily encouraged'.[66] Again, the charge is one of inconsistency: it is wrong to kill the unbaptized unborn (because they are unbaptized), but not wrong to kill unbaptized infidels. Yet the latter, too, are denied baptism.

(c) Her third objection to Catholic teaching is that in the case of abortion the Church abrogates to itself an authority which, in other circumstances, it is content to allocate to God. In some cases it leaves it to God to decide just who is in a state of grace, and who isn't. Thus in the case of victims of the Inquisition, the criminal who is guillotined, and the soldier dead on the field of battle:

> the Church leaves the matter to the grace of God; it admits that man is only an instrument in His hands and that the salvation of a soul is settled between that soul and God. Why then should God be forbidden to receive the embryonic soul in heaven? If a Church council should authorize it, He would no more object than He did in the glorious epochs when heathens were piously slaughtered.[67]

As perceived by Beauvoir, then, the Church feels that in the matter of abortion, it must issue the condemnation, rather than leave it to God's discretion. This is not consistent with its practice in other controversial cases, and it is, in addition, an affront to God's authority.

The religious objection, she claims, is little more than a front for 'a masculine sadism',[68] one 'that has nothing to do with morality'.[69] Such a sadism is epitomised by a book published in 1943, dedicated to Pétain. The author, a doctor Roy, had lamented the dangers of abortion, but, she says:

> nothing seems to him more hygienic than a caesarean delivery. He favours regarding abortion as a crime rather than a misdemeanour; and he would have it forbidden even as a therapeutic measure – that is, when the pregnancy threatens the life or health of the mother. It is immoral to make a choice between one life and another, he declares, and, fortified by this argument, he advises sacrificing the mother.[70]

Beauvoir is not impressed, identifying the following inconsistency in the doctor's argument:

> He asserts that the foetus does not belong to the mother, it is an independent being. When these 'right-thinking' physicians are lauding maternity, however, they state that the foetus forms part of the mother's body, that it is not a parasite living at the latter's expense.[71]

She concludes:

> How lively anti-feminism still is can be judged by the eagerness of certain men to reject everything favourable to the emancipation of women.[72]

These arguments relate to abortion both as an issue in personal morality and as an issue in social morality. Whether the law should treat abortion as a crime, as a misdemeanour, or as a right is one question, and there can be no doubt about Beauvoir's answer to this question. Whether the foetus is an individual in its own right, or whether it is inseparable from its mother, is another question having implications both for social and for personal morality. At this stage of her disquisition, Beauvoir clearly holds that a mother should never be sacrificed for the sake of a foetus. She gives precedence to the mother not just when her life is in danger, but also when a continuation of the pregnancy would threaten her health.

Beauvoir describes the experience of back-street or 'lay abortion' in vivid detail. In the cities, she writes:

> women help one another out. But it is not always easy to find a lay abortionist, still less to get the necessary money together. So the pregnant woman appeals to a woman friend, or operates on herself. These non-professional surgeons are often incompetent; they are prone to cause perforation by probe or knitting needle ... Crudely begun and poorly cared for, the abortion is often more painful than normal childbirth, it may be accompanied by nervous upsets that can verge on an epileptic fit, it is capable of giving rise to serious internal disorders, and it can induce a fatal haemorrhage.[73]

What makes back-street abortion a particularly unpleasant experience, she observes, is the peculiar combination of illegality and physical suffering which accompanies it. What this means *in practice* she then describes as follows:

> A social worker told me ... that in her area the women exchanged advice, lent one another instruments, and assisted one another, as simply as if it were a matter of removing corns from the feet. But they have to endure severe physical pain; the hospitals are obliged to receive a woman whose miscarriage has begun, but she is *punished* sadistically by the withholding of all sedatives during her pains and during the final operation of curetting. It appears that this persecution does not arouse the indignation of women only too habituated to pain; but they are sensitive to the humiliations heaped upon them. The fact that the operation they have undergone is clandestine and criminal multiplies its dangers and gives it an abject and agonizing character. Pain, illness and death take on the appearance of a chastisement: we all know how great is the

difference between suffering and torture, accident and punishment; through all the risks she takes, the woman feels herself to be blameworthy, and this interpretation of anguish and transgression is particularly painful.[74]

A woman experiences two distinct kinds of turmoil in relation to abortion, writes Beauvoir, one social, the other moral. Both of these experiences serve to further distance women from men. So far as its social and legal aspects are concerned, women are forced to beg and cringe, and seek the collusion of other parties in a clandestine and illegal practice. Few men have this experience visited upon them; as she puts it herself:

> they beg for an address, they beg a doctor and a midwife to take care of them; they risk being haughtily turned down, or they expose themselves to a degrading complicity. The deliberate invitation to another to commit an illegal act is an experience unknown to most men, and one that a woman undergoes in a confusion of fear and shame.[75]

Planning to have, or having, an abortion is also liable to cause a woman moral anxiety, she continues. Such anxiety is brought on by an awareness that abortion is, for moral purposes, situated somewhere between contraception and murder. For this reason, Beauvoir herself labels it 'an ambiguous act'; to be precise, she speaks of 'the ambiguous act she is engaged in'. As I read it, what Beauvoir means is that the moral status of abortion is unclear, since abortion is situated somewhere between contraception [which is unambiguously morally good] and murder [which is morally reprehensible], and that it is this uncertainty about its moral status which is the cause of the woman's anxiety. But Parshley, her translator (with whom I disagree) takes Beauvoir to be making the stronger point that abortion is a morally *dubious*, i.e. suspect, act and that it is because this cloud of moral suspicion hangs over abortion that the woman contemplating abortion is troubled.[76]

Psychologically speaking, Beauvoir paints an even grimmer picture of the post-abortion woman. She first of all cites the circumstance of miscarriage or *spontaneous abortion*, though Parshley's translation does not immediately make it clear that it is a spontaneous abortion she is writing about. The published English translation of the passage I have in mind goes as follows:

> Some women will be haunted by the memory of this child which has not come into being. Hélène Deutsch cites the case of a married woman, otherwise psychologically normal, who was twice compelled, because of her physical condition, to lose a foetus of

three months and who felt obliged to erect a small tombstone for each of them.[77]

If the miscarriage (*'la fausse couche'*) is not spontaneous but induced (*'a été provoquée'*), then, according to Beauvoir, the woman will have more reason to entertain the feeling that she has committed a sin (*'d'avoir commie un péché'*). She explains that the remorse which in childhood may have followed the jealous wish for the death of a newborn brother is revived, and the woman feels herself guilty of having really killed a baby (*'se sent coupable d'avoir réelement tué un enfant'*). Pathological states of melancholy may express this feeling of culpability. Other women may gain from abortion the sense of having destroyed a part of themselves (*'avoir été mutilée d'une part d'elles-memes'*) and feel resentment against the man who has agreed to or requested this mutilation (*'cette mutilation'*).

Beauvoir begins to conclude by contrasting men's and women's attitudes to abortion, and in doing so offers some valuable ideas for a feminist ethics. Feminist ethics will argue that there are specifically feminine values, in particular the values of nurturance, care and the bringing of children into the world. Some of these values will be reserved for women since they alone are capable of putting them into effect. She writes:

> Men tend to take abortion lightly; they regard it as one of the numerous hazards imposed on woman by malignant nature, but fail to realise fully the values involved.[78]

On the other hand:

> The woman who has recourse to abortion is disowning feminine values, her values, and at the same time is in the most radical fashion running counter to the ethics established by men.[79]
>
> *'La femme renie les valeurs de la feminité, ses valeurs, au moment ou l'éthique mâle se conteste de la façon la plus radicale.*[80]

'Her whole moral universe', continues Beauvoir:

> is being disrupted. From infancy woman is repeatedly told that she is made for childbearing (*'qu'elle est fait pour engendrer'*), and the splendours of maternity are for ever being sung to her. The drawbacks of her situation – menstruation, illnesses and the like – and the boredom of household drudgery are all justified by this marvellous privilege she has of bringing children into the world. And now here is man asking woman to relinquish her triumph as female in order to preserve his liberty, so as not to handicap his future, for the benefit of his profession.[81]

The 'disruption' of the woman's moral universe comes, not from within that universe but from outside. It is imposed upon her by 'the masculine moral code'.[82] The pregnant woman finds herself trapped between two moral codes. One informs her that a child is 'a precious treasure', that to give birth is 'a sacred function',[83] and that she is privileged to be able to bring children into the world. On the other hand, there is not nearly enough positive support given to women who become pregnant: 'Poverty, crowded quarters, and the need for women to work outside the home are among the most frequent causes of abortion'.[84] The social oppression and isolation of the unmarried mother, the crushing stigma attached to pregnancy and, by implication, to sex outside marriage, also conspire to drive the woman to abortion:

> illegitimate motherhood ('*la maternité illégitime*') is still so frightful a fault that many prefer suicide or infanticide to the status of unmarried mother: which means that no penalty could prevent them from 'getting rid' of the unborn baby ("*de 'faire passer l'enfant'*").[85]

The upshot of this entire drama is that the pregnant woman is the locus of a war between two rival moral codes: a life-affirming, nurturant, natalist code on the one hand, and, on the other, an anti-natalist ethic that damns pregnancy and motherhood in any context other than marriage. According to Beauvoir, the woman herself *experiences* this drama as follows:

> Even when she consents to abortion, even desires it, woman feels it as a sacrifice of her femininity: she is compelled to see in her sex a curse, a kind of infirmity, and a danger. Carrying this denial to one extreme, some women become homosexual after the trauma of abortion.[86]

> ('Même consentant à l'avortement, le désirant, la femme le ressent comme un sacrifice de sa feminité: il faut que définitivement elle voie dans son sexe une malédiction, une espèce d'infirmité, un danger. Allant au bout de ce reniement certaines femmes deviennent homosexuelles à la suite du traumatisme de l'avortement'.[87])

The 'hypocrisy' of 'the masculine code' is that:

> Men universally forbid abortion, but individually they accept it as a convenient solution of a problem; they are able to contradict themselves with careless cynicism.[88]

But a woman finds it impossible to remain indifferent to these contradictions and, in agonising over them, she 'overcompensates' as well for male hypocrisy. Beauvoir explains:

But woman feels these contradictions in her wounded flesh; she is as a rule too timid for open revolt against masculine bad faith; she regards herself as the victim of an injustice that makes her a victim against her will, and at the same time she feels soiled and humiliated. She embodies in concrete and immediate form, in herself, man's fault; he commits the fault, but he gets rid of it by putting it off on her; he merely says some words in a suppliant, threatening, sensible, or furious tone: he soon forgets them; it is for her to interpret these words in pain and blood.[89]

So, women:

learn to believe no longer in what men say when they exalt woman or when they exalt man: the one thing they are sure of is this rifled and bleeding womb (*'ce ventre fourragé et saignant'*), these shreds of crimson life, this child that is not there (*'ces lambeaux de vie rouge, cette absence de l'enfant'*). It is at her first abortion that woman begins to 'know'. For many women the world will never be the same. And yet, for lack of widely available contraceptives, abortion is today in France the only recourse for women unwiling to bring into the world children doomed to misery and death.[90]

IV

Concluding Comments

At the outset, I distinguished between two questions about abortion:

(1) The *social* question: Should abortion be legalised? (or, How should the law and the Health Services respond to the demand for abortion?);

(2) the *personal* question: Is it morally permissible to procure an abortion, or for someone else to assist in the procurement of an abortion?

I now conclude that Beauvoir's answer to the social question is an emphatic 'Yes'. Her position on the social question of abortion is, essentially, that free, safe and legal abortion should be available to every woman. The alternative to legal abortion is backstreet abortion, which often has dire consequences for women, such as haemorrhaging, septicaemia, and death itself. Placing a legal ban on abortion also has, as its consequence, that many unwanted children get born, many of whom end up in orphanages, prison, and in psychiatric institutions. In her later writings on this topic for the pro-choice organization *Choisir*, Beauvoir claims that the law itself is behaving in a criminal fashion when it forces women to bring unwanted children into the world, and, she further maintains, a law against abortion is an essential part of a social system designed for the oppression of women.

Beauvoir's position on the morality of abortion is much less clear when it is considered as an issue in *personal morality*. She advances the following arguments in defence of the practice:

(i) By means of contraception *and* abortion, woman is no longer at the mercy of biological fate: reproduction can now be brought under woman's own control.

(ii) Traditional Catholic objections to it are unsound.

(iii) A mother should never be sacrificed for the sake of her foetus.

(iv) There is a crushing stigma attached to pregnancy outside marriage.

(v) Abortion is not murder, even if it is not contraception either.

(vi) Without abortion, there will be far more children who are doomed to misery and death in later life.

She also cites the following arguments *against* the practice:

(i) It is an especially desperate remedy for a crisis pregnancy.

(ii) It is morally ambiguous, in a way that contraception isn't. Morally speaking, it lies somewhere between contraception and murder.

(iii) The woman may experience post-abortion remorse for the creature whose life she has ended.

(iv) She may even feel that she has destroyed or mutilated a part of herself.

(v) The woman who has recourse to abortion is disowning 'feminine values'.

(vi) The woman herself experiences the abortion as a sacrifice of her femininity.

(vii) Abortion is contrary to her 'instinctive tendency' to have the baby.

There isn't much between these two sides of the argument, tilting it decisively to one side or the other. For this reason, it is much less certain where Beauvoir stands on the issue of abortion considered as an issue in personal morality. Still and all, I am inclined to think that, by a small enough margin, she comes down in favour of it. I base this conclusion on the following three considerations:

(i) Her claim that abortion is not murder.

(ii) The fact that it is not always clear whether she is expressing her own views on the matter, or simply documenting the thoughts and feelings of women who have had the abortion experience. This observation relates mostly to the *negative* remarks she makes about abortion.

(iii) In her later writings for *Choisir*, she focusses exclusively on the pro-abortion side of the argument. For example, in her *Preface à l'Avortement: une loi en procès. L'Affaire de Bobigny*, she says the following:

> (i) Correctly carried out, an abortion is, medically speaking, as harmless as a tooth extraction.

> (ii) It is less dangerous than giving birth.

> (iii) Unwanted children end up abandoned and dependent on the Social Assistance Service.

> (iv) Most delinquents, and many criminals, had this sorry start in life, and often they end up in psychiatric institutions.

> (v) To think that a foetus is a human being is to adopt a *metaphysical* attitude, one which is extensively contradicted by social practices: when a woman miscarries in hospital, the administration throws the foetus in the bin, and the Church approves; it does not even consider giving this 'human person' a Christian burial. 'It treats it as mere waste'.[91]

> (vi) The law against abortion is an essential part of the system that society has put in place for the oppression of women (*'pour opprimer les femmes'*[92]).

Some will hear, in her narrative of the rifled and bleeding womb, the echoes of a Catholicism beckoning to her from afar. There is, I believe, a small measure of truth in such a reading: there is a distinctly Catholic resonance to the claim that when a woman consents to an abortion, even desires it, she feels it as a *sacrifice of her femininity*. Yet contrary to the emphasis in Catholic teaching, Beauvoir's abiding focus is on the woman, not on the unborn child, nor on the putative rights of this child. She is, in fact, endeavouring to construct a new feminist ethics in *The Second Sex*, one which affirms and defends feminine values (*'les valeurs de la feminité*). This feminist ethics will enjoin on us a way of life which will be life-giving, life-affirming, nurturant, and self-empowering. The life which is guided by such an ethics will be characterised, not by submission to biological fate, but by control of one's biological destiny. In accordance with this ethics, a woman will give life, and support life, on *her* terms, not at the behest of the State, nor the Church, nor a husband, or partner, or parents. Woman is confronted by powerful forces: by a strong biological instinct to reproduce, by a natalist State, by a male ideology that exalts motherhood but also condones backstreet abortion as a convenient solution to an inconvenient problem. If a woman is to take charge of her biological destiny, if she is to give life on her terms, then she needs, in addition to contraception, a free, safe and legal abortion service available to her. This is the core of the feminist ethics proposed in *The Second Sex*.

Notes

1　'I no longer believe in God', I told myself, with no great surprise ... from now on His name would have to be a cover for nothing more than a mirage ... I was not denying Him in order to rid myself of a troublesome person: on the contrary, I realized that He was playing no further part in my life and so I concluded that He had ceased to exist for me', *Memoirs of a Dutiful Daughter*, p. 137.

2　'Personal morality' is a general expression for a range of questions relating to what, morally speaking, an individual moral agent may or may not do. 'Social morality' is a general expression which refers to a range of questions relating to public policy on morally controversial practices, such as abortion, prostitution, and drug-use.

3　See 'Archbishops' onslaught against abortion "evil"', *The Guardian*, 24 January 1980.

4　H. Davis, *A Summary of Moral and Pastoral Theology*, 1952, pp. 63, 64.

5　*The Guardian*, 24 January 1980.

6　*Ibid*.

7　J.Whale, 'The Tensions of John Paul II', *The Sunday Times*, 6 April 1980.

8　'Bishops say new pro-life poll now needed', *The Irish Times*, 27 May 992.

9　*Ibid*.

10　*Ibid*.

11　*Ibid*.

12　*Ibid*.

13　'Bishops accept both "Yes" and "No" votes', *The Irish Times*, 6 November 1992.

14　*Ibid*.

15　*Ibid*.

16　*Ibid*.

17　*Ibid*.

18　*Catechism of the Catholic Church*, p. 489.

19　*Ibid*.

20　*Ibid*.

21　*Ibid*.

22　'"Information" means aiding in abortion, say bishops', *The Irish Times*, 9 March 1995.

23　*Ibid*.

24　*Ibid*.

25　*Ibid*.

26   'Bishops see Supreme Court rulings in X case to be a corruption of law', *The Irish Times*, 1 July 1995.

27   *Ibid.*

28   *Simone de Beauvoir, A Feminist Mandarin*, p. 101.

29   *Ibid.*

30   *Simone de Beauvoir*, p. 21.

31   *Ibid.*, p. 65.

32   *Simone de Beauvoir*, p. 53.

33   *Ibid.*, pp. 53, 54.

34   *Ibid.*, pp. 289, 290.

35   *Ibid.*, p. 337.

36   *Ibid.*, pp. 337, 338.

37   *Ibid.*, p. 340.

38   *Ibid.*, p. 341.

39   *Ibid.*

40   *Ibid.*

41   *Ibid.*

42   *Simone de Beauvoir, A Biography*, p. 552.

43   *Ibid.*, p. 547.

44   *Ibid.*

45   *The Second Sex*, p. 150.

46   *Ibid.*

47   *Ibid.*

48   *Ibid.*

49   *Ibid.*

50   *Ibid.*, p. 151.

51   *Ibid.*

52   *Ibid.*

53   *Ibid.*

54   *Ibid.*

55   *Ibid.*, p. 152.

56   *Ibid.*, pp. 151, 152.

57   *Ibid.*, p. 501.

58   *Ibid.*, pp. 501, 502.

59   *Ibid.*, p. 502.

60   *Ibid.*

61   *Ibid.*

62   *Ibid.*

63   *Ibid.*, p. 503.

64   *Ibid.*

65   *Ibid.*

66   *Ibid.*

67   *Ibid.*, p. 504.

68   *Ibid.*

69   *Ibid.*

70   *Ibid.*

71 *Ibid.*

72 *Ibid.*

73 *Ibid.*, p. 506. For a detailed medical account of back-street abortion, see J. Irving, *The Cider House Rules*, chapter 2, 'The Lord's Work', pp. 56–97.

74 *Ibid.*, p. 507.

75 *Ibid.*

76 The original passage is as follows: '*Cette intervention qu'elle réclame, souvent dans son coeur elle la repousse. Elle est divisée à l'intérieur d'elle meme. Il se peut que son désir spontanée soit de garder cet enfant qu'elle empeche de naître; meme si elle ne souhaite pas positivement la maternité, elle ressent avec malaise l'ambiguité de l'acte qu'elle accomplit. Car si'il n'est pas vrai que l'avortement soit un assassinat, il ne saurait non plus etre assimilée à une simple pratique anticonceptionelle; un evènement a eu lieu qui est un commencement absolu et dont on arrète le dèveloppement'.*, *Le Deuxième Sexe*, Vol. II, p. 340. Parshley translates this passage as follows: 'In her heart she often repudiates the interruption of pregnancy which she is seeking to obtain. She is divided against herself. Her natural tendency can well be to have the baby whose birth she is undertaking to prevent; even if she has no positive desire for maternity, she still feels uneasy about the dubious act she is engaged in. For if it not true that abortion is *murder*, it still cannot be considered in the same light as a mere contraceptive technique; an event has taken place that is a definite beginning, the progress of which is to be stopped'., *The Second Sex*, pp. 507, 508.

77 *Ibid.*, p. 508.

78 *Ibid.*

79 *Ibid.*

80 *Le Deuxiéme Sexe*, p. 341.

81 *The Second Sex*, pp. 508, 509.

82 *Ibid.*, p. 509.

83 *Ibid.*

84 *Ibid.*, p. 505.

85 *Ibid.*, pp. 505, 506.

86 *Ibid.*, p. 509.

87 *Le Deuxième Sexe*, pp. 341, 342.

88 *The Second Sex*, p. 509.

89 *Ibid.*

90 *Ibid.*

91 *Les Ecrits de Simone de Beauvoir*, p. 507. (My translation)

92 *Ibid.*

Chapter Eight

SIMONE DE BEAUVOIR, ALBERT CAMUS AND THE THEORY OF PUNISHMENT

In this chapter I propose to seek answers to the following questions:

(1) What is Simone de Beauvoir's theory of punishment?

(2) Does she make a convincing case for punishment?

(3) Does she make a convincing case for capital punishment?

(4) How does her theory of punishment, and in particular her stance on the death penalty, compare with that of Camus?

(5) Does her essay on punishment synchronise with her other ethical writings of the 1940s?

The main textual basis of the chapter will be Beauvoir's post-war essay 'Oeil pour Oeil', published in the journal *Les Temps modernes* in February 1946. It was subsequently published in the collection of essays *L'Existentialisme et la sagesse des nations* in 1948. I shall also make extensive use of Tony Judt's *Past Imperfect: French Intellectuals 1944–1956*, in the early sections where I sketch the historical and cultural backdrop to Beauvoir's essay. Where very detailed, or very technical information was required, I have consulted Pierre Assouline's *L'Epuration des intellectuels, 1944–45*. In the section devoted to Camus I shall present a detailed reconstruction of his views on the death penalty, making extensive use of his 1957 essay *Réflexions sur la guillotine* for that purpose. I also draw on Camus' essay both when offering a critique of Beauvoir's theory of punishment, and when presenting a comparative overview of their respective contributions to the debate on the death penalty.

I

Beauvoir's essay 'Oeil pour Oeil'[1] was written at the height of those events known collectively, and even temporally, as *l'épuration*. 'In the circumstances of postwar France', observes Tony Judt:

> the drive to expel from the community all those associated with the Vichy years was understandable and inevitable. The last months of the Occupation had been the worst, both in material deprivation and in the punishments and revenge exacted by the Germans and the Milice for the growing audacity of the Resistance. The mass murder of the citizens of Oradour took place in June 1944. But even before then the Conseil National de la Résistance had made clear, in two of the first demands of its original charter, that the liberation of France would be followed by legal and economic sanctions against those who had collaborated. The shape and extent of those sanctions remained undefined, but as the war drew to an end it was clear to all that there would be a demand for revenge.[2]

In itself, the concept of a purge was unproblematic. As Judt explains:

> French history since the Revolution is studded with such things, undertaken after the fall of a regime and usually confined to the wholesale replacement of officials or the selective punishment or exile of politicians and ministers from the losing side. The most recent such exercise had actually been taken under Daladier, in October 1939, when the Interior Minister, Albert Sarraut had sought to pursue a nationwide purge of Communists in the wake of the Moscow Pact.[3]

Serious crimes of collaboration could be prosecuted under Article 75 of the 1939 Penal Code which made it a capital offence:

> (1) For any French citizen to take up arms against France, and (2) For any French citizen to enter into secret communication with a foreign power with a view to pressing it to enter into hostilities against France, or who facilitates France's enemies, whether by aiding and abetting hostile armies to invade France, by undermining the loyalty of France's soldiers, or by any other means whatever.[4]

However, as Judt points out, Article 75 basically addresses the crime of *treason*, and it was therefore necessary to introduce other categories of offence to cover the larger number of people to be prosecuted. The shape of the new jurisprudence can be gleaned from Ordinance No.45–

1089 of 30 May 1945, which instituted a national committee charged with purging intellectuals and artists of all hues who:

(1) approved of any of the enemy's actions ('Soit favorisé les entreprises de toute nature de l'ennemi'), or

(2) who opposed France's war effort and that of her allies ('Soit contrarié l'effort de guerre de la France et de ces Alliés'), or

(3) who hindered the efforts of the Resistance, especially by denouncing such efforts ('ou entravé la résistance des Francais, notamment par des dénunciations'[5]). Official trials for collaboration, or treason, were held from 1944 until the beginning of the 1950s:

> and tribunals, courts of justice, and the High Court would eventually sentence to death nearly 7,000 people (3,900 in absentia). Of these, fewer than 800 were eventually executed.[6]

The purge was pursued with particular ferocity against *intellectuals*. 'The treatment of writers and artists who had collaborated', notes Judt:

> was notoriously unfair – not so much because some of them did not deserve the punishment they received (many did), but because it was so selective ... intellectuals were singled out for much more attention than was ever given to lawyers, generals, businessmen, and high civil servants whose services to the occupying authorities had been unquestionably more significant.[7]

Three reasons have been given for the severe treatment of intellectuals:

(1) As de Gaulle later noted in his memoirs, in literature as in everything else, talent is a responsibility. Judt takes up the point as follows:

> The capacity to express a point of view in a way calculated to convince others, the skill in dressing up an unacceptable act in respectable moral clothing, confer on the writer a power but also a duty. The abuse of such responsibilities calls down on the guilty party greater blame than would attach to someone who merely reads the writer's words or acts upon them. That is why newspapers and their erstwhile owners and editors were so severely sanctioned at the Liberation, losing not only their names and their positions but also the vey property itself.[8]

(2) Collaboration issuing from the pen had a distinct advantage over other forms of collaboration from the point of view of the jurist:

> It left an unambiguous record, open to examination and cross-examination. An individual could deny that he or she ever worked for the Germans or for Vichy or could claim that such work was a cover for clandestine opposition. Such a claim was hard to disprove, and if the accused could obtain corroborative evidence or a friendly witness, it was hard to secure a conviction, once the first flush of field justice had passed. But an article, a letter, a book, play, or

poem could not be denied. The decision to let one's name appear in a tainted journal or on the list of a publisher who accepted German censorship or (worse) who published openly collaborationist writers was an error that could not readily be undone. This was especially the case in a time when words, as it was now asserted, had *mattered* so.[9]

(3) Finally, the purge was undertaken by intellectuals themselves. 'This meant', explains Judt:

> that the significance to be assigned to a person's words was now being weighed by men and women for whom words were everything and who were seeking, both philosophically and in the political realm, to establish the historicity and centrality of intellectual choice.[10]

Two official bodies were instituted for the self-policing activities of the intellectuals, both of them emanating from the *Comité Nationale des Ecrivains (CNE)*, which had been formed under the aegis of the Resistance. Both operated under the terms of the 30 May 1945 ordinance (*Ordonnance No.45–1089 du 30 mai 1945*), which established a framework for defining procedures for purging '*les gens de lettres*'. The *comité d'épuration* had the task of deciding who among the names it investigated was 'more or less compromised', as distinct from those who were subject to the law and found guilty of '*indignité nationale*'. The latter would, in principle, be the concern of the courts; the former would be named by the commission.

> It was then for writers, artists, scholars, journalists and others to decide whether they wished to be associated with these people in any way. Such a boycott, if successful, would effectively expunge 'guilty' people from the intellectual community, since newspapers would not print their articles; publishers would not take their books; and theaters, film studios, and orchestras would deny them work.[11]

Among the initial members of this commission were Jacques Debû-Bridel, Raymond Queneau, Paul Eluard, Gabriel Marcel and Vercors (Jean Bruller). There was also established a *Comité d'épuration de l'édition*, with Jean-Paul Sartre sitting on it as the representative of the CNE. 'These examining bodies', comments Judt:

> though clearly partisan, were not drawn exclusively from any one side or interest group within the intellectual community. During the autumn of 1944 they put out a series of lists, placing those whose names appeared there in the uncomfortable position of being presumed guilty until proved innocent. There was some internal dissent within the CNE over the makeup of these lists ... But on 27 September the CNE unanimously voted to clarify matters somewhat by announcing that anyone who supported Pétain after the

occupation of the southern zone (in November 1942) was a prima
facie candidate for national indignity.[12]

At this point the published lists of names included everyone from
Robert Brasillach and Pierre Drieu la Rochelle, active collaborators by
any standard, to Pierre Andreu and Jean Giono, whose sin was at best
one of omission, of having failed to make a clear break with the Vichy
regime and its goals. 'As a symbol, a representative of intellectual
collaboration', writes Judt:

> Brasillach was almost too perfect. After a gilded youth that took
> him from the Ecole normale supérieure to *Je suis partout*, he moved
> comfortably within the literary and journalistic circles of Occupied
> France, writing, speaking, and visiting Germany in the company of
> other collaborators. Born in 1909, he was of the same generation as
> Merleau-Ponty, Mounier and the rest, but unlike them he had not
> abandoned his youthful interest in the extreme Right. He never
> made any effort to hide his views, which included a virulent and
> often expressed anti-Semitism. Although it became fashionable after
> his death to cast aspersions upon his gifts as a writer,
> contemporaries of all parties had credited him with a major talent;
> he was not just a gifted and dangerous polemicist but a man of
> acute aesthetic insight and real literary talent. In short, an
> intellectual, *première classe*.[13]

Brasillach was tried in January 1945, and found guilty of treason under
the second clause of Article 75, which makes it a capital offence for any
French citizen to enter into a secret communication with a foreign
power with a view to pressing it to enter into hostilities against France,
or who facilitates France's enemies, whether by aiding and abetting
hostile armies to invade France, by undermining the loyalty of France's
soldiers, or by any other means whatever. In his trial it was established
at the outset (with Brasillach's agreement) that he had been pro-Vichy
and was anti-Communist, anti-Jewish, and an admirer of Maurras.
'Not', notes Judt:

> that these traits were unique to the accused; during the trial
> Brasillach remarked that anyone seeking to read an anti-Semitic,
> anti-national tract at least as vicious as anything he had ever written
> had only to turn to Louis Aragon's poem, *Feu sur Léon Blum*![14]

What was at issue, however, was whether he was a traitor. Here the
prosecutor adduced evidence in accordance with the closing section of
regulation II of article 75, placing the emphasis on Brasillach's
responsibility as an influential writer. 'How many young minds did
you, by your articles, incite to fight the *maquis*? For how many crimes
do you bear the intellectual responsibility?'[15] In a language which all

would understand, observes Judt, Brasillach was baptised 'the intellectual who betrayed'.[16]

Brasillach was found guilty of treason under Article 75, and sentenced to death. A petition was circulated, due largely to the efforts of François Mauriac, seeking clemency for Brasillach. It asked for mercy for Robert Brasillach, citing in his favour the sole fact that his father had died for France on 13 November 1914. There were 59 signatories, including Paul Valéry, François Mauriac, Georges Duhamel, Roland Dorgelès, Albert Camus and Gabriel Marcel. Simone de Beauvoir refused to sign the petition, and Jean-Paul Sartre also refused. De Gaulle rejected the petition, and Brasillach was executed by firing squad on 6 February 1945. This is the background to Simone de Beauvoir's essay 'Oeil pour Oeil', in which she explains and seeks to vindicate her decision to refuse to sign the petition on behalf of Robert Brasillach.

In the next section I shall offer a summary of Beauvoir's essay, based on my own translation. Then I shall answer the questions posed in the opening paragraph, concluding with an attempt to locate the essay 'Oeil pour Oeil' in relation to Beauvoir's other ethical writings of the 1940s.

II

Before the war, says Beauvoir, they had lived without wishing misfortune on any of their contemporaries: words of revenge and expiation had no meaning for them. They had *scorned* their political and ideological adversaries more than they had detested them. As for those considered noxious by society – murderers, thieves and such like – they hadn't considered such people as enemies; their crimes had seemed merely accidents for which society itself was to blame, because it had deprived these people of a real opportunity in life.

Since June 1940, however, they had learned to be angry and they had learned to hate. They had come to wish death and humiliation on their enemies. 'And today', she says:

> each time that a tribunal condemns a war criminal to death, we, too, take responsibility for that verdict. It's in our name that judgement is delivered and punishment is meted out. We congratulated ourselves on the death of Mussolini, on the hanging of Kharkov's executioners. Their punishment expresses our values and our reasons for living.[17]

She adds that their attitude towards 'ordinary', everyday criminals hadn't changed, because at this end of things the social order had not become less unjust. 'But to the extent that that the social order rejected tyranny', she maintains, 'and strives to recover a lost human dignity (*'de rétablir l'homme dans sa dignité'*) we claim it as ours'.[18]

The role of judge and executioner came easily during the Occupation. Then hatred was easy. When they had read the articles published in *Je suis partout*, heard about the torturers in Buchenwald, they had said to themselves 'They will pay for it'. They had paid for it, they would continue to pay for it, they were paying for it every day. And yet, says Beauvoir, people were still not satisfied.

To some extent this was due to circumstances. The purge had not been totally sincere; not all the guilty had been caught. But none of this could explain the fact that a revenge which they had so bitterly desired had left them feeling so dissatisfied. In fact, she says, what is at stake here is the concept of punishment itself.

The characteristic of punishment, she claims, is that it aims exclusively at the person who is punished. The aim is not to prevent him committing further crimes, for if it is lawful to punish him, it is because he can no longer do any harm. Nor is it for the purposes of deterrence that he is punished: it would be absurd to suppose, she says, that Mussolini was executed as a warning to future dictators! Punishment is not justified, therefore, on pragmatic grounds. Rather it is a response to a fundamental emotion, one capable of taking precedence over all pragmatic concerns. She develops this point as follows:

> Man doesn't live by bread alone; we have spiritual appetites as well which are just as important. The thirst for vengeance belongs here. It is a response to one of the metaphysical needs of humanity (*'elle répond à une des exigences métaphysiques de l'homme'*).[19]

To gain a better understanding of the meaning of punishment, says Beauvoir, it is necessary to see it operating in a *spontaneous* way. In the immediate aftermath of the Liberation there were summary executions and lynchings of Vichy militia, SS functionaries, and so on. The punishments involved here were not aimed at distant objectives. The aim was rather to catch up with these people by means of death and suffering; and the sole justification for what was inflicted on them was the hatred they had inspired. One doesn't hate a hailstorm, or a plague: 'it is human beings alone who are hated (*'on ne hait que les hommes'*)'.[20] And they are not hated because they are the material cause of material havoc, but because they have been the *conscious* perpetrators of real evil. A soldier who kills in combat isn't hated, because he is following orders, and because his adversary can use similar methods of warfare against him. We are not appalled until one human being treats other human beings as objects (*'du moment ou un homme traite ses semblables comme des objets'*), when by means of torture, humiliation, subordination or assassination he denies their status as human beings. 'Hatred', she writes:

> is the seizure of another's liberty, when that same liberty has been used to bring about that absolute evil (*'ce mal absolu'*) which is the degradation of human beings into disposable objects (*'la dégradation de l'homme en chose'*).[21]

'They will pay for it'. That word says a lot, says Beauvoir, since to pay for something is to furnish an equivalent for what one has received. The desire for equivalence is captured by the old *jus talionis*: an eye for an eye, a tooth for a tooth. This law is a response to a deep-seated human need. 'I once heard a maquisard explain', she says:

> how he had applied this law to a Vichy policeman who had tortured a woman. 'He understood', he had commented soberly.[22]

The suffering inflicted in punishment, revenge, and so on, cannot undo the harm already done, she allows, but what it can accomplish is to recover the totality of the situation, namely, where one independent consciousness finds itself facing another. 'An object for another, each of us is a subject for herself (*'Objet pour autrui, chaque homme est sujet pour soi'*) , and we unceremoniously insist on getting this recognition for ourselves'.[23] This respect which we demand for ourselves we then extend to others, and finally to all human beings, and this, she says, 'is the metaphysical source of the idea of justice'.[24] It is this respect which vengeance tries to re-establish against the tyranny of a liberty which tries to force itself on others.

However, she continues, there are two major probems associated with vengeance. The first is that the person who is punished must experience himself as a victim, and violence alone is not sufficient to make him think in this fashion. What one wants is what she calls 'a magical transformation' of this hostile liberty, in particular a free recognition of past excesses, an honest confession of past mistakes, and a genuine feeling of remorse for them. But vengeance alone cannot achieve these ends: if, for example, the punishment is very severe, the prisoner's mind will drown in suffering and never, as a consequence, get to make these appraisals. On the other hand, if we economise on the punishment, the prisoner may recover his autonomy and even experience a kind of well-being. That is why historically, she explains, truly vindictive men have gone to great lengths to devise 'exquisite' means of punishment for their captives.

The other problem with vengeance, when we set out to avenge the dead, is that one of the relevant parties will contest the meaning of the gesture, while the other, being dead, remains for ever absent. So where, then, does the punishment get its meaning? An outsider cannot intervene except at the level of this universal human essence (*'cette essence universelle d'homme'*) which has been damaged in the person of the victim. As a consequence, he must approach the punishment at a universal level. Yet no third party is qualified 'to defend the universal rights of man'[25] (*'les droits universelles de l'homme'*). Whoever attempts to do so runs the risk of elevating himself into a sovereign conscience for all, thereby becoming himself a tyrant in turn. This is the reason, observes Beauvoir, that we are always troubled by private acts of retribution; vengeance runs the constant risk of substituting one scandal, one evil, for another. It is for this reason that society refuses to authorise private acts of vengeance. From the very start of the Liberation, an ordinance was issued which strictly forbade private acts of violent retribution. The task of punishment was delegated to specially authorised bodies. 'It was declared that there should be punishment without hatred, in the name of universal principles (*'on déclare qu'il faut punir sans haine, au nom de principes universels'*)'.[26] So, wonders Beauvoir, if vengeance ultimately leads to failure, does 'social justice' (*la justice sociale'*) fare any better?

Social justice, maintains Beauvoir, does not concern itself with restoring a moral equilibrium or balance. Nor does physical torture have any place here. The remaining sanctions of prison, degradation, national disgrace and death, all share the characteristic of simply removing the culprit from society. In truth, she says, the judges do not concern themselves with a past which is incapable of being restored; they think instead of the future:

> Their aim is to restore a human community which conforms to its own idea of itself (*'une communauté humaine conforme à l'idee qu'elle s'est forgée d'elle même'*); their aim is to maintain the values which have been rejected by the crime.[27]

Social justice, she maintains, demands two things: a guilty verdict, and an act of punishment. Without the punishment the verdict is little more than a verbal comedy; yet it is the verdict which counts for more in the final analysis. It is the *willingness* to execute the guilt party that matters more than his actual death. For example, she says, it was plausible to affirm this willingness at a certain stage in the trial of Pétain, to condemn the man to death even if there was no intention of actually *taking* his life.

This extreme case demonstrates, she claims, how far vengeance and social justice are from each other. In the case of Pétain, the High Court was prepared to distinguish between Pétain the traitor and Pétain the old man, condemning the one while pardoning the other. Here, she says, the High Court vividly demonstrated one of the defining characteristics of social justice, namely, its reluctance to consider the guilty party in the totality of his person (*'dans la totalité de son être'*), its refusal 'to engage in a metaphysical struggle with a free consciousness imprisoned in a body'.[28] Rather it condemns him in so far as his behaviour is a reflection, or a token, of certain evil deeds (*'certains actes mauvais'*). In this sense punishment takes on the character of 'a symbolic manifestation', and the condemned man is not too far from being considered an expiatory victim.

Is it fair, then, she wonders, to judge a person on the basis of a single moment in his life, on the basis of just one side of his personality? Since he is no longer the same person as the one who committed the crime (he is now a vulnerable prisoner in the dock), can we continue to hate him, and what good is served by punishing him? The concept of Christian charity emerges in discussion of this objection to social justice, she says, and it does so with a greater urgency than any other cosideration because it finds in the notion of original sin (*'la décheance originelle'*) a defence which is available to all sinners: that the same putrefaction is to be found in the soul of all human beings, and that grace alone is capable of saving us (*'seule la graçe peut nous permettre de la surmonter'*[29]). God alone is capable of deciding the extent of the temptation, and of the mistake. On this view, 'the only sins are sins against God, and He alone has the right to punish (*'et d'ailleurs in n'y a de faute qu'envers Lui; Lui seul a le droit de punir'*[30])'. As for us mere mortals, we are all brothers in sin and misery, and crime is not necessarily to be seen as an earthly scandal since everything on the face of the earth is scandalous in the eyes of God; it was on that basis that He chose to redeem us. So, 'we should forgive each other as God has forgiven us (*'ils doivent se pardonner les uns les autres afin que Dieu leur pardonne'*)'.[31]

The argument from Christian charity has much to recommend it, she comments. People often do things without understanding what they are doing, and indeed one can say that they never understand exactly what it is they are doing. For example, one would not consider hating those members of the Hitler youth who were only sixteen years of age, and were so savagely Nazi in their behaviour, yet never got the opportunity to criticise this ideology. It is better to re-educate children and ignorant populations rather than punish them. Nor does one judge an act without also judging the person whose act it is, for one hasn't meaning without the other.

But nonetheless, she continues, there are cases where no redemption is possible because the evil perpetrated is 'an absolute evil' (*'un mal absolu'*[32]). In such cases, Christian charity is not an adequate response. One can make allowances for misdemeanours and even for those crimes of an anti-social nature; but when someone deliberately sets about degrading another human being, reducing that other human being to the level of a thing, a scandal erupts for which no amends can be made. What we have here is the one inexcusable sin against a human being (*'péché contre l'homme'*), and when it occurs no toleration can be permitted. In cases of this type, punishment is always deserved.

It is lawful, she continues, for a Christian to opt for charity, because Christians believe in the existence of a supreme legislator; but this response is not available to those who favour an intra-mundane, human ethics, to those who stand by human values. Undoubtedly, human beings have their pathetic side, but they are also free and, as such, capable of resisting the greatest temptations. For human life to have meaning, human beings must be held responsible for the evil they do as much as for the good. 'That', she says, 'is why I refused to sign the petition for Robert Brasillach' (*'C'est pour ces raisons que je n'ai pas, quant à moi, signé la pétition en faveur de Robert Brasillach'.*).[33] Brasillach, she clearly believes, *deserved* to die, as does anyone else who is guilty of 'absolute evil'. She leaves us in no doubt about this, since she says:

> Society solemnly rejects those who are responsible for the crimes which society rejects, and when these crimes are particularly abominable only one punishment can restore the equilibrium, and that punishment is death.[34]

It is, I think, worth adding the following biographical note to the above summary of Beauvoir's essay on the death penalty. It is based on the closing pages of her account of her first trip to the United States, published under the title *America Day by Day*.[34a] During her four-month stay in America in 1947, she was taken on a guided tour of Chicago's county prison. Having visited the men's section, then the women's section, the visiting section, the kitchen, the hospital, the library, and the chapel ('which is painted a tender toothpaste pink and decorated with gilt plaster – a chapel for nuns with childlike hearts'[34b]), she is brought through a metal door and enters the section 'where the longest sentences are served'. The prisoners here include men who are having their death sentence appealed. If their appeal is rejected, they will be 'transferred to the area reserved for the prisoners condemned to death'.[34c] She then describes the Death Row section, including the Execution Chamber where:

> behind a glass, like a dentist's chair exhibited for sale in a display window, is the chair, with its ingenious apparatus for holding the patient and bringing his blood to boiling point in a minute and a half.[34d]

She concludes her account of her visit to Death Row with the following sentence: 'I have to admit, there's nothing to criticize in such a beautiful prison, aside from the fact that it's a prison'.[34e]

III

Beauvoir's disquisition on punishment is a fascinating blend of jurisprudence, existentialism and moral theology (with her continuous use of words and phrases such as 'sin', 'pardon', 'expiate', and 'resist temptation'). Nevertheless, I do have some reservations about it. In the first place, I am uneasy about the distinction between anti-social crime and crimes against humanity, the latter identified with atrocities committed under the canopy of war. Surely it is possible to degrade human beings into disposable objects on other occasions? Second, the theory, in my view, adheres too rigidly to the principle of equivalence, even if Beauvoir herself wants to deny that this is the case.

She maintains that her social justice theory is not an equivalence theory when she writes:

> Society solemnly rejects those who are responsible for the crimes which society rejects, and when these crimes are particularly abominable only one punishment can restore the equilibrium and that punishment is death. This is not an application of the law of equivalence, which carries no weight from the point of view of organised justice; besides, neither Brasillach, nor Pétain, nor Laval, themselves directly killed anyone. Yet death alone is capable of expressing the violence with which we want to reject certain actions.[35]

There are three main parts to this argument:

(i) Death alone can atone for killing and other crimes of a comparable magnitude;

(ii) This is not an application of the principle of equivalence;

(iii) Those who are morally responsible for crimes of this magnitude, even if they didn't themselves actually carry them out, are guilty and therefore deserving of death.

I find it difficult here to avoid concluding that propositions (i) and (ii) contradict each other. Proposition (i) looks suspiciously like a restatement of the principle of equivalence, a suspicion supported by her statement that 'only one punishment can restore the equilibrium, and that punishment is death'. In addition, Beauvoir makes no attempt to explain why our abhorrence of killing and other comparable crimes cannot be expressed by other forms of punishment besides execution, such as by depriving the guilty party of liberty, of a *worthwhile life*, for the remainder of his days. Her contemporary Camus vehemently rejected the proposition that killing merits death by execution, even the most debauched killing. He replies that:

> If murder is in the nature of man, the law is not intended to imitate or reproduce that nature. It is intended to correct it.[36]

Camus also reminds us that:

> Beheading is not simply death. It is just as different, in essence, from the privation of life as a concentration camp is from prison. It is a murder, to be sure, and one that arithmetically pays for the murder committed. But it adds to death a rule, a public premeditation known to the future victim, an organization, in short, which is in itself a source of moral sufferings more terrible than death. Hence there is no equivalence. For there to be equivalence, the death penalty would have to punish a criminal who had warned his victim of the date at which he would inflict a horrible death on him and who, from that moment onward had confined him at his mercy for months. Such a monster is not encountered in private life.[37]

In short, the system of justice should not itself stoop to evil, while the death penalty, in the form in which the justice system imposes it, inflicts a punishment more terrible than death, and one which had not been imposed on the original victim of the crime.

Camus acknowledges that 'certain men are irremediable in society',[38] and that such individuals constitute

> a permanent danger for every citizen and for the social order, and that therefore, before anything else, they must be suppressed.[39]

Indeed it is this sole fact, he asserts, that legitimates discussion of the death penalty. But the death penalty itself, he maintains, is not the correct way of dealing with pathological killers. He would have it replaced with what he calls:

> hard labor – for life in the case of criminals considered irremediable and for a fixed period in the case of others.[40]

Hard labour for life has two redeeming features, as he sees it: it imposes a severe and lengthy punishment, and, less obviously, it 'leaves the condemned man the possibility of choosing death, whereas the guillotine offers no alternative'.[41] Here Camus is not *advocating* suicide, merely remarking that suicide is a lesser evil than capital punishment, and that hard labour for life gives the option of suicide, whereas capital punishment does not.

My argument here is not that Camus is correct, and that Simone de Beauvoir is mistaken, in their respective stances on the morality of capital punishment; rather, and simply, that Camus is much more prepared to argue for his position, and meet his opponents with counter-argument. Beauvoir's tone is dogmatic and peremptory when it comes to discussing the death penalty, and she tends to give precedence to intuition over analysis. Intuitively, the proposition 'absolute evil deserves absolute punishment' looks sound, but under examination it begins to look less compelling and, more importantly, we see that it is susceptible not just to one, but to several interpretations.

Finally, Christian teaching, or at any rate current Christian teaching, does not require of Christians that they abjure all forms of punishment (forgiving others as God has forgiven us, etc.); indeed the most recent statement of Catholic teaching does not require a public authority to abjure *any* form of punishment, not even the death penalty. *The Catechism of the Catholic Church* (1994) says:

> Preserving the common good of society requires rendering the aggressor unable to inflict harm. For this reason the traditional teaching of the Church has acknowledged as well-founded the right and duty of legitimate public authority to punish malefactors by means of penalties commensurate with the gravity of the crime, not excluding, in cases of extreme gravity, the death penalty.[42]

But, significantly, it immediately adds that:

> If bloodless means are sufficient to defend human lives against an aggressor and to protect public order and the safety of persons, public authority should limit itself to such means, because they better correspond to the concrete conditions of the common good and are more in conformity to the dignity of the human person.[43]

There are repeated references to capital punishment in Camus' writings, but by far the most sustained and analytical discussion of the topic is that which is to be found in his 1957 essay *Réflexions sur la guillotine*. In this section I shall quote from Justin O'Brien's translation, 'Reflections on the Guillotine' (1960).

Camus' essay has two broad purposes:

(1) to argue philosophically against the death penalty, and

(2) the political objective of having death by guillotine abolished for ever in France.

Of course, Camus sought an end to the death penalty *as such*, in France and elsewhere, but if all else failed he was prepared, as a preliminary step, to settle for an end to the guillotine. As he puts it himself:

> If the French State is incapable of overcoming habit and giving Europe one of the remedies it needs, let France begin by reforming the manner of administering capital punishment. The science that serves to kill so many could at least serve to kill decently. An anaesthetic that would allow the condemned man to slip from sleep to death would assure his elimination, if you insist, but would put a little decency into what is at present but a sordid and obscene exhibition.[44]

Camus begins his essay with the story of the shattering effect which the experience of having witnessed a public execution had had on his own father. He concludes, perhaps too hastily, that:

> When the extreme penalty simply causes vomiting on the part of the responsible citizen it is supposed to protect, how can anyone maintain that it is likely, as it ought to be, to bring more peace and order into the community?[45]

But Camus' attention is directed for the most part in his essay, not towards the witnesses to execution, but towards the individual who is executed, and the means used to bring about his death. The true awfulness of the experience, he begins, is heralded by the fact that 'no one dares speak directly of the ceremony'. Instead, it is spoken about, by those who are forced to speak about it, such as journalists, in a kind of coded language, such as that the condemned man 'has paid his debt to society', or that 'at five a.m. justice was done'.

Camus, for his part, says he will talk about it 'crudely'. Such plain talking is necessary, he declares, for:

when silence or tricks of language contribute to maintaining an abuse that must be reformed or a suffering that can be relieved, then there is no other solution but to speak out and show the obscenity hidden under the verbal cloak.[46]

To be blunt about it, he says;

if people are shown the machine, made to touch the wood and steel and to hear the sound of a head falling, then public imagination, suddenly awakened, will repudiate both the vocabulary and the penalty.[47]

With this purpose in mind, Camus directs his attention to the deterrence theory, or as he himself phrases it, to the argument from the exemplary value of punishment. This is the argument that:

Heads are cut off not only to punish but to intimidate, by a frightening example, any who might be tempted to imitate the guilty.[48]

Camus replies that society does not follow this theory in practice, and that:

there is no proof that the death penalty ever made a single murderer recoil when he had made up his mind, whereas clearly it had no effect but one of fascination on thousands of criminals.[49]

If society followed the deterrence theory in practice, then it would 'exhibit the heads'. He elaborates:

Society would give executions the benefit of the publicity it generally uses for national bond issues or new brands of drinks. But we know that executions in our country, instead of taking place publicly, are now perpetrated in prison courtyards before a limited number of specialists.[50]

This argument is not as potent as Camus supposes. At most it demonstrates that the criminal justice system is lethargic and inconsistent in its adherence to the deterrence principle. It does not demonstrate that capital punishment does not deter, even when carried out behind closed doors. It remains a possibility that it deters by virtue of being carried out at all. And as we shall see, the criminal justice system could have other reasons – not necessarily good ones – for not executing in public.

In the following pages Camus gives graphic scientific and anecdotal accounts of death by guillotine, accounts, he maintains, which would be publicised if the State *really* believed in the deterrent powers of execution. He concludes that it cannot really believe in the deterrence principle, since otherwise it would publish graphic accounts of the event. However, there could be other reasons for not doing so, such as the brutalising effects of doing so on the population at large. It might, then, be considered counter-productive to do so, and anyway simply not necessary: it might be sufficient to simply advertise the fact that an execution was scheduled to occur at such and such a time, or had just occurred.

It should be added that Camus himself was of the opinion that the real reason the (French) State did not graphically exploit the imagery of the execution experience was that it feared:

> provoking revolt and disgust in the public opinion ... The man who enjoys his coffee while reading that justice has been done would spit out at the least detail.[51]

Camus could well be on the right track here: a State that believes in the efficacy of the death penalty would clearly be unwise to publicise its method of execution if this would lead to a public outcry against it. Yet it hardly follows that it should abandon this method of punishment altogether.

Camus next examines the putative effects of the law permitting, or requiring, capital punishment for certain categories of crime, on the mind and behaviour of the actual, and would-be criminal. He argues that such a law deters neither the impulsive killer, nor the hardened criminal. The impulsive killer, because 'he doesn't know that he is going to kill', because he 'makes up his mind in a flash and commits his crime in a state of frenzy or obsession'.[52] It will not deter the hardened criminal since the majority of men sentenced to death had themselves witnessed a public execution, when records of such events were actually kept. Of course, men do fear death: 'The fear of death, arising from the most obscure depths of the individual, ravages him'.[53] But the fear of death, observes Camus:

> has never sufficed to quell human passions. Bacon is right in saying that there is no passion so weak it cannot confront and overpower fear of death. Revenge, love, honor, pain, another fear manage to overcome it.[54]

Indeed, the instinct to live, he adds, is matched by another, the death instinct:

> which at certain moments calls for the destruction of oneself and of others. Man wants to live, but it is useless to hope that this desire will dictate all his actions. He also wants to be nothing; he wants the irreparable, and death for its own sake. So it happens that the

criminal wants not only the crime but the suffering that goes with it, even (one might say, especially) if that suffering is exceptional. When that odd desire grows and becomes dominant, the prospect of being put to death not only fails to stop the criminal, but probably also adds to the vertigo in which he swoons. Thus, in a way, he kills in order to die.[55]

In reply to the argument that no record can be kept of all the murders the penalty succeeded in preventing – since, *ex hypothesi*, they never took place – but which it did prevent, or at least could have prevented, Camus says':

Thus, the greatest of punishments ... rests on nothing but an unverifiable possibility. Death, on the other hand, does not involve degrees or probabilities. It solidifies all things, culpability and the body, in a definitive rigidity. Yet it is administered among us in the name of chance and a calculation. Even if that calculation were reasonable, should there not be a certainty to authorize the most certain of deaths? However, the condemned is cut in two, not so much for the crime he committed but by virtue of all the crimes that might have been and were not committed, that can be and will not be committed. The most sweeping uncertainty in this case authorizes the most implacable certainty.[56]

Camus moves on to evaluate the theory of retribution, that the criminal deserves to be punished, and that the punishment should fit the crime; as he himself phrases it:

Whoever has done me harm must suffer harm; whoever has put out my eye must lose an eye; and whoever has killed must die.[57]

Camus has two arguments, basically, against retributivism, the second of which he develops at great length. The first is that retribution is nothing more than retaliation, which itself is nothing more than a natural instinct. But the law should not allow itself sink to such a primitive level:

Law, by definition, cannot obey the same rules as nature. If murder is in the nature of man, the law is not intended to imitate or reproduce that nature. It is intended to correct it.[58]

The second argument against retribution is that capital punishment is *far worse* than death (occurring due to murder). To begin with:

for there to be equivalence, the death penalty would have to punish a criminal who had warned his victim of the date at which he would inflict a horrible death on him and who, from that moment onward, had confined him at his mercy for months. Such a monster is not encountered in private life.[59]

In the case of the man condemned to death, 'the horror is parcelled out ...' Part of that horror is that:

> Torture through hope alternates with the pangs of animal despair. The lawyer and chaplain, out of mere humanity, and the jailers, so that the condemned man will keep quiet, are unanimous in assuring him that he will be reprieved. He believes this with all his being and then he ceases to believe it. He hopes by day and despairs of it by night. As the weeks pass, hope and despair increase and become equally unbearable. According to all accounts, the color of the skin changes, fear acting like an acid.[60]

In this way, the condemned man ceases to be actively human, reduced instead to the level of a parcel that is handled by others:

> He is no longer a man but a thing waiting to be handled by the executioners ... When the officials whose job it is to kill that man call him a parcel, they know what they are saying. To be unable to do anything against the hand that moves you, is this not indeed being a parcel, or a thing, or, better, a hobbled animal?[61]

Then, finally, comes the day that his being an object comes to an end:

> During the three quarters of an hour separating him from the end, the certainty of a powerless death stifles everything else; the animal, tied down and amenable, knows a hell that makes the hell he is threatened with seem ridiculous.[62]

Following further pages of prose in the same vein, Camus reaches the following conclusion:

> No, what man experiences at such times is beyond all morality. Not virtue, nor courage, nor intelligence, nor even innocence has anything to do with it. Society is suddenly reduced to a state of primitive terrors where nothing can be judged. All equity and dignity have disappeared ... A man is undone by waiting for capital punishment well before he dies. Two deaths are inflicted on him, the first being worse than the second, whereas he killed but once. Compared to such torture, the penalty of retaliation seems like a civilized law. It never claimed that a man who gouged out one of his brother's eyes should be totally blinded.[63]

This is a strong argument against the criminal justice system, it may be objected, but not against capital punishment *per se*. It would lose much, if not all its force, if the sentence was carried out immediately following its being pronounced, or even shortly afterwards. But, of course, this doesn't happen, in order to allow the prisoner exercise his right of appeal, for the process of judicial review to be invoked, and so on. These delays are undoubtedly agonising, but they may save a life and prevent a miscarriage of justice.

Camus concedes that 'The death penalty definitively eliminates the condemned man'.[64] But he reminds us quickly, that it has been known, through judicial error, to have eliminated some innocent men as well. Compassion should also be given its place, for 'There's a solidarity of all men in error and aberration'.[65] Of course, 'compassion does not exclude punishment, but it suspends the final condemnation'.[66] Certain juries, he observes, are aware of this:

> for they often admit extenuating circumstances in a crime that nothing can extenuate. This is because the death penalty seems excessive to them in such cases and they prefer not punishing enough to punishing too much.[67]

What, then, about major criminals whom all juries would condemn at any time and in any place whatever? Such persons (and Camus even uses the word 'monsters' here) 'must be kept from doing it again'. The only remaining question is whether this imperative necessitates killing them. Indeed, so far as Camus is concerned, 'On this frontier, and on it alone, discussion about the death penalty is legitimate'.[68]

At this juncture Camus advances his own ideas against capital punishment, as distinct from simply replying to the arguments advanced by those who defend it. Generally stated, his argument will be:

> the abolition of the death penalty ought to be asked for by all thinking members of our society, for reasons both of logic and of realism.[69]

What Camus calls reasons of logic (for opposing the death penalty) are these:

> (i) imposing the death penalty on a man deprives him of the opportunity of making amends, and absolutely no man should be denied the opportunity of adding to the sum of his actions 'a little of the good that will make up in part for the evil we have added to the world'.[70]

> (ii) Only someone who is abolutely innocent is entitled to be made 'supreme judge' and no human being is absoluely innocent:

> > we have all done wrong in our lives even if that wrong, without falling within the jurisdiction of the laws, went as far as the unknown crime.[71]

So, 'precisely because he is not absolutely good, no one among us can pose as an absolute judge and pronounce the definitive elimination of the worst among the guilty'. More profoundly, he adds that:

Capital punishment upsets the only indisputable human solidarity –
our solidarity against death – and it can be legitimized only by a
truth or a principle that is superior to man.[72]

Reference to a principle which is superior to man invites mention of the
divine, and, indeed, Camus immediately proceeds to say that:

In fact, the supreme punishment has always been, throughout the
ages, a religious penalty. Inflicted in the name of the King, God's
representative on earth, or by priests or in the name of society
considered as a sacred body, it denies, not human solidarity, but the
guilty man's membership in the divine community, the only thing
that can give him life.[73]

It is possible to furnish a justification of capital punishment from a
purely religious perspective for two reasons:

(a) it gives the guilty man the opportunity to make amends, and

(b) 'The real judgment is not pronounced, it will be in the other world'.[74] In
other words, it does not prevent the guilty man from meeting his Maker,
who will deliver the final judgment.

On this basis Camus observes that:

capital punishment is for the believer a temporary penalty that
leaves the final sentence in suspense, an arrangement necessary
only for terrestrial order, an administrative measure which, far from
signifying the end for the guilty man, may instead favor [sic] his
redemption.[75]

Turning his attention to Catholicism specifically, he adds the following:

I am not saying that all believers agree with this, and I can readily
imagine that some Catholics may stand closer to Christ than to
Moses or St. Paul. I am simply saying that faith in the immortality of
the soul allowed Catholicism to see the problem of capital
punishment in very different terms and to justify it.[76]

The main problem, however, with the religious defence of the death
penalty was that society is no longer religious; in Camus' words, its
institutions and customs have lost all contact with the sacred. It follows
that:

When an atheistic or skeptical or agnostic judge inflicts the death
penalty on an unbelieving criminal, he is pronouncing a definitive
punishment that cannot be reconsidered. He takes his place on the
throne of God, without having the same powers and even without
believing in God.[77]

The Court abrogates to itself the power of a God in whom it does not believe, which is hypocritical, and it delivers a final judgment, which only a God is entitled to do.

By such reasoning Camus is brought to the conclusion, repeated over and over in the closing pages of his essay, that 'our society must now defend herself not so much against the individual as against the State'.[78] Forbidding a man's public execution, he declares:

> would amount to proclaiming publicly that society and the State are not absolute values, that nothing authorizes them to legislate definitively or to bring about the irreparable. Without the death penalty, Gabriel Péri and Brasillach would perhaps be among us. We could then judge them according to our opinion and proudly proclaim our judgment, whereas they now judge us and we keep silent.[79]

Casting his eye over Europe, Camus remarks that:

> On our continent, all values are upset by fear and hatred between individuals and between nations. In the conflict of ideas the weapons are the cord and the guillotine. A natural and human society exercising her right of repression has given way to a dominant ideology that requires human sacrifices.[80]

For all these reasons he concludes that:

> in the unified Europe of the future the solemn abolition of the death penalty ought to be the first article of the European Code we all hope for.[81]

There are fascinating similarities and differences between Beauvoir's and Camus' approaches to the issue of the death penalty, prescinding entirely from the totally different conclusions they reach. Beauvoir develops a theory of punishment, first of all, one which justifies punishment in terms of social justice. The aim of social justice is to restore, and maintain, a truly human community, one in which the human status of each individual is fully recognised. From this perspective there is but one absolute evil, namely, the abject degradation of another human being to the level of a thing. Death alone, she argues unconvincingly, can atone for such an evil.

Camus, too, believes in moral absolutes, not least the absolute value of the human individual, but concludes, very differently, that it is precisely for this reason that the State must never be permitted to repudiate that absolute value. When it does so, it makes an absolute of itself, and such an absolute, he contends, is not worthy of recognition. Ironically, then, from the same basic ethical position Beauvoir and

Camus are driven to opposite conclusions: she supporting the death penalty, he deploring it. She wanted Brassillach dead, whereas Camus greatly regretted his death, not least because it seemed to give the dead Brassillach a moral advantage over his contemporaries. In any event, Beauvoir and Camus reach their very opposite conclusions, it seems to me, because she is mesmerised by the original crime and its victim, whereas Camus' eyes are focussed on the prisoner. What makes capital punishment more a moral dilemma than a straightforward moral issue is that there are two lives at stake: the victim (of the original crime) and the prisoner (sentenced to death for that same crime). While Camus unquestionably offers a more comprehensive discussion of the ethics of the death penalty, neither author, it could be said, takes into consideration the full dimensions of the practice.

V

The essay 'Oeil pour Oeil' comes at about the mid-way point of Simone de Beauvoir's writings in the 1940s, the most explosive and important stage of her writing career. It comes after *She Came to Stay, Pyrrhus et Cinéas, The Blood of Others, and Who Shall Die?*, while it precedes *All Men Are Mortal, The Ethics of Ambiguity,* and *The Second Sex*. It is chronologically very close, then, to what I would regard as her two most important works: *The Second Sex,* and *The Ethics of Ambiguity. The Second Sex* is now a feminist classic, while *The Ethics of Ambiguity*, despite its author's own reservations about it expresssed in her memoirs, may nonetheless be considered the single, most sustained and most substantial contribution to have been made to the elaboration of an existentialist ethics.[82]

The essay 'Oeil pour Oeil' was not written as a preface, so to speak, to the later, much more substantial pieces of prose just cited. Its central theme, that of crime and punishment, was born out of the atrocities of the Second World War and the reprisals which followed, and the essay remains strongly focussed throughout on these events. Nonetheless, in exploring and sharpening her moral thought, as she does in this essay, Beauvoir may be said to be doing further preparatory work for the full-scale ethical treatise which was to follow, viz. *The Ethics of Ambiguity,* as well as constructing the philosophical context within which *The Second Sex* would be written. According to Michèle le Doeuff, that context is 'existentialist morality'.[83] Let me explore a little what she means. A central proposition of *The Second Sex* is that women are relegated to the category of the Other, that is, to the category of the inessential, the subordinate and the secondary. But women are human beings and, as the present essay informs us, this makes a world of a difference to the way they ought to be perceived and treated:

> An object for another, each of us is a subject for herself, and we unceremoniously insist on getting this recognition for ourselves. This respect which we demand for ourselves we then extend to others and finally to all human beings, and this is the metaphysical basis of the idea of justice.[84]

But, as *The Second Sex* so graphically illustrates, the rule of justice is systematically flouted in the way that women are treated, by their relegation to the category of the Other. This proposition, which underpins the whole of *The Second Sex*, owes as least some of its meaning to the post-war essay on punishment. The sub-text is that relegation to the category of the Other is dehumanising, and this is the worst thing one can do to a human being.

It can be argued that had one not known otherwise, one would never have guessed that the essay 'Oeil pour Oeil' had been written by an existentialist. The ease and frequency with which Beauvoir makes use of the Catholic vernacular (e.g. her many references to sin, redemption, expiation, atonement and the virtue of charity), her frequent recourse to neo-Scholastic terminology (e.g. a universal human essence, totality of being, social justice) and above all, perhaps, the grim certainty of her moral convictions – none of these features would normally be considered remotely existentialist. But this is because existentialism is standardly identified with Sartrian existentialism, which in turn Beauvoir is still commonly considered to have replicated in a diluted form. I have myself argued at length against this orthodoxy, as have other Beauvoir specialists, in the 1990s. I maintain that Beauvoir made her own distinctive contribution to existentialism, especially in the form of an existentialist ethics, and there is, demonstrably, some support for this thesis in the essay 'Oeil pour Oeil'. The concepts of an absolute evil, of a universal moral standard, of human rights and a universal human essence were all alien to Sartre's philosophy at this time: either they are entirely absent from, or else they are formally repudiated in the three works containing his formal contribution to ethical theory: *The War Diaries* (1939–1940), *Existentialism and Humanism* (1946), and *Notebooks for an Ethics* (1947–1948).

In *The Ethics of Ambiguity*, Beauvoir says such things as:

> (i) 'A freedom which is interested only in denying freedom must be denied'[85];

(ii) that it is by way of such cumbersome procedures as tribunals 'that the "sacred character" of human life gets restored'[86];

(iii) 'The freedom of a single man must count for more than a cotton or a rubber harvest'[87];

(iv) 'The individual as such is one of the ends at which our action must aim'[88];

(v) and 'an action which wants to save man ought to be careful not to forget him on the way'.[89]

This ethics, she says in the conclusion to this work, is:

> individualism in the sense in which the wisdom of the ancients, the Christian ethic of salvation and the Kantian ideal of virtue also merit this name.[90]

Here Beauvoir explicitly aligns her ethical theory with mainstream Western philosophy and Christian thought. The high moral tone, even absolutism, of the essay *Oeil pour Oeil*, is not, then an aberration, an atypical, knee-jerk episodic reaction to a burning issue. It synchronises comfortably with her later, more important writings.

Notes

1   There is no published translation, so I have made my own translation as appropriate.
2   T. Judt, *Past Imperfect*, p. 57.
3   *Ibid.*, pp. 57, 58.
4   A translation from one of the Appendices in P. Assouline, *L'Epuration des intellectuels 1944-45*, p. 158.
5   *Ibid.*, p. 164.
6   Judt, *op. cit.*, p. 59.
7   *Ibid.*, p. 60.
8   *Ibid.*
9   *Ibid.*, pp. 60, 61.
10 *Ibid.*, p. 61.
11 *Ibid.*
12 *Ibid.*, p. 62.
13 *Ibid.*, p. 65.
14 *Ibid.*
15 *Ibid.*
16 *Ibid.*
17 *L'Existentialisme et la sagesse des nations*, p. 109.
18 *Ibid.*

19 *Ibid.*, p. 113.
20 *Ibid.*, p. 114.
21 *Ibid.*
22 *Ibid.*, p. 115.
23 *Ibid.*, p. 116.
24 *Ibid.*
25 *Ibid.*, p. 121.
26 *Ibid.*, p. 122.
27 *Ibid.*, p. 123.
28 *Ibid.*, p. 125.
29 *Ibid.*, p. 133.
30 *Ibid.*
31 *Ibid.*, p. 134.
32 *Ibid.*, p. 135.
33 *Ibid.*, p. 136.
34 *Ibid.*, pp. 123, 124.
34a I am working from a recent translation by Carol Cosman, published by University of California Press, 1999.
34b *America Day by Day*, pp. 365, 366.
34c *Ibid.*, p. 367.
34d *Ibid.*
34e *Ibid.*, pp. 368, 369.
35 *L'Existentialisme et la sagesse des nations*, p. 124.
36 Camus, *Resistance, Rebellion, and Death*, p. 198.
37 *Ibid.*, p. 199.
38 *Ibid.*, p. 211.
39 *Ibid.*
40 *Ibid.*, p. 231.
41 *Ibid.*, pp. 231, 232.
42 *Catechism of the Catholic Church*, p. 488.
43 *Ibid.*
44 *Resistance, Rebellion, and Death*, p. 233.
45 *Ibid.*, p. 176.
46 *Ibid.*, p. 177.
47 *Ibid.*
48 *Ibid.*, p. 179.
49 *Ibid.*, p. 180.
50 *Ibid.*
51 *Ibid.*, p. 187.
52 *Ibid.*, p. 188.
53 *Ibid.*, p. 189.
54 *Ibid.*, p. 190.
55 *Ibid.*, p. 192.
56 *Ibid.*, pp. 193, 194.
57 *Ibid.*, p. 198.
58 *Ibid.*

59   *Ibid.*, p. 199.
60   *Ibid.*, pp. 200, 201.
61   *Ibid.*, p. 201.
62   *Ibid.*, p. 202.
63   *Ibid.*, pp. 204, 205.
64   *Ibid.*, p. 210.
65   *Ibid.*, p. 217.
66   *Ibid.*
67   *Ibid.*, pp. 217, 218.
68   *Ibid.*, p. 219.
69   *Ibid.*, p. 220.
70   *Ibid.*, p. 221.
71   *Ibid.*
72   *Ibid.*, p. 222.
73   *Ibid.*
74   *Ibid.*
75   *Ibid.*, p. 224.
76   *Ibid.*
77   *Ibid.*, p. 225.
78   *Ibid.*, p. 227.
79   *Ibid.*, p. 228.
80   *Ibid.*, p. 229.
81   *Ibid.*, p. 230.
82   I have argued at length for this claim in my book *Existentialism, Feminism and Simone de Beauvoir*, especially pp. 68–87.
83   *Hipparchia's Choice*, p. 90.
84   *L'Existentialisme et la sagesse des nations*, p. 116.
85   *The Ethics of Ambiguity*, p. 91.
86   *Ibid.*, p. 107.
87   *Ibid.*, p. 113.
88   *Ibid.*, p. 135.
89   *Ibid.*, p. 153.
90   *Ibid.*, p. 156.

Chapter Nine

LE BON DIEU

For someone who so vehemently rejected God, Simone de Beauvoir wrote an extraordinary amount about Him. She did so in her memoirs, short stories, journal articles and philosophical monographs. The psychological origins of this obsession were many and varied, and its consequences constitute a rich and substantial theology. Psychologically, Beauvoir's God fulfils many functions: at times He is someone to cling to – especially when she has been spurned by her father – at times He is the object of her sexual reveries. At times she even aspires to be God, a writer-god, as when she says:

> If at one time I had dreamed of being a teacher it was because I wanted to become a law unto myself; I now thought that literature would allow me to realize this dream. It would guarantee me an immortality which would compensate for the loss of heaven and eternity; there was no longer any God to love me, but I should have the undying love of millions of hearts.[1]

In this chapter I propose to present a detailed account of Simone de Beauvoir's understanding of God. She *had* this understanding of God during childhood and adolescence, and much later in life she presents it in the more refined, sophisticated prose of a major, established author. I will begin with the first volume of her memoirs, *Memoirs of a Dutiful Daughter*, which contains her most extensive, and most important, reflections on God. Then I will look at the ideas of God which are presented in the collection of short stories, *When Things of the Spirit Come First*. Third, I will examine the concepts of God which are invoked in her (untranslated) philosophical monograph *Pyrrhus et Cinéas,* and, to a lesser extent, the view of God which is contained in the later, more substantial philosophical work, *The Ethics of Ambiguity.* Finally, I will conclude with some reflections on Simone de Beauvoir's theology.

My argument in this chapter is not, of course, that Simone de Beauvoir had a lifelong *belief* in God, that she was, in effect, some kind of closet Catholic. Clearly she believed in God as a child, as well as for at least a portion of her adolescence, and equally it is beyond doubt that she did not believe in God thereafter. But it is worth clarifying the meaning of the word 'belief' in these contexts. Believing in God is not like believing there are people in this room, since the former belief is reflected in and sustained by a litany of practices, whereas little, if anything, hinges on the latter belief. Thus the person who *believes* in God will do such things as pray, bless herself, go to Church, attend the sacraments, have her children baptized and confirmed, call for a priest at the approach of death, and so on. One might call such a belief a religious belief in God, and for a long stretch of her life Simone de Beauvoir did not have this religious belief. As she put it herself when writing about Lourdes, the truths of religion are convincing only to those who are already convinced, and she herself was no longer convinced.

On the other hand, there are marked contrasts between Beauvoir's writings about God, and those of Sartre. Beauvoir's writings of the 1940s, for example, do not contain the same shrill, aggressive statements of atheism as Sartre's. Unlike Sartre, she does not attempt to demonstrate that the concept of God is self-contradictory. She introduces, and comments at length, on a wide range of ideas about God, and clearly finds some of these ideas more congenial than the others. Like Camus, she is fiercely critical of the idea of an impersonal, silent and immutable God (what Stephen Eric Bronner in his *Camus: Portrait of a Moralist* calls Camus' 'religious atheism'), but unlike Camus she finds far more acceptable the idea of a dependent, contingent God, because this allows scope for human agency. Finally, while she herself does not have a religious belief in God, she is prepared to write about those who do. These portraits are not flattering, to put it mildly; that of Anne's (Zaza's) mother, for instance, represents such people as narrow-minded, obsessive, driven and tyrannical. But they also allow such people to speak for themselves, and the rest of us to hear them. She allows us to see and hear *how the world looks* to such people, and what sustains them as they journey through life. There is much that is theologically incisive in these narratives.

God in the Memoirs

In the first volume of her memoirs (hereafter *Memoirs*), Simone de Beauvoir presents at least ten different concepts of God, visions of God such as she had perceived Him during an intensely-lived Catholic childhood and adolescence. She had perceived God as Creator, as Providence, as Supreme Moral Being, as Supreme Moral Authority, as omnipotent, as loving, as Christ or God the Son, as perfection and as immanence. The idea of God the Creator, and in particular as the giver of life, emerges in her account of how the facts of human reproduction were to be understood. This was a puzzle to which she had spent many years seeking a solution. At first she was told that parents purchased their children in a shop. But gradually, she confides, this explanation was forgotten, and she contented herself with what she is pleased to call 'a vaguer solution'. This is an explanation to the effect that 'It is God who makes children. He had created the earth out of chaos, and shaped Adam out of clay: so there was nothing unusual in the idea that He could produce a baby from an empty cradle'.[2] According to this account of God, it is God who makes children, not their parents; God did not make the earth out of nothing, but out of chaos; and neither did He make Adam out of nothing, but out of mud or clay. Kirkup's translation of the sentence *'rien d'extraordinaire `a ce qu'il fît surgir dans un moïsse un nourisson'* is a little misleading: it is not that it was not beyond God to produce a baby from an empty cradle, but that it was not beyond God to produce a baby in a cradle which had hitherto been unoccupied; or to produce a baby in a cradle where hitherto there had been neither baby nor cradle.

She re-visits the idea of God the Creator in her account of her own early adolescence. Here God is seen as the Creator who is present in His creations, but more obviously so in the countryside than in the city. As she herself puts it:

> Yet, much more strongly than in Paris, I could feel all around me the presence of God; in Paris He was hidden from me by people and their top-heavy preoccupations; here I could see blades of grass and clouds that were still the same as when He had snatched them out of primal Chaos, and that still bore His mark. The harder I pressed myself against the earth, the closer I got to Him, and every country walk was an act of adoration.[3]

These words resonate with details of the nineteenth-century cultural debates about cities, in particular the claim that cities divinise man because everywhere he is surrounded by human creations, whereas in the countryside, an intact, unsullied Nature speaks continuously to us of God, the true Divine. [See my 'Engels and the Question about Cities' for extensive coverage of these nineteenth-century debates].

With reference to His creation, Beauvoir attributes to God a 'sovereign' but not an infinite or unlimited power. All creation, on this view, derives from God, but it is human creatures alone who can fully *experience* the fullness of God's creation. It is not that God does not have knowledge of His own creation, since God 'knew all things after His own fashion'. But God lacks a body, and for this reason, she concluded, 'it seemed to me that He needed my eyes in order that trees might have their colours'.[4] For how, she plausibly reasons:

> could a pure spirit have experienced the scorching of the sun, the freshness of the dew, if not through the medium of my own body?[5]

God had created the earth for humans so that they could give witness to the glories of His creation. Children, moreover, made better witnesses than adults:

> Deprived of my presence, Creation sank into a shadowy slumber; by waking it to life again, I was accomplishing the most sacred of all tasks, whereas grown-ups, the indifferent ones, took God's laws into their own hands.[6]

In his discourse on religion entitled *Religion, If There is no God*, Leszek Kolakowski echoes some of Marx's points about the consolations of religion when he writes:

> people who are able to absorb their misery, thanks to their strong belief in a purposeful order wherein everything is ultimately given a meaning, are better prepared to sustain the inevitable blows of destiny and not to succumb to despair.[7]

This observation can be usefully applied to Simone de Beauvoir's invocation of God as Providence, as her Protector, and Protector of those who were nearest and dearest to her. The occasion was the outbreak of World War I, when her father was called up. Georges Bertrand de Beauvoir, unlike his wife, had long since ceased to practise his religion, and, indeed, openly mocked a number of Catholic pieties. As his daughter on more than one occasion observed:

> Papa didn't go to Mass, he smiled when Aunt Marguerite enthused over the miracles at Lourdes: he was an unbeliever.[8]

But she immediately adds that 'This scepticism did not affect me, so deely did I feel myself penetrated by the presence of God'.[9] When

Georges de Beauvoir left for the Front, he was accompanied to the Metro by his wife and elder daughter. His wife cried, but his daughter, on her own admission, had no idea – other than a vaguely abstract idea – of the real dangers posed by war. As she explains:

> I never realized that my father was in danger. I had seen wounded men; I knew there was a connection between war and death. But I could not conceive that this great collective adventure could possibly concern *me*.[10]

This conviction was strengthened by her faith, by her absolute trust in God, who would not allow any harm to befall her father:

> And besides I was convinced that God would protect my father very specially for me: I was incapable of imagining any misfortune happening to him.[11]

This, in fact, is a rather sophisticated translation of a sentence which has, arguably, a much less sophisticated, but far more intriguing and provocative philosophical meaning. What Beauvoir actually writes is: *'j'étais incapable d'imaginer le malheur'*, which translated literally means that she was incapable of imagining *any* misfortune (and not just harm befalling her father). A faith so strong that it eclipses all fear, and undermines the power of imagination, is very strong indeed. It could be argued that a faith which was that strong induces an ill-advised complacency, for if you are *incapable* of imagining any misfortune you are unkikely to take steps to avoid misfortune before it strikes. Yet her point seems to be, not that misfortune won't strike, but that it won't strike the person who puts all her trust in God. God will protect, and so strong is this conviction that no human depravity will prevail against it.

The concept of God as Supreme Moral Authority has at least two distinct meanings:

> (i) God alone knows everything, and therefore His moral teaching is faultless;

> (ii) God alone is owed complete submission and respect.

In this latter sense, God is the Supreme Moral Being. Simone de Beauvoir invokes the second of these two meanings in writing about her early childhood. The precise context is her transition from a petulant infancy to a more reflective childhood, acompanied by her often unsuccessful attempts at engaging her parents in meaningful conversation. She had metamorphosed into 'a good little girl', so much so that 'there was not much occasion to reprimand or twart me'. In addition, she was now of a mental age and disposition that she was able to ask for reasons for a particular parental decision when it did not appeal to her. All too often, however, she was met by a stubborn, peremptory refusal to discuss the matter any further. Nonetheless, she was still at an age to remain convinced that her parents sought only what was best for her, and, furthermore, that they *knew* what was best. They knew what was best because 'it was the will of God their lips gave utterance to', and God had to be obeyed on all occcasions. God merited this obedience because:

> He had created me; He had died for me; He was entitled to my total submission. I felt I bore upon my shoulders the reassuring yoke of necessity.[12]

Here two distinct reasons are given for submission to God:

(a) God created us;

(b) God, in the person of His son, Jesus Christ, died for us.

Since God created us, we literally owe everything to God, since without God's intervention we would not even exist; we would be *nothing*. Second, since God made the ultimate sacrifice for humanity, by laying down His life for us, we owe Him our undying thanks and respect. Beauvoir doesn't speculate further on why God chose to be the Redeemer, still less on why He chose to create us in the first place.[13] She simply reminds us that God bestowed on us the greatest gift it is possible to possess, namely, life itself, and that He also made the ultimate sacrifice on our behalf, by dying for us. The combination of these two facts about God, she maintains, in the first volume of her memoirs, entitles God to an absolute, unfailing respect to which no one else is entitled.

'There was nothing He did not know'.[14] This means, in the first place, that nothing *escapes* God, or, as Beauvoir herself phrases it in French, '*Il n'en laissait rien échapper*'. In particular, what doesn't escape God are the faults and virtues of His creatures. She points out that He was familiar with her own virtues and vices as a schoolgirl, to a far greater extent than her teachers – and *they* kept meticulous records of such matters. But she did not fear the wrath of God since, as she explains, her faults and errors 'were washed so clean in the waters of repentance that they shone just as brightly as my virtues'.[15] She derived immense happiness from the *thought* of God's omniscience: knowing that God knew how good she really was:

> consoled me for all my earthly shortcomings and failures; it saved me from the indifference, from the injustice and the misunderstandings of human nature.[16]

God, she was convinced, was always on *her* side, and the reassurance which she derived from this conviction developed in her a self-belief of unearthly proportions:

> If I had done wrong in any way, at the very instant that I dropped upon my knees to ask His forgiveness He breathed upon my tarnished soul and restored to it all its lustre. But usually, bathed as I was in His eternal radiance, the faults I was accused of simply melted away; His eternal judgement was my justification. He was the supreme arbiter who found that I was always right. I loved Him with all the passion I brought to life itself.[17]

She took these reflections with her when she went on retreat for several days each year. She evidently desired to grow even closer to God, she notes in her meditations, but did not know how to go about it. Good behaviour would not bring her any closer to God, she reckons, since 'My conduct left so little to be desired that I could hardly be any better than I already was'.[18] Besides, God surely was not interested in petty misdemeanours, only in significant Sin. By way of this whole train of thought Beauvoir comes to expatiate on the demands of God's moral teaching. As she herself experienced it, God forbade a great many things:

> but never asked for anything positive apart from a few prayers or religious practices which did not change my daily course in any way.[19]

Indeed, what struck her as most peculiar, she confesses, was the sight of people who had just received Communion plunging straight back into the ordinary routine of their lives, as if nothing had happened. She was no exception herself, she admits, but she still found it embarrassing. The mystery was that believers and non-believers alike 'led just the same kind of life', and for this reason, she says:

> I became more and more convinced that there was no room for the supernatural in everyday life. And yet it was that other-worldly life that really counted: it was the only kind that mattered.[20]

On this view of the moral life, Christian ethics makes no practical difference to the way each moral agent behaves, since non-Christian moral agents behave no differently. What this means, in effect, is that Christian and secular ethics are no different in the demands they make on us as moral agents, nor in their influence on us as moral agents, since non-Christian moral agents are indistinguishable, so far as their general behaviour goes, from their Christian counterparts. But not only is the evidence for this claim both limited and anecdotal, the claim itself seems greatly exaggerated. First of all, the parallels hold, if they hold at all, only between devout Christians and non-believers who are already committed to leading a good life – basically, ordinary, decent citizens. The comparison does not extend to those who flout the most basic laws of society, nor to those with different religious outlooks, nor to those who live on the margins. Christian ethics also offers a very different *basis* for morally good conduct, namely, that God created each one of us, and that God also died for us. Beauvoir says that she experienced Christian ethics as a series of prohibitions, but does not seem to see that every statement of a rule that *forbids* a practice can also be reformulated in terms that *advocate* the very opposite practice. Thus the injunction on spouses *not to commit adultery* can also be presented as a rule enjoining spouses to remain *faithful* to each other. It is possibly easier to *understand* the negative rule, but that is a different matter. Beauvoir also probably underestimates the extent to which some of the basic Christian precepts – such as the prohibition on killing, and the commandment to love one another – have permeated social consciousness over the centuries, so that what appears secular is, in a sense, no more than a scaled-down Christian ethics in disguise.

Simone de Beauvoir meditates on God the Son, or Jesus Christ, as a preface to writing about God as Supreme Moral Authority. She was, she declares, very pious during the rising years of her childhood [9–11 years], and she then itemises what Catholic piety means in practice. She went to Confession twice a month to Abbé Martin; she went to Communion three times a week, while each morning she read a complete chapter of *The Imitation of Christ*. Between classes, she continues, she used to slip into the school chapel and, with her head in her hands, she would 'offer up lengthy prayers'.[21] Indeed, often in the course of the day, she says, she would lift up her soul to God ('*j'élevais mon âme à Dieu*'[22]). But it was God made flesh, Jesus Christ, who truly fascinated her. She adored Christ to distraction ('*éperdument*'), she says. She had read the narratives which were used to supplement the gospel, in which Christ featured as the hero, and working from there she imagined His 'grave, tender, handsome face' ('*son beau visage tendre et triste*'), 'with the eyes of a lover' ('*avec des yeux d'amoureuse*'). She continues in this vein as follows:

> I would follow, across hills covered with olive groves, the shining hem of his snow-white robe, bathe His naked feet with my tears; and He would smile down upon me as He had smiled upon the Magdalen. When I had had my fill of clasping His knees and sobbing on His blood-stained corpse, I would allow Him to ascend into heaven.[23]

Having ascended into heaven, she concludes, Christ became one with that more mysterious Being:

> to whom I owed my existence on earth, and whose throne of glory would one day, and for ever, fill my eyes with a celestial radiance.[24]

> ('Il s'y fondait avec l'être plus mystérieux à qui je devais la vie et dont un jour, et pour toujours, la splendeur me ravirait'.[25])

This concept of God is theological rather than philosophical. Jesus Christ is one of the three persons in God, who takes a bodily form while He exists on earth. When He ascends into heaven, following the Resurrection – if we adopt the New Testament version – or at the conclusion of one of Simone de Beauvoir's reveries, He becomes one with God once again, with God the Father, that is. In the person of His Son, Jesus Christ, God takes on a form which is not only recognisably human, but is also eminently suitable for the purposes of prose fiction.

The idea of God as Providence emerges during one of her earliest meditations on death. She had been blessed with parents who adored her; she also lived the closetted life of a young *bourgeoise*. In the Luxembourg Gardens, she was forbidden to play with little girls who did not belong to her social circle. And:

> Unlike the vulgar race of boys and girls ('*comme le vulgaire*') we did not have the right to drink from the metal goblets that were chained to the public fountains; grandmama had made me a present of an opalescent shell, a mother-of-pearl chalice from which I alone might drink ...[26]

Few things were capable of disturbing her equanimity, she writes, except perhaps *death*. But death itself did not fill her with terror, since, as she explains, 'my faith protected me from the terrors of death'.[27] ('*contre la mort la foi me défendait*'.[28]) When the time came for her to depart this world she would close her eyes, 'and in a flash the snowy hands of angels would transport me to the celestial regions'.[29] All that separated her from 'paradise resplendent with the true light' was 'a thin azure curtain'. So, time and time again, she would dispose her limbs upon the carpet, join her hands in prayer, 'and command my soul to make her escape'.[30] She acknowledges that these antics amounted to no more than a game, and that had she *been* on her deathbed she would have been terrified. But the *idea* of death, of personal extinction, did not frighten her. It did not frighten her because she had nothing to fear from it. She had nothing to fear because 'God had given me the promise of eternity'.[31] ('*Dieu me promettait l'éternité*'.[32]) She understood eternity to mean she would never cease to see, to hear, to talk to herself: '*jamais je ne cesserais de voir, d'entendre, de me parler'.*[33] There would be no end: *'Il n'y aurait pas de fin'.*[34]

This concept of God as the One who guarantees immortality to the faithful is exceedingly familiar to anyone raised in a Catholic milieu. It also helps to explain the enduring attractions of religious belief for the elderly, as well as for parents and children, i.e. among those who are closest to death, or who are particularly vulnerable, or those who have immense duties of care. Faith reduces, in the end, to trusting in God[35]; indeed, who *wouldn't* trust in a God who offers protection from death itself? So there is nothing unusual about Beauvoir's meditations in these pages on death and eternity; all devout Catholics have that same total trust in God, who has promised them life everlasting.

The concept of God as infinite, or as infinite perfection, emerges on that troubling occasion when Simone de Beauvoir loses her faith, i.e. loses that absolute trust in God that immunises the faithful against the terrors of death. She had disowned her spiritual director, Abbé Martin, for having masqueraded as God's representative when, in reality, he was nothing more than her mother's spy. Momentarily, she had doubted God, for 'perhaps God Himself was as fussy and narrow-minded as an old church-hen'.[36] But when she left the chapel, 'God had been restored to His position of omniscient majesty'.[37] Yet the episode had already sown the seeds of doubt. To begin with, she could no longer accept any priest as 'sovereign Judge', as someone whose authority derived from God. Indeed, she concluded, 'No one on earth was the exact incarnation of God'.[38] (*'Personne sur terre n'incarnait exactement Dieu'.*[39]) Without an intermediary, she found herself facing God 'alone before Him'. She was also left with troubling questions, such as 'who was He? What did He really want? On whose side was He?'[40] The conflict between *secular* and *theological* reason emerges at its sharpest at this juncture; and at the same time, the limitations of theological reason begin to manifest themselves. Theological reason gives her the means of defending the truths of religion against attack. But theological reason will not suffice to restore her faith. So, she had:

> subtle arguments to refute any objection that might be brought against revealed truths; but I didn't know one that could prove them.[41]

She explains that:

> The allegory of the clock and the clock-maker did not convince me. I was too ignorant of human suffering to find in it an argument against Providence; but there was no very obvious harmony in the world.[42]

She found herself trapped between these two extremes: on the one hand she retained a sense that 'there was no greater disaster than to lose one's faith'[43] (*'je pensais qu'il n'y a pas de plus grand cataclysme que de perdre la foi'*[44]); on the other hand, 'The facts of religion were convincing only to those who were already convinced'.[45] (*'Les faits religieux n'étaient convaincants que pour les convaincus'*.[46]) The loss of faith was the greatest loss anyone could sustain, but that conviction alone could not help her retain her faith. Moreover, the truths of religion were not independently verifiable; these truths could be compelling only to someone who was already disposed to find them compelling.[47]

How did Simone de Beauvoir resolve this crisis of faith? She informs her readers that for a long time her concept of God had become increasingly abstract and rarified, sublimated:

> to the point where He no longer had any countenance divine, any concrete link with the earth or therefore any being.[48]

God as she now imagined Him had become *so* perfect that it had become impossible for Him to actually exist: *'Sa perfection excluait sa realité'*.[49] Divested of all the features that had once given God a human, or recognisable apearance, the refining exercises of the mind had ended up by refining God out of existence. 'That', says Beauvoir:

> is why I felt so little surprise when I became aware of His absence in heaven and in my heart ... I realized that He was playing no further part in my life and so I concluded that He had ceased to exist for me.[50]

> (*'C'est pourquoi j'éprouvai si peu de surprise quand je constatai son absence dans mon coeur et au ciel ... je m'aperçus qu'il n'intervenait plus dans ma vie et j'en conclus qu'il avait cessé d'exister pour moi'*.[51])

II

When Things of the Spirit Come First[52]

In a specially prepared preface to the English translation of *Quand prime le spirituel*, Simone de Beauvoir informs her readers that she started work on these short stories 'a little before I was thirty', and that unlike her previous truncated attempts at prose fiction, she sought on this occasion 'to speak about the world I knew ...'.[53] This world was a socially closed milieu permeated by Catholicism, a Catholicism 'that was in the air I breathed during my childhood and early youth'.[54] Several of her friends, she continues:

> had never broken away from it: willingly or unwillingly they had undergone the dangerous influence of that kind of spiritual life.[55]

She had decided, she continues, 'to tell their stories and also deal with my own conversion to the real world'.[56] Simone de Beauvoir, I argue throughout this book, did indeed convert to 'the real world', but not as comprehensively as she would have us believe. As is abundantly clear from these short stories, the closed, suffocating world of the Catholicism she had imbibed during her childhood and adolescence remains intensely familiar to her, though whether this is due to her prodigious powers of retention and recall, or to the fact that she had remained, to some extent, on familiar terms with that world, is another matter. At all events, these narratives draw extensively on the Catholic vernacular, as well as on Catholicism's more arcane dogmatic teachings. They provide an object representation of the devotional life of the truly Catholic citizen. 'For my part, I am too far from Catholicism', confides the eponymous heroine of the story *Chantal*. This is the impression which Beauvoir herself so often wished to convey; but in her prefatory notes to these short stories, she writes that:

> Chantal's inner monologue and her diary showed her both as she longed to be and as she really was. I had succeeded in conveying that distance between a person and himself which is the essence of bad faith.[57]

All of these stories are autobiographical, but the one that comes closest to pure autobiography is the final story *Marguerite*. Beauvoir herself describes it as 'a satire on my youth', and adds that she gives Marguerite 'my own childhood at the Cours Désir and my own adolescent religious crisis'.[58] So here again we encounter the same familiar visions of God: as Christ:

> then coming home to a creamy cup of chocolate still talking to the Christ who had come down into me[59]:

as Supreme Moral Being ('I offered God my life so that He should grant our soldiers the victory'[60]), and as omnipotent:

> when you have been living in a world peopled with angels and saints, under the eye of an all-powerful being, it is strange suddenly to find yourself alone amidst mere blind things[61].

In the story entitled *Anne* we are introduced to God as Providence ('Once again God had listened to her prayer'[62]), as omniscient ('Only

God knows what point you my have reached by now'[63]), and as Supreme Moral Authority ('and we have no right to judge'[64]).

In the first volume of her memoirs Simone de Beauvoir confesses that she 'adored Christ to distraction'.[65] That she means this quite literally is evident from the adjoining sentences:

> As supplements to the Gospels, I had read disturbing novels of which He was the hero, and it was now with the eyes of a lover that I gazed upon His grave, tender, handsome face; I would follow, across hills covered with olive groves, the shining hem of His snow-white robe, bathe His naked feet with my tears; and He would smile down upon me as He had smiled upon Mary Magdalen. When I had had my fill of clasping His knees and sobbing on His blood-stained corpse, I would allow Him to ascend into heaven.[66]

This infatuation with the handsome Jesus develops, in the short story *Marcelle*, into a clearly recognizable sado-masochistic *mise en scène*. In fact, in her prefatory notes to the English edition of these short stories, Beauvoir writes that she:

> had come to realize that when I was a child, there was a very close connection between my piety and the masochism of some of my games.[67]

Marcelle identifies herself with a heroine who was fond of:

> quivering with repentance at the feet of a sinless, beautiful and terrible man. He had the right of life and death over her, and she called him 'Lord'.[68]

This same Lord, she now confides:

> made her strip herself naked before him, and he used her body as a step when he mounted his splendidly decked charger.[69]

But not content with these humiliations, Marcelle:

> With a sensuous delight ... drew out this moment of feeling the harsh spur flay her servile back as she knelt there, her head bowed, her heart full of adoration and passionate humility. And when the stern-eyed avenger, vanquished by pity and by love, laid his hands on her head as a sign of forgiveness she clasped his knees in an exquisite swoon.[70]

The short story *Anne* represents for Beauvoir herself her most successful attempt in prose fiction 'at bringing back to life Zaza, the friend who had meant so much to me'.[71] In this short story, she says, she drew 'a more faithful and a more engaging portrait of her than I had done in the earlier versions'.[72]; but it is the portrait which she draws of Anne's

(Zaza's) mother that interests me for present purposes. Anne's mother was a devout Catholic, who communicated, at length, with God as she knew Him. Her devotional monologues introduce an entirely new God to the reader, whom I propose to call the God of the Faithful. He is addressed as 'Lord' by His 'servants', who 'worship' and 'love' Him, who are so 'humble' and 'unworthy' that they do not even deserve to *stand* before Him, and so 'prostrate' themselves at His feet. The God of the Faithful has entrusted His faithful with the care of their children's souls, and they believe that one day they will be called to account for their stewardship. But they can turn to God for 'guidance', 'help' and 'protection'. This is precisely what Anne's mother does when the future she has mapped out for any of her children appears to be threatened. Such is the case with her daughter Anne, who is carrying on a secret correspondence with a student at the Sorbonne; there can, she reasons, be no doubt about this since 'no young man of our world would presume to write to a daughter of mine'.[73] She acknowledges that her daughter prays with great intensity ('fervently'), and that all through Mass she keeps her face buried in her hands. Yet 'she is letting herself be carried away by weakness'. For this reason the mother beseeches the Lord to:

> Enlighten, oh Lord, this straying conscience; she is letting herself be carried away by weakness; inspire her to make a sincere confession.[74]

She draws a contrast between her own ineffectual policing of her daughter's behaviour, and God's harshness in dealing with His own son:

> It is absurd that she has not yet spoken to me of her own free will: I have been weak with her: Lord, give me the strength to be hard. Thou didst not spare Thy own Son![75]

With mounting anguish she reminds her Lord that she had kept her daughter:

> so pure for thee, oh Lord! She had in her the makings of a saint and for a while I thought that Thou wouldst do us the great honour of reserving her for Thyself.[76]

But she now perceives her daughter to be the prey 'of an unbeliever and a stranger', and she implores the Lord to 'Save her from them!'

Anne's mother then concisely documents the prospects and the progress of her other daughter Lucette, before returning to the subject of Anne, whom she thinks she may send abroad for year 'to a convent where she will be supervised and where she can perfect her English'.[77]

In particular she wants her daughter to have no further contact with Chantal Plattard (aka Simone de Beauvoir):

> this pretentious little intellectual, a girl who hangs about cafes with men, who has no family, and who does not believe in God or the Devil, and who has lost her social position.[78]

Anne's mother is amused at the idea that Chantal's male friends are interested in her mind rather than her body; she knows better, since 'These so-called pure relationships between men and women, it's the promiscuity of savages and wild animals'.[79] Unless they are sanctified by the grace of God, 'men are only filthy beasts'.[80] Chantal, she is convinced, 'is no longer a virgin; she has no principles; she looks like a woman used to dissipation'.[81] The mother vows that she 'shall not let them sully my little Anne, my pure treasure'. She acknowledges that God has given her 'such beautiful children, with healthy bodies and such clean souls', and that she has, perhaps, been a 'presumptuous mother'. She implores God:

> not to punish me too severely: Thy will be done; but if it is possible, take this cup from me. Speak, oh God; I shall obey.[82]

So the God of the Faithful appears in many guises. He is a Lord and Master, He helps and protects, He enlightens and saves; He is a Father whose will is always done. A mother can entrust herself to Him; she can confide her innermost thoughts, feelings and anxieties to Him, and He can lighten the burdens of parenting. It is not remotely an equal relationship, since the God of the Faithful must always be obeyed, since the faithful are not fit to even stand before Him, and since His will must always be done. But a Catholic mother can have a relationship with this God which she is incapable of having, or so it seems, with a spouse, a priest, or any of her children. It is a very private relationship in which intimacies and confidentialities can be confidently exchanged, and in which favours can be granted. This God of the Faithful is an intimate confidant, a man of unrivalled power, a sympathetic ear, an ally. He is an immensely seductive individual.

III

God in the Philosophical Monographs

There is virtually no resemblance between the God of the Faithful – such as we encounter Him in the short story *Anne* – and the God of the philosophers, such as He is presented in the philosophical monographs. We are introduced to this God of the philosophers for the first time in *Pyrrhus et Cinéas*, where we are informed that God's will cannot be surpassed (*'on ne dépasse pas la volonté de Dieu'*[83]), but the impersonal tone of this sentence (in contrast to 'Thy will be done') very accurately portends the kind of philosophical prose which follows. She elaborates in these words:

> If God is infinite, and a plenitude of Being, then there is no distance between His project and His reality. What He wills simply is; He wills things things as they are. His will is simply the foundation of static being; one could hardly call it a will. Such a God is not a particular individual: He is the universal, the immutable and eternal being. And the universal is silence. Such a being doesn't entreat us to do anything, it doesn't promise anything, it demands no sacrifice, it dispenses no rewards or punishments, it cannot justify anything, it offers no basis either for hope or for despair. It exists, nothing further can be said about it. The perfection of its being leaves no space for human agency.[84]

This passage concludes with a variation on the concept of God which we last met during the narrative of Simone de Beauvoir's adolescent crisis of faith. On that occasion we were told that God's perfection excluded His reality. In the first philosophical monograph, however, Beauvoir is attempting to lay an anthropological basis for an ethics, and so she shifts her focus from God to the relationship between God and human agency. If God is infinite, she reasons, then there is no place for human agency. Human agency is laborious by contrast with God's effortless use of His powers, but, more importantly, the human will cannot compete with the will of God. Whatever God wills automatically obtains, regardless and independently of the desires of any human being.[85]

Of more immediate interest, however, is the way that the God of the philosophers has been divested of all *personal* characteristics – unlike the God of the Faithful, who behaves like a mentor, a psychiatrist, a lover and a patriarch all wrapped in one. The infinite God, by contrast, scarcely possesses a will, since His will is automatically done. He is a plenitude of Being, such a Totality that there is no room in such a being for disappointment, hope or disapproval. Small wonder, then, that Beauvoir inclines towards saying that He is not an individual at all, since He lacks all the usual markers of individuality. He is the universal, but never the particular; He is the immutable and eternal being; He is silent; He neither commands, entreats nor admonishes; He makes no demands; He neither rewards nor punishes. He is beyond all human contact. It is not possible to have a relationship with such a God, and corroborative proof of this datum is provided by the very personal characteristics attributed, of necessity, to the God of the Faithful. If the God of the Faithful didn't exist, it would have been necessary to invent Him.

In *Pyrrhus et Cinéas* Beauvoir is concerned to lay the basis for an existentialist ethics, an anthropological foundation for an ethics of this kind. Having discarded the premise of the *futility* of all human agency (both in its secular and in its theological versions), she opts instead for the premise of the *necessity* of human agency in the creation of a human world. Good and evil are grounded in the fact that humans have a capacity to act on the world and transform it for better or for worse. The only good is the good that is *done,* the only evil that which is perpetrated. To phrase the point, as does Beauvoir herself, in the terms of virtue ethics, the only good is the good that is done by the virtuous, the only evil that which is done by the wicked.[86]

At this stage she introduces another God who is situated somewhere between the Silent, Eternal Totality of the philosophers, and the patient, seductive, psychiatrist-God of the Faithful. This God has created human agents, but cannot realise His plan for their salvation without their cooperation. These creatures are a special creation, or have a privileged place in God's creation. They alone are endowed with free will. They do not act, or obey, of *necessity;* if they did, it would not have been necessary to have created them in the first place: either *any* creature could have executed the divine plan, or it would have needed no execution at all. God is now seen to need an ally: human agents who *freely* carry out His wishes. This God is a Partner (what Beauvoir herself calls a neighbourly God[87]): we need Him, for otherwise we would not have existed in the first place, but He also needs us if His plans are to be realised.[88] Beauvoir remarks that Christians now find themselves, once again, in the presence of a personal and living God, on whose behalf they can act.[89] Such a God, she further observes, is no longer absolute, because He depends on us. But such a God is our ally, or partner, in a joint enterprise.

Beauvoir returns to the subject of God in her second, post-war philosophical monograph, *The Ethics of Ambiguity.*[90] She does so in the opening pages, where she is intent on providing a defence of existentialist ethics against the many objections which have been brought against it. It is held against existentialism, she says, that it is a philosophy of the absurd and of despair, that it encloses us in a sterile anguish, in an empty subjectivity. She concedes that, *prima facie,* there may be some merit in these observations; indeed:

> Does not Sartre declare, in effect, that man is a 'useless passion', that
> he tries in vain to realize the synthesis of the for-itself and the in-
> itself, to make himself God?[91]

There are two ways of reading this passage, having dramatically
different implications. On the first reading, the concept of God is the
concept of a synthesis between Nothingness and Being. But as such a
concept is self-contradictory, it cannot denote any existing thing.
Therefore there cannot *be* such a God and, as such, it is an exercise in
futility for any human being to attempt to be God, or to emulate God.
On the second reading, only God can be God; only God can achieve a
perfect synthesis of consciousness and Being, and it is a vain pretence
for any mere mortal to attempt to achieve such a synthesis. This latter
reading tallies much better with her theology. It is also, demonstrably,
the meaning which she had in mind. One of the logical requirements of
an ethics, she goes on to argue, is that the agents for whom it is
proposed are susceptible to *failure*; indeed, 'without failure, no ethics'.[92]
This is why 'One does not offer an ethics to a God'.[93]:

> for a being who, from the very start, would be an exact coincidence
> with himself, in a perfect plenitude, the notion of ethics would have
> no meaning.[94]

Ethics, a code of conduct, in other words, is designed for beings who
are both imperfect, but have some prospect of reducing their
imperfections. Ethics is never envisaged for God, who is already
perfect, and can never be anything less than perfect. In the words of C.
Stephen Evans:

> God is seen as a personal being, supreme in power, knowledge and
> moral worth, who created all other existing beings out of nothing.[95]

IV

Concluding Comments

There is much that is surprising to the philosophical mind in the details
of Simone de Beauvoir's Catholic theology, not least the fact that she
had developed such a theology. And there is multiple irony in the fact
that a woman whose most important work was banned by the Catholic
Church had such a tenacious grasp of the rudiments, as well as the
refinements, of the Catholic faith. Her theology, in effect, is a paean to
the power of faith. Faith precedes reason, first of all, since the truths of

religion are convincing only to those who are already convinced, i.e. who already place all their trust in God. Second, faith precedes philosophy, since the content of faith provides a more reliable guide to the nature of God than do the conclusions of the philosophers. The God of the Faithful is the only God with whom any member of the faithful could have a relationship; in particular, the God of the Faithful is a God for *mothers*. This God appears in many guises. He is a Lord and Master. He helps and protects. He enlightens and saves. He is a Father whose will always gets done. A wife can confide in Him things she could never repeat to her husband. He is that close to her.

The God that Beauvoir herself seems most comfortable with is the God whose powers are in some way limited by His reliance on His human creatures. She quotes with approval, in her *Pyrrhus et Cinéas,* the words of the mystic Angelus Silesias, who said 'God needs me, just as I need Him'.⁹⁶ This concept of a sovereign, but dependent God, makes many appearances in her writings. For example, in the first volume of her memoirs she allows that God knows all things after His own fashion; but owing to His lack of corporeal characteristics, it seems to her that 'He needed my eyes in order that trees might have their colours', i.e. in order that their colours might be seen and appreciated. And in *Pyrrhus et Cinéas* she develops the idea of God as the one who has created human agents, but cannot realise His plan for their salvation unless they agree to cooperate with Him. It is, I think, worth noting that the God who features in Beauvoir's account of her own crisis of faith, and her subsequent loss of faith, is a God who is so perfect that He can no longer exist for her. He is not *'le bon Dieu',* but *'le tout immuable et Éternel'.*

Notes

1   *Memoirs,* p. 142.
2   *Ibid.,* p. 19.
3   *Ibid.,* p. 125. See also p. 79: 'the purple beech, the blue cedars, and the silvery poplars would be sparkling with the primal freshness of the first morning in Eden: and I was the only one awake to the beauty of the earth and the glory of God.'.
4   *Ibid.,* p. 125.
5   *Ibid.*
6   *Ibid.,* p. 126.
7   *Religion,* p. 35.
8   *Memoirs,* p. 41.

9   *Ibid.*

10   *Ibid.,* p. 30.

11   *Ibid.*

12   *Ibid.,* p. 31. *'il m'avait créée, il était mort pour moi, il avait droit à une absolue soumission. Je sentais sur mes épaules le joug rassurant de la necessité'., Mémoires,* p. 34

13   See Kolakowski, *op. cit.,* p. 49.

14   *Memoirs,* p. 74. *'Il n'en laissait rien échapper.', Mémoires,* p. 74.

15   *Memoirs,* p. 74.

16   *Ibid.*

17   *Ibid.*

18   *Ibid.*

19   *Ibid.,* p. 75.

20   *Ibid.*

21   *Ibid.,* p. 73. *'et je priais longtemps.', Mémoires,* p. 74.

22   *Ibid.*

23   *Memoirs,* p. 73. For more on 'the sexual subtexts of many Catholic Liturgies', see A. Mahon 'Pierre Klossowski and the "Morality of Evil"', *Journal of Cultural Studies,* No. 5, 2002, pp 23–36

24   *Ibid.*

25   *Mémoires,* p. 74.

26   *Memoirs,* p. 47.

27   *Ibid.,* p. 48.

28   *Mémoires,* p. 50.

29   *Memoirs,* p. 48.

30   *Ibid.*

31   *Ibid.*

32   *Mémoires,* p. 51.

33   *Ibid.*

34   *Ibid.*

35   See Kolakowski, *op.cit.,* pp. 30, 31.

36   *Memoirs,* p. 135.

37   *Ibid.*

38   *Ibid.,* p. 136.

39   *Mémoires,* p. 136.

40   *Memoirs,* p. 136.

41   *Ibid.*

42   *Ibid.*

43   *Ibid.*

44   *Mémoires,* p. 137.

45   *Memoirs,* p. 136.

46   *Mémoires,* p. 137.

47   This is a pervasive refrain in some recent philosophy of religion. See P.J. McGrath, *Arguing about God* (1996); L. Kolakowski, *Religion, If there is no God* (1982, 1993); and C.S. Evans, *Philosophy of Religion* (1885). See also R. Jolivet, *The God of Reason,* 1958.

48   *Memoirs*, p. 137.
49   *Mémoires*, p. 138.
50   *Memoirs*, p.137.
51   *Mémoires*, p.138.
52   *Quand prime le spirituel*, 1979.
53   *When Things of the Spirit Come First*, p. 7.
54   *Ibid.*
55   *Ibid.*
56   *Ibid.*
57   *Ibid.*, p. 8.
58   *Ibid.*
59   *Ibid.*, p. 160.
60   *Ibid.*
61   *Ibid.*, p. 163.
62   *Ibid.*, p. 123.
63   *Ibid.*, p. 119.
64   *Ibid.*
65   *Memoirs*, p. 73.
66   *Ibid.*
67   *When Things of the Spirit Come First*, p. 7.
68   *Ibid.*, p. 11. *'car elle aimait frissonner de repentir aux pieds d'un homme beau, pur et terrible. Il avait droit de vie et de mort sur elle et elle lui disait 'Seigneur'., Quand prime le spirituel*, p. 6.
69   *Ibid.* *'il la faisait mettre nue devant lui et, pour monter sur son cheval richement caparaçonné, il se servait de son corps comme d'un marchepied'., ibid.*
70   *Ibid.* *'Elle prolongeait avec volupté ce moment où la tête courbée, le coeur empli d'adoration, d'une humilitè passionnée, elle sentait un dur èperon ecorcher sur son dos d'esclave. Quand, vaincu par la pitié et par l'amour, le justicier aux yeux sévères posait la main sur sa tête en signe de pardon, elle embrassait ses genoux en défaillant délicieusement'., ibid.*
71   *When Things of the Spirit Come First*, p. 8.
72   *Ibid.*
73   *Ibid.*, p. 111.
74   *Ibid.*
75   *Ibid.*
76   *Ibid.*
77   *Ibid.*, p. 112.
78   *Ibid.*
79   *Ibid.*, p. 113.
80   *Ibid.*
81   *Ibid.*
82   *Ibid.*, pp. 113, 114. In the recent surprise hit film in France, *The Girl from Paris* (*Une hirondelle a fait le printemps*, 2001), the elderly farmer Adrien visits his local church and invokes the help of a provident God in the same way. He apologizes for not having visited the church very

often, but asks God to give him a little longer on earth, so that he can do some things he still had to do.

83 *Pyrrhus et Cinéas*, p. 36.

84 This is my own translation of the following passage: '*Si Dieu est l'infinité et la plénitude de l'être, il n'y a pas en lui de distance entre son projet et sa réalité. Ce qu'il veut est. Sa volonté n'est que le fondement immobile de l'être; à peine peut-on encore l'appeler volonté. Un tel Dieu n'est pas une personne singulière: il est l'universel, le tout immuable et éternel. Et l'universel est silence. Il ne réclame rien, il ne promet rien, il n'éxige aucun sacrifice, il ne dispense ni châtiment ni récompense, il ne peut rien justifier, ni rien condamner, on ne saurait fonder sur lui ni optimisme, ni désespoir: il est, on ne peut rien en dire de plus. La perfection de son être ne laisse aucune place a l'homme*'.,ibid.

85 For a more extended treatment of this point, see my *Existentialism, Feminism and Simone de Beauvoir*, pp. 4, 5.

86 '*Rien n'est bon que le vertu, le mal c'est le péché*', *Pyrrhus et Cinéas*, p. 39.

87 '*Il est pour l'homme un prochain*'., ibid., p. 40.

88 '*Il a crée l'homme pour qu'il existe un être qui ne soit pas un donné mais qui accomplisse son être, selon le désir de son créateur*', ibid., p. 39.

89 '*Le chrétien se trouve alors devant un Dieu personnel et vivant pour qu'il peut agir*'., ibid., p. 40.

90 *Pour une morale de l'ambiguïté.* Gallimard, 1947.

91 *The Ethics of Ambiguity,* p. 10.

92 *Ibid.*

93 *Ibid.*

94 *Ibid.*

95 *Philosophy of Religion,* p. 32.

96 '*Dieu a besoin de moi comme j'ai besoin de lui*'., *Pyrrhus et Cinéas*, p. 40.

Chapter Ten

SIMONE DE BEAUVOIR ON DEATH

A preoccupation with death is a notable and well-known feature of Simone de Beauvoir's writing, but it is a feature particularly of her memoirs and, for obvious reasons, of her tome on old age. In this chapter I propose to focus on her thoughts on death in the first three volumes of her memoirs, that is, in her *Memoirs of a Dutiful Daughter*, in *The Prime of Life*, and in *Force of Circumstance*. I shall also give special attention to her short memoir of her mother's dying, *A Very Easy Death*. Her lengthy meditation on death has a number of truly special features. First of all, it is rooted in her response to the death of particular people who were close, and sometimes very close to her, such as her uncle Gaston, the young Algerian student Bourla, and, of course, Jean-Paul Sartre. Second, she considers the religious perspective on death on a number of occasions, but increasingly comes to doubt the power of its consolations. 'Religion could do no more for my mother than the hope of posthumous success could do for me', she writes, adding that:

> Whether you think of it as heavenly or as earthly, if you love life immortality is no consolation for death.[1]

In the third place, she focusses with particular intensity on the tragedy of *premature death*. When Bourla was murdered during the Occupation, following another roundup of Jews, Sartre did his best to convince her that death at nineteen is fundamentally no more absurd than death at eighty, but she remained inconsolable. Premature death is especially tragic since it deprives a person of his or her future. Fourth, while Beauvoir was terrified of death from an early age ('I used to choke with dread whenever I thought of mortal death'), her singular achievement was to have demonstrated why it is such a *rational* thing to fear it. She offers the following reasons:

(1) Death separates the dead from the living, and does so eternally.

(2) It is a return to Nothingness.

(3) 'It is a departure to no destination'.

(4) It ends all experience, not just painful experience.

(5) It is an endless night.

(6) We go to a world where the word 'together' no longer has any meaning.

(7) When someone dies, several other individuals die with him: the child he was, the adolescent, the young man or woman, and so on.

(8) He dies also in the sense that he will be remembered by some people as a child, by others as an adolescent, and by others still as a young man. The reason is that 'everyone weeps for the one who was dear to him'.

(9) Death separates you from those you love, and doesn't allow any opportunity to explain things to a remaining partner. Finally,

(10) The dead are always dead for others, never for themselves.

In the fifth and final place, I hold that Beauvoir makes a substantial contribution to the existentialist debate about death, a debate whose main features I have documented elsewhere. She sides with Sartre against Heidegger in this debate, though much of her discussion ranges far beyond their particular contributions. She formally adopts the Sartrian view of death as 'an unrealizable'. Death is not a possible project for us as human beings. As she puts it, 'death is the external limit of my possibilities, and not a possibility of my own'; in other words, it is the end of all projects, and as such cannot itself be a project.

I

Memoirs of a Dutiful Daughter

In the first volume of her memoirs, *Memoirs of a Dutiful Daughter*, Simone de Beauvoir tells us how, in her early childhood, she learned to distinguish between death and personal extinction, that is, between death and *her* death. She was terrified, she confesses, by the thought of personal extinction, but fortunately she could derive immense comfort and reassurance from the promise of eternal life which, as a devout young Catholic, she had been given by God. As she phrases it herself:

> God had given me the promise of eternity: I could not ever cease to see, to hear, to talk to myself. Always I should be able to say: 'Here I am'. There *could* be no end.[2]

(This last sentence is worth repeating in its original form: '*Il n'y aurait pas de fin*'.[3]) It is interesting to note that in these sentences Beauvoir adopts a Wittgensteinian notion of death, understood as the end or cessation of all experience. To be dead is not to be able to see, not to be able to hear, not to be able to talk to oneself, and so on. Later in her life she would visualise death as 'nothingness', as 'the void', and as an 'eternal night'. Wittgenstein, according to D.Z. Phillips, wanted to make the point that death was not a possible object of experience: death was the end of all experience, and one cannot, logically, experience the end of all experience.[4] It is doubtful, to say the least, that Simone de Beauvoir had such a sophisticated idea in mind during her early childhood, however precocious she may have been; but she does appear to have reached this Wittgensteinian conclusion later in life when, influenced by Sartre, she came to the view that death is an 'unrealizable': that it is not a possible project for us as human beings. And this idea, in turn, is one of the possible meanings ascribable to her strange aphorism that death is not a *natural* occurrence. I propose to analyse these, and other claims about death, at greater length, at a more advanced stage of this chapter. For the moment, I wish merely to draw attention, once again, to the solace which Simone de Beauvoir, as a devout young Catholic, was able to draw from her faith in God. God, she was certain, would not let death befall her; there could be no death for someone who had received the promise of eternal life. These words are still echoed in *The Litany of the Saints*: 'Bring N to eternal life, first promised to him/her in baptism/ Lord, hear our prayer'.

The harrowing events of World War I gave Simone de Beauvoir further cause to harbour morbid thoughts about death. War was responsible for two forms of *separation*: first of all, it separated young men from their families, and then it separated those who were killed at the Front from those who survived, and those who remained at home. On this occasion, moreover, Beauvoir is unable to draw the same consolations from her religion. As she puts it herself:

> Through books, communiqués, and the conversations I heard, the full horror of the war was becoming clear to me: the cold, the mud, the terror, the blood, the pain, the agonies of death. We had lost friends and cousins at the front. Despite the promises of heaven, I

used to choke with dread whenever I thought of mortal death which separates for ever all those who love one another.[5]

Of course, death, be it in war or at any other time, separates the dead from *all* of the living, not just from those of the living who were loved. But death as separation is the dominant idea here. The separation involved is that of the dead from the living. The reference to *physical* death, *la mort qui sur terre*,[6] hints at another kind of separation, namely, that of the soul from the body. This latter form of separation is still the defining feature of death as it is understood in Catholic teaching, which remains premissed on a kind of Platonic substance dualism.[7]

The concept of death as separation, as eternal separation, reappears with a particularly poignant intensity in Simone de Beauvoir's narrative of the first dying she ever witnessed. This was the dying of her uncle Gaston, whose death-throes lasted a whole night. She gives the following account:

> Aunt Marguerite sat holding his hand, and saying things he couldn't understand. His children, my parents, my sister, and I were with him when he died. He gave the death-rattle, and vomited up some blackish stuff. When he stopped breathing his jaw sagged, and a scarf was tied round his head to keep it up. My father was sobbing openly: I had never seen him weep before. The violence of my own despair surprised everyone, including myself. I was very fond of my uncle, and I cherished the memory of our early morning hunting expeditions at Meyrignac. I was very fond of my cousin Jeanne and I couldn't bring myself to say: she's an orphan. But neither these regrets nor my compassion could explain the storm of grief that swept over me the next two days: I couldn't bear to think of that despairing glance which my uncle had cast at his wife just before he died, and in which the irreparable was already an accomplished fact ... [8]

This account of dying focusses as much on the living as on the dying. Death will separate the living from the dying, and it will do so with a crushing finality. The living will have to live with this thought, while the dying have to die with it. In this sense death harms *both* the living *and* the dead. Beauvoir seems to think that what caused her uncle Gaston such despair was the thought that he would never see his wife again. But the depth of his despair suggests also that he was terrified by the thought that he would not see anyone or anything ever again. At all events, Beauvoir focusses here on the effects of death on the closest human relationships, and the havoc it causes. Her fear of death is now the fear that it will terminate the closest, most intimate relationship she herself will have in the future. For she adds, 'Perhaps one day, I too, would see that look in the eyes of a man whom I had loved all my life'.

The dying and death of her paternal grandfather evokes a very different kind of response in Simone de Beauvoir from anything she has narrated thus far. The difference in his case was that he was of an age to die. As she phrases it herself, 'he was very old, his death seemed natural now, and I could feel no sadness about it'.[9] A natural death, on this view, is a death which occurs at an advanced chronological age. There is, as it were, no more living left to be done, and as such it is not an object of marked sadness or grief. Nevertheless, she travelled to Meyrignac for the funeral, 'dressed in heavy mourning, wearing a hat swathed in black crepe georgette'.[10] 'The whole family, she reports:

> had gathered at Meyrignac; it was perhaps because of this great upheaval that I'd remained unmoved by the sight of grandpa's dead body, the house and the garden. When I was thirteen, I had wept at the thought that one day I would no longer feel at home at Meyrignac; that day had come; the property belonged to my aunt and cousins; this summer I would visit them as a guest, and very soon, no doubt, I would never return there; but I didn't heave a single sigh of regret. My childhood and adolescence and the sound of cows' hooves kicking the stable door as I leaned out into the starlit night – all that was far, very far behind me.[11]

In this passage we find Beauvoir striking a most mundane, almost legalistic note, as she chronicles the social and legal consequences of death when it is the death of an elderly male member of the petty landed aristocracy. Death in such cases not only separates the dead from the living, it also separates them from their landed estate. This property then passes, by inheritance, into new ownership within the family, in accordance with inheritance law and family tradition. In this very clear sense, some people literally profit from the death of others. Yet a third kind of separation associated with death is the manner in which it closes a chapter in the narrative of the life of those who survive. Parents and grandparents loom giant-like in the experiences and recollections of children, and this kind of spectral presence is really extinguished in later life only by death, the shrinkage of advanced age, and terminal illness. With the death of her paternal grandfather, the Meyrignac phase of Simone de Beauvoir's life, and its wealth of associations with the comfortable, pampered existence of the landed gentry, for all practical purposes comes to an end. Someone else's death thus marked a rite of passage from childhood to adulthood, from a fondly remembered past to a present which could have no further association with that past.[12]

The Prime of Life

Beauvoir's next sustained reflection on death occurs, not with the death of her close friend Zaza, but when her father died during the Occupation. Later, in her most moving memoir of her mother's dying – *A Very Easy Death* – she will draw a stark contrast between her father's attitude to death – which she characterises as one of indifference – and her mother's, which was essentially one of rebellion. Her father, she says in *The Prime of Life:*

> faced death with an indiffference that amazed me, though he had often said that it mattered little to him whether he died on one day rather than another, since death was in any case inevitable.[13]

This reported attitude is eerily reminiscent of Meursault's in *l'Etranger*, especially when he claims that since we must all die, it obviously doesn't matter when or how. But it seems from the remainder of her narrative of her father's dying that he was not so much indifferent to death as weary of life, ill at ease and profoundly unhappy with the modern world. Not feeling that he belonged to the modern world, he had no regrets about leaving it. As Beauvoir herself puts it:

> Besides, he had little in common with this new world of ours, and very few reasons for continuing to stay alive in it. He did not struggle: I was amazed at the peaceful way he returned to nothingness ... I sat with him through his last moments, and watched the grim, protracted struggle with which life finally extinguishes itself, vainly trying to grasp the mystery of this departure to no destination.[14]

Beauvoir tends to put a totally negative construction on death in these sentences: it is a return to nothingness, a departure to no destination. But her father's death was, in one sense, a positive experience for him: it cut short the misery of having to live in a world which had become completely alien to him, whose values were not his. Death offered permanent relief from the discomfort of not belonging anywhere. It took him out of a world to which he did not belong, even if it did not transport him anywhere else.

Not long afterwards, when Sartre and Beauvoir were on a cycling trip in the Free Zone, where Sartre obtained his demobilization papers, Beauvoir herself had her own brush with death. Her bicycle – whose brakes were barely functioning – skidded when she attempted to avoid two other cyclists on a descent, and she suffered various minor injuries. Reflecting on her experience a few days later, she was surprised to discover that her great fear of death had greatly diminished. The 'terror' which death had always aroused in her had vanished because, in a variation of Wittgenstein's argument, death amounted to precisely nothing. Death was *nothing* because there was no one there to experience it. 'It was at that moment', she confides:

> that I emotionally accepted the truth of what I had once read in *Lucrèce*, and to which my rational mind had long since assented – that, in the most literal and precise sense, death is *nothing*. A *person* never is dead; there is no longer a 'person' to sustain the concept of 'death'. I felt I had finally exorcized my fears on that score.[15]

In other words, a person never experiences death, since a dead person, by definition, is incapable of experiencing anything. Here Beauvoir identifies one of the logical requirements of an experience, namely, that there must be someone who is capable of *having* the experience. But that someone no longer exists once death strikes. It follows that death cannot be experienced, and that therefore it is rational not to fear it. It evidently hasn't yet occurred to Beauvoir to reflect at length on the full implications of *post mortem* existence, on the full meaning of death as 'nothingness'. This will change when she comes to write about the death of friends and acquaintances of her adult years.

The first such death was that of a young Algerian Jew of Spanish descent she calls 'Bourla' in her memoirs. He had been in Sartre's philosophy class at the Lycée Pasteur during the spring of 1941, and at the time of his death, he had been 'involved' with Lise Oblanoff, a former pupil of Beauvoir's at Passy. The two of them had been living together in what Beauvoir calls 'my hotel on the rue Dauphine'. 'I always took what he said seriously', she writes, 'since he never advanced any proposition without first testing its truth himself'.[16] 'It was charming', she continues:

> to see the two of them walking along side by side: Lise so tall and blonde, a majestic peasant, and Bourla so dark and lithe, eyes and hands perpetually moving, alert. He found me somewhat over-rational, but liked me very much all the same. Lise insisted on my going and chatting to them when they were in bed at night. I would kiss her; whereupon he would put his own forehead up for my attention, saying, 'What about me? Don't I get a kiss?' So I would kiss him as well.[17]

Towards the end of the war Bourla and his father were rounded up by the Germans and 'carted off' to Drancy, the detention centre for French Jews. Despite frantic efforts to have them released they were both killed, presumably shot, though it appears that the bodies were never recovered. 'I was shattered', writes Beauvoir:

> both by Lise's grief and on my own account. There had been plenty of other deaths to sicken me, but this one touched me intimately. Bourla had been a close neighbour of mine, and I had taken him to my heart: besides, he was only nineteen. Sartre did his honest best to convince me that in a sense *every* life is complete at its end, and that death at nineteen is fundamentally no more absurd than death at eighty; but I did not believe him. How many places and people that boy might have seen and loved, which now he would never know! Every morning, simply by opening my eyes, I robbed him of the world.[18]

There are several claims made about death in this passage. One is that *premature* death is particularly tragic, that there is, in fact, no proper comparison between premature death – such as death at the age of nineteen – and death in old age – such as death at the age of eighty. Not even Sartre's attempt to persuade her otherwise could dispel this thought from her mind. The reason given for this difference between premature and 'natural' death is that premature death deprives the individual of a future, of all the experiences she or he would otherwise have had. Each morning, when she looked afresh at the world, she would realise just how much he was missing. In this sense, she robbed him of the world. Beauvoir would react in basically the same way to the news of Camus' 'premature' death in a car crash.

Beauvoir continues her meditation on Bourla's death as follows:

> But the most awful thing was that I did not rob a *person*; there was no one to say, 'The world has been snatched from me'. No one. Nor was this emptiness anywhere given embodiment: there was no grave, no body, not even so much as a bone. It was as though nothing had happened, absolutely nothing. A note of his was found, scribbled on a scrap of paper: 'I am not dead. We are only separated'. It was a voice from another age. Now there was no one there to say, 'We are separated'. This nothingness terrified me.[19]

Beauvoir returns in this passage to the earlier quasi-Wittgensteinian refrain that death is not an event in life, that we do not live to experience death. She also identifies death with emptiness, and, thirdly, draws our attention, once again, to the phenomenon of death as a social event. Part of the awfulness of a missing body is that close friends and relations cannot pay their last respects to the dead, and this leaves a permanent vacuum in their lives.

Beauvoir concludes her meditation on Bourla's disappearance and death with the following words:

> Why had things turned out this way? Why had his father been convinced he ran no danger? Why had we believed him? ... These were useless questions, but they still tormented me. There was one other that I asked myself, in a scared sort way. He had said, 'I won't die because I don't want to die'. He had not gone to his death willingly; it had come to him, without his consent. Had he stood for an instant and seen his end, looked death in the face? And who had been the first to go, he or his father? If he was conscious, I felt certain, he must have cried No! aloud or in his heart, a last frantic, terrible spasm that was all for nothing – and remained thus, rooted in eternity. He had cried No! and then there had been – nothing. I found the very thought unbearable; but I had to bear it.[20]

Three things stand out in this passage. The first is the distinction she draws between actions and events, and the relegation of death to the latter category. The second is the distinction between circumstances over which one does have control and those over which one has no control, and the fatalistic relegation of death, once more, to the latter category. Finally, there is the Dylan Thomas-like call to rebel against death, much akin to the Camusian call to rebel against the absurd. She will later preface her memoir of her mother's death with the haunting words of the Dylan Thomas poem.

Beauvoir concludes *The Prime of Life* with a very long, essentially six-stage meditation on death, a meditation in which autobiographical and formal philosophical details intermingle. From an early age she had found the thought of death terrifying. Once again, it wasn't so much death *per se* that had terrified her as:

> the thought of that utter non-being – *my* utter non-being – that would descend on its appointed day, for ever and ever.[21]

The idea of *personal* annihilation filled her with such terror that she could not, she says, imagine herself facing it courageously.

On the other hand, she confesses, fear never prevented her doing anything she had wanted to do – fear, that is, that death might be the consequence. Her innate optimism, in part, had been responsible for this failure of fear to intimidate her. Nor for that matter did she fear the prospect of death, since it would, in a sense, be simply one further experience. She does not see any contradiction between the idea of death as one further experience one has – and, to that extent, not something to be afraid of – and the Wittgensteinian idea that death cannot be experienced since, *ex hypothesi*, there is no one there to experience it. She derived mental comfort from the former, plausible idea, notwithstanding the fact that she herself had drawn the Wittgensteinian conclusion on several occasions. On this occasion, she recalls, thinking of death as an *experience* shielded her from thinking of death as 'an endless night'. In her own words:

> It would be the final point of life for me, true, but still *a part* of life; and on the occasions when I believed myself face to face with it, I surrendered myself calmly to this lively adventure, never giving a thought to the void that yawned for me on the farther side.[22]

She distinguishes at this stage between the *idea* of death as an endless night, and the *reality* of death as an impossible experience. Since there will be no one to experience death, it follows logically that nothing will be experienced, and it is in that sense irrational and time-wasting to fear something that cannot be experienced. The paradox of death is that it can be experienced only prior to death. As she puts it herself:

> What I rejected, with all my heart and soul, was the horror of that endless night, which, since it did not exist, would never *be* horrible, but held infinite horror for me, who *did* exist.[23]

She strikes an even more positive note at the start of the next paragraph when she observes that the alternative of death always guarantees us against an excess of suffering. It is the kind of option available to those who have voluntary euthanasia (or physician-assisted suicide) available to them as a legal and medical option, and it is the option, furthermore, which is *advocated* by those who argue and campaign for these alternatives. Beauvoir herself puts it more abstractly: '"Rather than endure that", I used to say, "I will kill myself"'.[24] The war, she adds, gave a very real substance to these thoughts, since 'misfortune became a daily reality, and so did death'.

She tried, she confides, on a great many occasions, to overcome death in her dreams. She dreamed of 'passing through death as Alice passed through the Looking Glass', so that once on the other side she could absorb it into herself instead of being annihilated by it. In this way she *would* survive death. She would then be able to say 'I am dead', despite being dead. Unfortunately, she would then wake up and, she says, the truth would catch her by the throat: 'When I am dead, that voice will speak no more'.[25]

Beauvoir turns to the theme of old age in the next paragraph. She was afraid of growing old, she admits:

not because my features would change and my powers diminish, but because of the ever stronger taste of death that would poison my every living moment, the black ruled line's slow but inexorable approach.[26]

Once again, she equates death with separation, and with nothingness:

In those days the line was still lost on the far horizon; but inevitably, sooner or later, the time of separation, of not being, could come.[27]

What particularly depressed her was the thought of a world in which there would be no trace of her to be found, and she says that Emily Brontë had the exact same thought:

Emily Brontë had stared at the moon, with its halo of reddish muslin, and thought: One day I shall see it no longer. It was the same moon that all our eyes reflected.[28]

Part of the awfulness of death is that it *isolates* us from all other human beings. 'Death is common to all of us, yet each individual faces it alone'.[29] Death marks a transition from a world in which there are common experiences to another world in which common experiences are quite impossible. We go to a world where the word 'together' no longer has any meaning.

III

Force of Circumstance

In the third volume of her memoirs, *Force of Circumstance*, published in 1963 when she was fifty-five years of age, Simone de Beauvoir recalls the afternoon that Claude Lanzmann rang to tell her about Camus' death in a car crash. She stood there, she says:

leaning against the window, watching night come down over Saint-Germain-des-Prés, incapable of calming myself or of giving way to real grief. Sartre was upset as well, and we spent the whole evening with Bost talking about Camus.[30]

Despite taking some sleeping pills, she found that she couldn't sleep that night; so she got up, put on some clothes, and went walking through the night. She was not grief-stricken for the Camus who opposed independence for Algeria, 'who had been struck out of my heart when he gave his approval to the crimes of France'.[31] No, the Camus for whom she grieved was:

> the companion of our hopeful years, whose open face laughed and smiled so easily, the young, ambitious writer, wild to enjoy life, its pleasures, its triumphs, and comradeship, friendship, love and happiness. Death had brought him back to life.[32]

She makes the profound point that when an adult dies, several other individuals die with him, namely, the child he was, the adolescent, and the young man (or woman as the case may be). He dies as well in the sense that he will be remembered by some people as a child, by others as an adolescent, and by still others as a young man. For 'everyone weeps for the one who was dear to him'.[33]

In the Epilogue to the third volume her thoughts, not surprisingly, become distinctly melancholy:

> Perhaps the people I pass in the street see merely a woman in her fifties who simply looks her age, no more, no less. But when I look, I see my face as it was, attacked by the pox of time for which there is no cure.[34]

Death, she reports, is no longer:

> a brutal event in the far distance; it haunts my sleep. Awake, I sense its shadow between the world and me: it has already begun.[35]

It had already begun in the sense that she was no longer able to do, and enjoy, many of the things she used to be capable of doing and enjoying. She was not saying goodbye to them, rather:

> it is they who are leaving me; the mountain paths disdain my feet. Never again shall I collapse, drunk with fatigue, into the smell of hay. Never again shall I slide down through the solitary morning snows. Never again a man.[36]

She concludes, miserably, that the only new experience that she can have at this hour of her life is 'misfortune'. That misfortune she then describes as follows: 'Either I shall see Sartre dead, or I shall die before him'.[37] 'It is appalling', she reflects, 'not to be there to console someone for the pain you cause by leaving him. It is appalling that he should abandon you and then not speak to you again. Unless I am blessed by a most improbable piece of good fortune, one of these fates is to be mine. Sometimes I want to finish it all quickly so as to shorten the dread of waiting'.[38] So the following further thoughts, then, are registered in these excerpts about death. First, that each stage of life brings about the death of a previous stage, or stages. Second, before ever you die, certain experiences become closed off to you anyhow. (I am reminded of Nancy Astor's remark that when she was young she dreaded growing old, because of all the things she would no longer be able to do. Now that she was old, she found that she didn't *want* to do them). Third, death separates you from those you love, or the person you love, in the most unjust fashion. Not only does death cause an irrevocable separation, it doesn't allow any opportunity to explain things to a remaining partner. These thoughts were sufficient to cause Simone de Beauvoir to entertain the idea of suicide. Yet, she maintains, 'I loathe the thought of annihilating myself quite as much now as I ever did'.[39]

IV

A Very Easy Death

One year after the publication of *Force of Circumstance,* Simone de Beauvoir published a slim, interim volume chronicling her mother's death from cancer. The tone of the book is set by the Preface, in which she quotes the famous lines from Dylan Thomas:

> Do not go gentle into that good night.
> Old Age should burn and rave at close of day;
> Rage, rage against the dying of the light ...

These words applied pre-eminently to her mother, first, because 'she was of an age to die',[40] and second, because 'she had an animal dread of death',[41] despite the fact that 'she believed in heaven',[42] and was afflicted by feebleness and poor health. Beauvoir had endowed her mother with the magical prestige of childhood (as she puts it in *Force of Circumstance),* but now she was obliged to confront her mother's naked body. As a child she had loved it dearly; as an adolescent it had filled her with an uneasy revulsion. But this body in a hospital bed provoked in her the most acute distress. It had this effect because it:

> hardly differed at all from a corpse – a poor defenceless carcass
> turned and manipulated by professional hands, one in which life
> seemed to carry on only because of its own momentum.[43]

In short, in confronting her mother's emaciated, wrinkled, shaven body, she found herself confronting a hastening death:

> For me, my mother had always been there, and I had never
> seriously thought that some day, that soon I should see her go. Her

death, like her birth, had its place in some legendary time. When I said to myself 'She is of an age to die' the words were devoid of meaning, as so many words are. For the first time I saw her as a dead body under suspended sentence.[44]

As her mother's condition worsened, Beauvoir found herself faced with two competing moralities: on the one hand, the heroic ethics of a medical profession, according to which life itself is the most precious possession and everything medically practicable should be done to preserve it; on the other hand, there was the humanitarian ethics of her sister Hélène, who was of the view that everything possible should be done to ease the dying of someone who was very close to death anyway. She sides with Hélène:

> Dr N passed by me: I stopped him. White coat, white cap: a young man with an unresponsive face. 'Why this tube? Why torture Maman, since there's no hope?' He gave me a withering look. 'I am doing what has to be done'.[45]

But when it came to a choice between operating to remove a cancerous intestinal obstruction that would have killed their mother within three days, and sparing their mother the trauma of surgery, the sisters agreed to the operation. A huge cancerous tumour was removed, but they decided between them to tell their mother she had had an emergency operation for peritonitis. A little later, watching her mother, 'her blue and hugely swollen arm ... swathed in bandages', Beauvoir reflects once again on the question of euthanasia.

> At the first trial I had given in: beaten by the ethics of society, I had abjured my own. 'No', Sartre said to me. 'You were beaten by technique! and that was fatal'.[46]

She agrees, but continues: 'There were only two things to choose between on that Wednesday – operating or euthanasia'.[47] I take it she means the choice lay between operating and not operating, i.e. between medical intervention and *passive* euthanasia. But then she says:

> Maman, vigorously resuscitated, and having a strong heart, would have stood out against the intestinal stoppage for a long while and she would have lived through hell, for the doctors would have refused euthanasia.[48]

This second reference to euthanasia is clearly a reference to *active* euthanasia, where her mother would have been given a lethal injection to cause immediate death and prevent further suffering. But whether her mother would have *wanted* active euthanasia, supposing that the doctors would have agreed (which they wouldn't), is a moot point. On the one hand, her mother 'clung ferociously to this world, and she had an animal dread of death'.[49] Following the operation, she had told one of her doctors that she was in no hurry to meet her Maker ('But I don't want to go and see Him right away'[50]). On the other hand, 'Maman', Beauvoir tells us:

> had an old relative who had been kept alive in a coma for the last six months. 'I hope you wouldn't let them keep me going like that', she had said to us.[51]

The two sisters noticed, and were surprised by the fact that their mother did not ask for the priest. It wasn't, muses Beauvoir, that she had lost her faith or anything like that, rather that she was reluctant to accept the earthly meaning of eternal life. She was reluctant to die with Christ, as current Catholic teaching has it. In her daughter's elegant phrasing of it, 'The earthly meaning of eternal life was death, and she refused to die'.[52]

When Beauvoir was in Prague a few days later, fulfilling a number of engagements, she received a telegram informing her that her mother was very ill once again. She recalls that she did not particularly want to see her mother once more before she died; at the same time, she observes, 'I could not bear the idea that she should not see me again'.[53] She notes, on the one hand, that it is irrational to invest a single moment with such importance, since, for the dying person, there would be no memory of it. 'There would not be any atonement either',[54] she continues, presumably meaning that the event of death would not have secured her own reconciliaton with God. Yet she concludes this sequence of thought with the following remarkable sentence:

> For myself I understood, to the innermost fibre of my being, that the absolute could be enclosed within the last moments of a dying person.[55]

This seems to mean that while there is no absolute *beyond* death, there can indeed be an absolute *in* death. If this reading is correct, then Simone de Beauvoir has not lost her sense of the absolute, though she now invests it with a deeply intra-mundane meaning.

Approaching the closing stages of this short memoir, Beauvoir contrasts the attitudes towards death displayed by her parents and grandmother. Her mother did not acquiesce in death, something which mystified her friends, owing to the strength of her faith. (If you are a devout Catholic, then you will go to Heaven, so why resist death?) Her mother, she says, was afraid of neither God nor the Devil, only of leaving this earth. Her grandmother, by contrast, was quite content to make her exit:

My grandmother had known perfectly well that she was dying. Contentedly she said, 'I am going to eat one last little boiled egg, and then I am going to join Gustave again.[56]

Similarly her father who, 'Ruined, embittered ... accepted the void with the same serenity that Grandmama accepted Paradise'.[57] Her mother, on the other hand, 'loved life as I love it and in the face of death she had the same feeling of rebellion that I have'.[58] She notes that well-intentioned readers of her most recent books had tried to assure her that she would enjoy a kind of surrogate immortality through her writings. But she was inconsolable:

> Inwardly I told them all that they were wrong. Religion could do no more for my mother than the hope of posthumous success could do for me. Whether you think of it as heavenly or as earthly, if you love life immortality is no consolation for death.[59]

This is an interesting choice of words; she does not deny immortality, she simply contends that it is no substitute for earthly existence.

Her mother had what she describes as 'a very easy death; an upper-class death'.[60] Nonetheless, she protests, 'when someone you love dies you pay for the sin of outliving her with a thousand piercing regrets'.[61] She located what she calls 'touching evidence' of the warmth of her mother's affection for her among her mother's papers, a discovery which is worth recording again:

> She had put aside two letters, the one written by a Jesuit and the other by a friend; they both assured her that one day I should come back to God.[62]

Simone de Beauvoir's parting words on death, in the final paragraph of the memoir *A Very Easy Death*, are as follows:

> There is no such thing as a natural death: nothing that happens to a man is ever natural, since his presence calls the world into question. All men must die: but for every man his death is an accident and, even if he knows it and consents to it, an unjustifiable violation.[63]

The key idea here is that death is not a natural occurrence because it belongs to the world of events, and not to the world of actions. Death is something that happens to you, and by that fact alone it is not properly human.

V

Old Age

In her book on old age (*La Vieillesse*, 1970) Simone de Beauvoir inevitably comes to talk about death, though she usually does so in the context of talking about the elderly. People usually prefer old age to death, she says, though at a distance 'it is death that we see with a clearer eye'.[64] We see death with a clearer eye because the threat of death is always present, even more so when one reaches old age. By comparison, 'no one ever becomes old in a single instant'.[65] There is a sense, she claims, in which death, unlike old age, is not a calamity. When one utters the words 'I shall no longer exist', the 'I' remains intact, and, she adds, in a footnote, 'This identity is all the more strongly guaranteed to those who believe they have an immortal soul'.[66] Thinking of oneself as (growing) old, by contrast, means thinking of oneself as *another* than oneself, and this can be frightening. It can be frightening:

> Because every metamorphosis has something frightening about it. When I was a little girl I was amazed and indeed deeply distressed when I realized that one day I should turn into a grown-up. But when one is young the real advantages of the adult status usually counter-balance the wish to remain oneself, unchanged.[67]

But no such advantage accrues to old age, since 'even among those who are thought well preserved, age brings with it a very obvious physical decline'.[68]

In chapter 6, entitled 'Time, Activity, History', Beauvoir reflects on the far-reaching consequences of death for the bereaved. The death of a friend or relation brings with it several distinct losses for the bereaved: the loss of a friend or relation, of course, but much less obviously, the loss of that image of themselves which the deceased possessed, so that 'with him there vanishes a part of youth or childhood that he alone remembered'.[69] The death of children brings with it an even more crushing kind of loss: as she explains:

> the death of a child, of a small child, is the sudden ruin of a whole undertaking; it means that all the hopes and sacrifices centred upon him are pointless, utterly in vain.[70]

The death of friends of one's own age, she adds, does not possess this character of bitter failure. But it constitutes a devastating loss, just the same, since it wipes out the relationship we had with them. She describes this loss as follows:

> When Zaza died, I was too intent upon the future to weep for my own past; I wept only for her. But I remember my distress, much later, at the death of Dullin, although indeed he and I had never really been intimate. It was a whole section of my life that had collapsed: Ferroles, the Atelier, the rehearsals of *Les Mouches* and those wonderfully gay dinners when he used to tell us his reminiscences – all these disappeared with him. Later our agreements and disagreements with Camus were wiped out: wiped out too my arguments with Merleau-Ponty in the gardens of the Luxembourg, at his home, at mine, at Saint-Tropez; gone those long talks with Giacometti and my visits to his studio. So long as they were alive memory was not called upon for our shared past to remain alive in them. They have carried it away with them into the grave; and my memory can recover only a frigid imitation of it. In the 'monuments to the dead' that stud my history, it is I who am buried.[71]

In the closing pages of this chapter she formally adopts Sartre's perspectve on death, viewing it as an 'unrealizable'. This means that death is not a possible project for us as human beings. Death is the end of all our projects and, logically speaking, the end of all projects cannot itself be a project. In her words, 'death is the external limit of my possibilities and not a possibility of my own'.[72] She also subscribes in these pages to the macabre Sartrean image of the dead, who are dead for *others*, but never for themselves. You never recognize your own death, it can be recognized only by others, and you 'live on', so to speak, only to the extent that they remember you. But this fate is not as frightening as it sounds. Death is absence from the world, but as more and more of one's contemporaries die off, a build-up of absences begins to occur. 'When total absence has swallowed everything', she reasons, 'it will not make so very great a difference'.[73]

I will conclude with the closing words of her farewell tribute to Sartre in her narrative of his dying entitled *Adieux, A Farewell to Sartre*. I will do so because it captures both the good and the bad features of death as poignantly as this has ever been done. Her words are:

> His death does separate us. My death will not bring us together again. That is how things are. It is in itself splendid that we were able to live our lives in harmony for so long.[74]

Death could not erase the splendid life they had together. It could succeed only in putting a temporal limit to their partnership.

Notes

1   *A Very Easy Death*, p. 81.
2   *Memoirs of a Dutiful Daughter*, p. 48.
3   *Mémoires*, p. 51.
4   See D.Z. Phillips, *Death and Immortality*, p. 13, where he discusses the following quote from Wittgenstein:'*Death is not an event in life: we do not live to experience death*'.
5   *Memoirs*, p. 64.
6   *Mémoires*, p. 66.
7   See *Catechism of the Catholic Church*, p. 227. See also T. Sheehan, 'The Dream of Karl Rahner', *The New York Review*, 4 February 1982.
8   *Memoirs*, pp. 215, 216.
9   *Ibid.*, p. 317.
10 *Ibid.*, p. 320.
11 *Ibid.*
12 In a later volume of her memoirs she records that Sartre was *persona non grata* at Meyrignac, a ban which inhibited her, even when she wanted to, from stopping off to visit her relations.
13 *The Prime of Life*, pp. 489, 490.
14 *Ibid.*, p. 490.
15 *Ibid.*, p. 497.
16 *Ibid.*, p. 528.
17 *Ibid.*, p. 529.
18 *Ibid.*, p. 578.
19 *Ibid.*
20 *Ibid.*, pp. 578, 579.
21 *Ibid.*, p. 601.
22 *Ibid.*, p. 602.
23 *Ibid.*
24 *Ibid.* It is possible that Beauvoir may intend no more than a reference to plain suicide here; but the conjunction of suffering and suicide is a very prominent feature of assisted suicide, better known as voluntary euthanasia.
25 *Ibid.*, p. 604.
26 *Ibid.*
27 *Ibid.*
28 *Ibid.*, p. 605.
29 *Ibid.*
30 *Force of Circumstance*, p. 496.
31 *Ibid.*, p. 497.
32 *Ibid.*
33 *Ibid.*
34 *Ibid.*, p. 673.
35 *Ibid.*
36 *Ibid.*

37 *Ibid.*
38 *Ibid., pp. 673, 674.*
39 *Ibid., p. 674.*
40 *A Very Easy Death, p. 12.*
41 *Ibid., p. 14.*
42 *Ibid., pp. 13, 14.*
43 *Ibid., p. 18.*
44 *Ibid., pp. 18, 19.*
45 *Ibid., p. 25.*
46 *Ibid., p. 50.*
47 *Ibid.*
48 *Ibid., pp. 50, 51.*
49 *Ibid., p. 14.*
50 *Ibid., p. 53.*
51 *Ibid., p. 46.*
52 *Ibid., p. 53.*
53 *Ibid., p. 55*
54 *Ibid.*
55 *Ibid.*
56 *Ibid., p. 81.*
57 *Ibid.*
58 *Ibid.*
59 *Ibid.*
60 *Ibid., p. 83.*
61 *Ibid., p. 82.*
62 *Ibid., p. 91.*
63 *Ibid.*
64 *Old Age, p. 11.*
65 *Ibid.*
66 *Ibid.*
67 *Ibid.*
68 *Ibid.*
69 *Ibid., p. 408.*
70 *Ibid.*
71 *Ibid., pp. 408, 409.*
72 *Ibid., p. 491.*
73 *Ibid., p. 495.*
74 *Adieux, A Farewell to Sartre, p. 127.*

WORKS CITED

Assouline, P. *L'Epuration des intellectuels, 1944–45*. Editions Complexe, 1990.

Bair, D. *Simone de Beauvoir, A Biography*. Cape/Summit Books, 1990.

Baty, P. 'The Essential Guide to Sexuality', *Times Higher Education Supplement*, 18 June 1997.

Bauer, N. *Simone de Beauvoir, Philosophy and Feminism*. Columbia University Press, 2001.

Beauvoir, Simone de.

> *Pyrrhus et Cinéas*. Gallimard, 1944.

> *Pour une morale de l'ambiguïté*. Gallimard, 1947.
> *The Ethics of Ambiguity*. The Philosophical Library, 1948.

> *L'Existentialisme et la sagesse des nations*. Nagel, 1948.

> *Le Deuxième Sexe*. Gallimard, 1949.
> *The Second Sex*. Jonathan Cape, 1953. Penguin Books, 1972.

> *L'Amérique au jour le jour*. Gallimard, 1954.
> *America Day by Day*. University of California Press, 1999.

> *Mémoires d'une jeune fille rangée*. Gallimard, 1958.
> *Memoirs of a Dutiful Daughter*. A. Deutsch, Weidenfeld and Nicolson, 1962. Penguin Books, 1965.

> *La Force de l'âge*. Gallimard, 1960.
> *The Prime of Life*. A. Deutsch, Weidenfeld and Nicolson, 1962. Penguin Books, 1965.

> *La Force des choses*. Gallimard, 1963.
> *Force of Circumstance*. A. Deutsch, Weidenfeld and Nicolson, 1966. Penguin Books, 1968.

> *Une Mort très douce*. Gallimard, 1964.
> *A Very Easy Death*. A. Deutsch, Weidenfeld and Nicolson, 1966. Penguin Books, 1969.

> *La Vieillesse*. Gallimard, 1970.
> *Old Age*. A. Deutsch, Weidenfeld and Nicolson, 1972. Penguin Books, 1977.

> *Quand prime le spirituel*. Gallimard, 1979.
> *When Things of the Spirit Come First*. A. Deutsch, Weidenfeld and Nicolson, 1982. Flamingo, 1983.

> *La Cérémonie des adieux*. Gallimard, 1981.
> *Adieux, A Farewell to Sartre*. A. Deutsch, Weidenfeld and Nicolson, 1984. Penguin Books, 1985.

'Bishops say new pro-life poll now needed', *The Irish Press*, 27 May 1992.

'Bishops accept both "Yes" and "No" votes', *The Irish Times*, 6 November 1992.

'Bishops see Supreme Court rulings in X case to be a corruption of law', *The Irish Times*, 1 July 1995.

Butler, J. 'Sex and Gender in Beauvoir's *Second Sex'*, in E. Fallaize (ed.), *Simone de Beauvoir: A Critical Reader*, pp. 29–42.

Camus, A. *Resistance, Rebellion, and Death*. Alfred A. Knopf, 1960. Vintage, 1995.

Catechism of the Catholic Church. Veritas, 1994.

Cixous, H. 'Sorties', in Marks and Courtivron (eds.), *New French Feminisms*, pp. 90–98.

Clear, C. 'Walls Within Walls: Nuns in Nineteenth-Century Ireland', in C. Curtin *et al.* (eds), *Gender in Irish Society*. Galway, 1987, pp. 134–51. Reprinted, in an edited version, in A. Hayes and D. Urquhart (eds), *The Irish Women's History Reader*. Routledge, 2001, pp. 126–132.

Cohen, G.A. *Karl Marx's Theory of History: A Defence*. Oxford University Press, 1978.

Davis, H. *Moral and Pastoral Theology: A Summary*. Sheed and Ward, 1952.

Evans, C.S. *Philosophy of Religion*. InterVarsity Press, 1982.

Evans, M. *Simone de Beauvoir, A Feminist Mandarin*. Tavistock, 1985.

Fallaize, E. (ed.). *Simone de Beauvoir: A Critical Reader*. Routledge, 1998.

Foot, P.

> 'Moral Beliefs', *Proceedings of the Aristotelian Society*, 1958–59, pp. 83–104. Reprinted in J.J. Thomson and G. Dworkin (eds.), *Ethics*, Harper and Row, 1968, pp. 239–260.

> *Natural Goodness*. Clarendon Press, 2001.

Francis, C. and Gontier, F. (eds.).

> *Les Ecrits de Simone de Beauvoir*. Gallimard 1979.

> *Simone de Beauvoir*. Sidgwick and Jackson, 1987.

Geach, P.T. *God and the Soul*. Routledge and Kegan Paul, 1969.

The Glenstal Book of Prayer. The Columba Press, 2001.

Hamer, D. and Budge, B. (eds.). *The Good, the Bad and the Gorgeous*. Pandora, 1994.

Hayes, A. and D. Urquhart (eds.). *The Irish Women's History Reader*. Routledge, 2001.

Hickman, B. 'Archbishops' onslaught against abortion "evil"', *The Guardian*, 24 January 1980.

Holland, M. 'The Pope's laws on love and test-tube babies', *The Observer*, 15 March 1987.

Hutton, D. 'Blessing in Disguise', *Vogue*, May, 1994.

'"Information" means aiding in abortion, say bishops', *The Irish Times*, 9 March 1995.

Irigaray, L. 'This Sex Which is Not One', in Marks and Courtivron (eds.), *New French Feminisms*, pp. 99–106. Originaly published as 'Ce sexe qui n'est pas un', in *Ce Sexe qui n'est pas un*, Minuit, 1977.

Irving, J. *The Cider House Rules*, Jonathan Cape, 1985. Black Swan, 1986.

Jolivet, R. *The God of Reason*, Burns and Oates, 1958.

Judt, T. *Past Imperfect: French Intellectuals, 1944–1956*. University of California Press, 1992.

Keegan, J. 'Faith is the real miracle', *The Sunday Independent*, 24 August 1997.

Kelly, A. 'Morning sickness halves the risk of miscarriage', *Independent on Sunday*, 11 June 2000.

Kemmy, J. *The Limerick Compendium*, Gill and Macmillan, 1997.

Kiernan, F. *Seeing Mary Plain: A Life of Mary McCarthy*. W.W. Norton, 2000.

Kolakowski, L. *Religion: If There is no God*. Fontana, 1982, 1993.

Kristeva, J.

> 'Woman can never be defined', in Marks and Courtivron (eds.), *New French Feminisms*, pp. 137–141. Originally published as 'La femme, ce n'est jamais ça', *Tel quel*, Autumn, 1974.

> 'Stabat Mater', in Suleiman (ed.), *The Female Body in Western Culture*, pp. 101–118. Originally published in *Tel quel*, No.74, winter 1977, under the title 'Hérétique de l'amour'.

Küng, H. 'Christianity: A Drama still unfolding', *The Irish Times*, 31 January 2000.

Le Doeuff, M. *Hipparchia's Choice: An Essay Concerning Women, Philosophy, Etc.* Blackwell, 1991.

McCarthy, M. *Memories of a Catholic Girlhood*, Heinemann, 1957. Penguin Books, 1963.

McCourt, F. *Angela's Ashes*. Harper Collins, 1996. Flamingo, 1997.

MacCurtain, M. 'Godly Burden: Catholic Sisterhoods in Twentieth Century Ireland', in A. Bradley and M.G. Valiulis (eds.), *Gender and Sexuality in Twentieth-Century Ireland*. Amherst, 1997, pp. 245–256. Reprinted, in an edited version, in A. Hayes and D. Urquhart (eds.), *The Irish Women's History Reader*, pp. 146–151.

McGahern, J.

> *The Barracks*, Faber and Faber, 1963. Quartet, 1977.

> *The Dark*. Faber and Faber, 1963.

McGrath, P.J. *Believing in God*. Millington in association with Wolfhound Press, 1995.

MacIntyre, A. *After Virtue*. 2nd edition. University of Notre Dame Press, 1984.

McNay, L. 'Sartre's sex slave?', review of Bauer, *Simone de Beauvoir, Philosophy and Feminism*, in *Times Literary Supplement*, 12 October, 2001.

Mahon, A. 'Pierre Klossowski and the "Morality of Evil"', *Journal of Cultural Studies*, No.5, 2002, pp. 23–36.

Mahon, J.

> 'Engels and the Question about Cities', *History of European Ideas*, Vol. 3, no. 1, 1982, pp. 40–73.

> *Existentialism, Feminism and Simone de Beauvoir*. Macmillan, 1997. St. Martin's Press, 1997.

Marks, E. and Courtivron, I.de. (eds.). *New French Feminisms*. University of Massachusetts Press, 1980. Harvester Press, 1981.

The New Testament in Today's English Version. 4th printing. Collins, 1981.

O'Brien, C.C. *Maria Cross: Imaginative Patterns in a Group of Catholic Writers*. Chatto and Windus, 1954. Burns and Oates, 1963.

O'Brien, E.

> *The Country Girls*. Hutchinson, 1960. Penguin Books, 1963.

> *Girl With Green Eyes*. Jonathan Cape, 1962. Penguin Books, 1964.

O'Brien, K.

> *The Land of Spices*. 1941. Virago, 1988.

> 'Memories of a Catholic Education', in J. Kemmy (ed.), *The Limerick Compendium*, pp. 26–28. Originally published in *The Tablet*, 4 December 1976.

Okely, J. *Simone de Beauvoir, A Re-reading*. Virago, 1986.

Phillips, D.Z.

> 'Does it Pay to be Good?' *Proceedings of the Aristotelian Society*, 1964–65, pp. 45–60. Reprinted in J.J. Thomson and G. Dworkin (eds.), *Ethics*, pp. 261–278.

> *Death and Immortality*. Macmillan, 1970.

Sheehan, T. 'The Dream of Karl Rahner', *The New York Review*, 4 February 1982.

Simons, M.A. *Beauvoir and the Second Sex*. Rowman and Littlefield, 1999.

Smedt, E.J. de. *Married Love*. Geoffrey Chapman, 1964. Originally published as *L'Amour conjugal*. Editions Ch. Bayaert, 1963.

Suleiman, S.R. (ed.). *The Female Body in Western Culture*. Harvard University Press, 1985.

Swain, H. 'A life less extraordinary', *Times Higher Education Supplement*, 2 June 2000.

Updike, J. *In the Beauty of the Lilies*. Alfred A. Knopf, 1996. Penguin Books, 1996.

Walsh, J. 'Illuminating the dark side of the Irish', *The Sunday Times*, 29 April 1990.

Whale, J. 'The Tensions of John Paul II', *The Sunday Times*, 6 April 1980.

Whitehouse, J.C. (ed.). *Catholics on Literature*. Four Courts Press, 1997.

abortion, 2, 7, 8, 105, 111–136

absolute
  evil, 147, 150, 158, 160
  innocence, 156
  judge, 156
absolutes, 158
abstinence, 28
absolutism, 112, 161
absurd, the 181, 195
adaptationist, 105
Adieux, A Farewell to Sartre, 204
adolescence, 84, 111, 165, 191
adoration, 36, 177
adultery, 41, 191
Advent, 23
aging, 9
agony, 85
Algeria, 118, 198
alienation, 101
All Men Are Mortal, 159
altar, 44
Altar of Repose, 37
allure, 81, 85
amends, make 156, 159
America, 44
America Day By Day, 147
L'Amérique au jour le jour, 207
anatomy, 59, 66
Angela's Ashes, 28
angels, 25, 173
Angels of the Passion, 23
Angelus, the 16
Angelus Silesius, 9
apostasy, 45
apostle(s), 4
application, 40
Aquinas, St. Thomas, 123
Aragon, Louis, 141
aristocracy, petty landed 191
Assouline, Pierre, 137
Astor, Nancy, 199
atheism, 52, 166
atonement, 158, 160, 201
authenticity, 139, 158
Authority, Supreme Moral 167, 189
autoeroticism, 65
A Very Easy Death, 2, 4, 187, 199–202

Bair, Deirdre, 48, 104, 121
Baptism, 31, 45, 80, 125
The Barracks, 17, 18
Baty, Phil, 64, 67
Bauer, Nancy, vii
beatification, 4, 21
Beauvoir, Hélène de, 29, 30, 200
Beauvoir, Sylvie le Bon de, viii, 29, 30, 200
Being and Nothingness, vii, viii
Benedictine(s), 46
Benediction, 2, 4, 10
Bernanos, Georges, 1
binarism, 60
biological
  destiny, 64, 133
  facts, 60, 61
  fate, 69, 124, 133
biologism, 67
birth control, 63, 118, 120, 123
Blessed Lady, Our 15
Blessed Sacrament, the 37
Blessed Virgin, the 6, 15
The Blood of Others, 159
Bloy, Léon, 1
bodies, 6
body, the 4, 59–74
bodies, 6
Boylan, Clare, 35
Brasillach, Robert, 141–2, 147–8, 158–9
Brontë, Emily, 197
burden, the reproductive 63
Butler, Judith, 66, 71–73

Calvary, 4, 19
Camus, Albert, 8, 137, 142, 149–59, 194, 197, 204
canonical hours, 36
canon law, 116, 123
capital offence, 138
capital punishment, 8, 151–59
care, 18, 114, 129, 174
Carmelite(s), 25, 98
Cathecism of the Catholic Church, 28, 76–81, 96, 116, Catholic
  acceptance, 51
  archbishops, 113, 191

attitudes, 5, 7, 76
author(s), 1, 2
childhood, 6, 14, 20, 34
children, 95
Church, 14, 16, 25, 49, 52, 78
education, 15, 27, 49
experience, 15, 27, 49
eyes, 5, 20, 76
faith, 14, 15
formation, 2, 5, 6, 7, 13–33
history, 44
home, 14
iconography, 15, 28
inheritance, 5, 27
initiation, 28
lexicon, 2, 4, 77
literature, 10
milieu, 14, 174
moral theology, 7, 76, 111
obsessions, 2, 7, 76, 111
school(s), 14
strictures, 4
teaching, 1, 3, 7, 112, 117, 123
tradition, 3
upbringing, 6, 20, 119
vernacular, 4, 5, 21, 76, 160, 176
virtue, 7, 23, 76
virtue ethics, 7
writing, 1, 10
celibacy, 67
charity, 4, 78–80, 147
chastity, 4, 80
chapel, the school 23–4, 37, 172
chaplain
  the convent, 38
  the school, 40, 56
Chicago, 147
childbirth, 63, 99, 102
childhood, 87, 129, 165, 191
child–rearing, 103
children, 30–1, 62, 69, 97, 102, 124, 131, 168
Christ Jesus, the 21
Choisir, 8, 112, 120–1, 131, 133
Christ, 19, 27, 30, 52, 176, 201
Christianity, 41

Francesco, Piettro della, 30
Francis, Claude, 119–121
freedom, 64, 98, 119, 124, 160
Free Zone, the 192
fruits of the Holy Spirit, 80
fruit of thy womb, 4

Gatens, Moira, vii
gay(s), 67, 68
Geach, Peter, 77, 80
gender, 6, 60, 66, 67, 71, 72
gentleness, 80
gentry, the landed 191
gestation, 101, 105, 107
gifts of the Holy Spirit, 80
girl(s), 46, 66, 69, 75
girlhood, 42, 43
The Glenstal Book of Prayer, 10
God, 5, 8, 9, 17, 25, 29, 36, 45, 50, 52, 54, 77, 78, 79, 95, 115, 117, 126, 146, 165–186, 202
God's will, 50, 54, 170, 179, 180
God's ordinance, 50
Gontier, Francis, 119–121
grace, 4, 17, 52, 125, 126, 146
Greene, Graham, 1
guillotine,the 151, 152

The Handbook of Mystical Theology, 54
hard labour, 150
hate/hatred, 30, 142, 143
Heart, the Sacred 15, 17
Heaven, 52, 79, 123, 173, 190, 199
Heidegger, Martin, 188
High Mass, 37
historical
    being, 61
    circumstances, 62
Holland, Mary, 4, 10
Holy, the 27
Holy Communion, 4, 15, 18, 24, 27, 28, 55
Holy Day of Obligation, 28
Holy Ghost, the 72
Holy Spirit, the 28, 78, 79, 80

Holy Week, 17
home, a pious 20
hope, 4, 29, 78, 79
host,the 19, 27
Hugo, Victor, 122
human
beings, 29, 112, 113
dignity, 143
nature, 111, 170
rights, 77, 160
solidarity, 157
humanitarianism, 125
humanity, 114
humility, 26, 30, 177
hymns, 25

ideology, male 133
The Imitation of Christ, 24, 172
Immaculate Heart of Mary, the 15, 28
immodesty, 4, 41, 75, 85, 86
immortal soul, 51
immortality, 157, 165, 174, 187, 202
impure action(s), 18
Incarnation, the 4
indecency, 75, 83
indiference, 170, 192
Infant Jesus, the 4, 23
infidels, 126
infinite, the 25, 174, 180
injustice, 45
Inquisition, the 126
instinct, death 153
instinct to live, 153
Institut Catholique, the 49
insubordination, 41, 75
intercourse, 123, 124
intimacy, 76, 85
Irigaray, Luce, 65
Irish
    Catholic home, 14, 17
    family life, 17
    lace, 24
irony, 2, 66
Irving, John , 136

je suis partout, 141, 143
Jesuit(s), 15, 21, 41, 45, 46, 48, 52, 53, 112, 202
Jesus, 17, 24, 28, 79, 170, 172, 177
Joan of Arc, 25

Jolivet, Régis, 184
jouissance, 65
joy, 76, 79
Joyce, James, 16
Judgement Sent, the 17
Judt, Tony, 137–142
jurisprudence, 148
justice, 77, 158, 160

Keegan, Jennifer, 33
Kelly, Fred, 10
Kiernan, Frances, 57
kindness, 80
Kirkup, James, 2, 3, 31, 167
knowledge, 70, 80
Kolakowski, Lezscek, 168, 184
Kristeva, Julia, 6, 30–1, 65, 70
Küng, Hans, 20

Ladies of the Sacrd Heart, 46
The Land of Spices, 34, 35, 41, 49, 50, 75
Latin hymns, 34
Lavin, Mary, 56
Le Doeuff, Michèle, 159
Lent, 16, 41
Lenten procession, 4
lesbian(s), 67, 68
Liberation, the 138, 139, 143, 145
liberty, 144, 149
lilies
    Easter, 44
    of the field, 1, 62
Limbo, 4, 123
Limerick, 6, 34, 95
litany(ies), 44
Lloyd, Genevieve, vii
logic, 25, 48
Lord, the 9, 17, 178
Lourdes, 2, 28, 166, 168
Lourdes, Our Lady of 15
love, 26, 30, 79, 89, 90

McCarthy, Mary, 6, 42–47, 48–58
McCourt, Frank, 28, 95
MacCurtain, Margaret, 56
McGrath, P.J., 184
MacIntyre, Alasdair, 13
McNay, Lois, viii